To my parents

THE VICARIOUS HUMANITY OF CHRIST AND THE REALITY OF SALVATION

TABLE OF CONTENTS

iii

ACKNOWLEDGMENTS

Gratitude is due to many people who have helped in immeasurable ways in this study.

The pastoral and theological insights of my mentors Dr. Ray S. Anderson and Dr. Geoffrey W. Bromiley of Fuller Theological Seminary, Prof. James B. Torrance, Emeritus Professor, University of Aberdeen, and Dr. Thomas F. Torrance, Emeritus Professor, University of Edinburgh have been invaluable. Drs. Anderson and Bromiley originally guided this project in its first incarnation as a dissertation submitted for the Ph.D. in Systematic Theology at Fuller Theological Seminary. Since then, much revision has taken place, although the essential argument and outline remains. Dr. Anderson has provided the unique combination of pastoral and theological sensitivities which will never allow me to divorce theology from the ministry of the church. Dr. Bromiley's example of Christian maturity and exacting scholarship will always stay with me. The enthusiasm, encouragement, and critical theological thinking which Prof. James Torrance, the external reader of my dissertation, brought to my subject has been a rare gift. The influence of Dr. Thomas F. Torrance on my study is self evident. Dr. Torrance, during a memorable month in 1981 when I served as his teaching assistant at Fuller Seminary, provided such a stimulus that I felt compelled to investigate the further implications of his doctrine of "the vicarious humanity of Christ." If this work encourages some to see the profound evangelical and ecumenical implications of Torrance's doctrine of the vicarious humanity of Christ, then it will have achieved its goal. But beyond his theology, the influence of Dr. Torrance on me as a person committed to Jesus Christ in every area of his life has been profound.

Many friends contributed to this study through reading and encouragement, including Todd Speidell, Dale C. Allison, Jr., and Warren and Kathleen Muller. Financial support at a strategic time supplied by Eastminster Presbyterian Church, Wichita, and its pastor, Frank Kik, was greatly appreciated. Words cannot express my thanks for the work of my friends Jim and Judy Naylor in helping me to prepare the manuscript for publication. Thanks are also due to the administration, faculty, and staff of Friends University.

At various stages of research, the facilities of and help of the librarians at McAlister Library, Fuller Theological Seminary, Speer Library, Princeton Theological Seminary, and Edmund Stanley Library, Friends University were indispensable.

Appreciation must be given to the Scottish Academic Press for permission to use material from my article "The Vicarious Repentance of Christ in the Theology of John McLeod Campbell and R. C. Moberly," in the *Scottish Journal of Theology*, 38, No. 4, 1986, pp. 529-543. Permission has also been granted by T. and T. Clark, Ltd. for use of citations from Karl Barth, *Church Dogmatics*.

Wichita, Kansas,
November, 1990

PREFACE

RASHKOLNIKOV'S QUESTION
AND
THE REALITY OF SALVATION

In Dostoyevsky's classic novel, *Crime and Punishment,* Rashkolnikov's meeting with Sonia leads him to believe that the girl is quite feeble-minded.[1] He believes that her belief in miracles and in God is an indication of insanity. Rashkolnikov prods her, "So you pray a lot to God, Sonia?" Sonia is silent, then quickly responds, "What should I be without God?" Rashkolnikov's suspicions are confirmed: "She's mad all right!" he thinks. But it is the next question which probes the deepest, the question which is at once the most wonderful and the most tortuous for every Christian, or for any theist: "And what does God do for you?" This is the question of reality, the reality of salvation.

Salvation. Certainly some religious words are so overused that their very usefulness seems often to be at an end. So it seems with "salvation." But some words perhaps become overused because they are so pregnant with meaning for authentic human existence. "Salvation" is one of these. For Christians, it means that their religion is a religion of God's intervention into the human predicament. But how can we speak of salvation in a "secular" age, a "world come of age," when the human predicament cries out, not for a plethora of religious "doublespeak," but for *reality,* the presence of salvation—the presence of God?

---

[1] Fyodor Dostoyevsky, *Crime and Punishment,* trans. by David Magarshack (Hammondsworth: Penguin Books, 1966), p. 339.

The question of the reality of salvation can be examined in many different ways. One can understand "reality" according to a definition, as "genuineness, or correspondence between what the thing appears or pretends to be and what it is."[2] But where do we look for the reality, i.e. the genuineness, of salvation in the world today? In the movement of history? Religious experience? Or maybe political progress?

But this is more than a question which can be satisfied with an academic definition. It is a question which coincides with my own theological and spiritual pilgrimage. I am a child of the "Jesus movement" of the early 1970's, the movement among young people, mostly "counter-culture," which exhibited a great deal of excitement about the work of God in our midst. And no wonder! For the first few years, we could visibly see the working of God in the many people who had conversion experiences and in the general spiritual excitement which we felt. But, as in all periods of spiritual revival in church history, the time came when the dramatic and the exciting was not so common. Where is the reality of salvation when one comes down from the mountain of the spiritual "high" and has to take up once again the mundane existence of the nine-to-five job?

The question of the reality of salvation does not simply rise from the mundane, however, but also from the tragic of life. The nation is still recovering from seeing the graphic spectacle of the crew members of the space shuttle Challenger destroyed in an instant on their take off from Cape Canaveral. In an age which goes to extraordinary lengths to deny the reality of death, the scene of this tragedy has brought home the reality of death to an entire nation, and an entire world. How can Christians speak of the reality of salvation in such a world as this? The cerebral palsied man, who visits the seminary campus almost every day, cries out for a friend who will accept him in his tragedy, despite his obvious humiliation. Where is the reality of salvation in his world? The endless enormity of human tragedy cries out: The couple whose four year old daughter dies suddenly, just as she was learning about Jesus in Sunday school; not to mention the millions of un-

---

[2] *Webster's Dictionary of Synonyms* (Springfield, MA: Merriam-Webster, 1984), p. 663

born infants who never had a chance at life because of the practice of abortion and the poor of the world who have never known a day in their lives without hunger. The list goes on interminably and almost unbearably. Is the Christian message of salvation a cruel joke for such a world as ours? In a sense, what we have here is the *inverse* of the problem of evil: Where is the reality of salvation to be found? Where do we find the reality of salvation in such a world?

We hasten to add that such a question cannot be *answered* at least by this writer, if by anyone else. But it has to be *faced.* Dietrich Bonhoeffer was one individual Christian who, in his own way, and in his own historical situation, wrestled with the problem of the reality of salvation. Bonhoeffer had to face the question in light of the nightmare of National Socialism. In one of his last works, the never-completed *Ethics*, he discussed "The Concept of Reality" in regards to ethics, but in a radical, Christian sense. Bonhoeffer distanced himself from the traditional questions of ethics—"How can I be good?" and "How can I do good?"— and instead asked the question, "What is the will of God?"[3] Bonhoeffer stated the problem boldly:

> If the ethical problem presents itself essentially in the form of enquiries about one's own being good and doing good, this means that it has already been decided that it is the self and the world which are the ultimate reality.[4]

This is very different from the Christian position, according to Bonhoeffer, which is that the ultimate reality is "the reality of God, the Creator, Reconciler and Redeemer."[5] Without God, all data, laws and standards become "abstract," for God is not an "idea," and to say that the ultimate reality is God is not to say that God is "the religious rounding-off of a profane conception of the

---

[3] Dietrich Bonhoeffer, *Ethics*, ed. Eberhard Bethge, trans. Neville Horton Smith (New York: Macmillan, 1965), p. 188.

[4] Ibid.

[5] Ibid.

universe. It is the acceptance in faith of God's showing forth of Himself, the acceptance of His revelation."[6]

But God as the ultimate reality is not to be separated from the world and the self, according to Bonhoeffer. The ethical question of the good is understood in terms of the real:

> Good is the real itself. It is not the real in the abstract,
> the real which is detached from the reality of God, but
> the real which possesses reality only in God.[7]

The Incarnation, the Word made flesh, makes it possible to speak of "the possibility of partaking in the reality of God and in the reality of the world, but not in the one without the other."[8] This is where Bonhoeffer provides a direction for us concerning the problem of the reality of salvation. The reality of salvation is not to be found in the self or the world, but only in God. But, for the Christian, God is known only in human form, in Jesus Christ. The Incarnation enables us to confess both God as the ultimate reality, and the world which the Word has entered as significant. To participate in the reality of God's self revelation means "that I never experience the reality of God without the reality of the world or the reality of the world without the reality of God."[9] But in what way are we to understand how the Incarnation relates to our world or, indeed, to our humanity?

Jesus Christ as true human being. Confessed by the church for centuries, the implications of the humanity of Christ for salvation have often been reduced to his adequacy as a victim in order to satisfy the wrath of God, or simply as a noble, moral example of what it means to be a good person. There are indications even in the New Testament of those who literally denied the humanity of Christ (I Jn. 4:2,3). But even when the church has confessed the humanity of Christ, its confession has often remained in word alone. The Scottish poet Edwin Muir observed that in the Church

---

[6]   Ibid., p. 189.

[7]   Ibid., p. 190. See the contrary view presented by Socrates in Plato's *Euthyphro,*
      10 ff., in *Five Dialogues,* trans. by G. M. A. Grube (Indianapolis: Hackett,
      1981), pp. 14 ff.

[8]   Ibid., p. 195.

[9]   Ibid.

of Scotland in his day "nothing told me that Christ was born in the flesh and had lived on the earth."[10] The coldness of the practical Christology of his day originated, in his opinion, in "King Calvin" and his "iron pen." Through Calvin's influence in Scotland, "the Word made flesh is made word again." In the same poem, Muir predicts the end result of such a Christology:

> The fleshless word, growing, will bring us down, Pagan and Christian man alike will fall.... Abstract calamity, save for those who can build their cold empire on the abstract man.[11]

While Muir's view of Calvin's doctrine of the humanity of Christ as "abstract man" is surely a caricature (one need think only of Calvin's emphasis on the "vivifying flesh" of Christ in the Lord's Supper), the practical phenomenon which he is describing has not been a rare occurrence in church history. The radical implications of the humanity of Christ are seldom seen in some quarters.

Resources in the history of Christian thought certainly exist for considering the radical implications of the humanity of Christ. Luther's statement that we can never draw God's Son deep enough into our own flesh, our own humanity, readily comes to mind.[12] As Otto Weber states, great significance is to be found in the self-disclosure of God as a human being, rather than simply as an "idea." Therefore, theology is not simply a study of "content" *about* God, but reflection upon God himself, in his self-revelation.[13] So also, ethics is integrally related to dogmatics, according to Weber, because the Word was made flesh. The personal nature of God's self-revelation is not abstract but intensely practical.[14] More recently, Ray S. Anderson has explored the implications of

---

10 Edwin Muir, *An Autobiography*, p. 277ff., cited in Bill Cant, "One Foot in Eden," *New College Bulletin* (September, 1982, No. 13), p. 2.

11 Edwin Muir, *Collected Poems*, p. 228, cited in ibid.

12 Cited in Martin Kähler, *The So-Called Historical Jesus and the Historic Biblical Christ*, trans. and ed. Carl E. Braaten (Philadelphia: Fortress Press, 1964), p. 46.

13 Otto Weber, *Foundations of Dogmatics*, Vol. 1, trans. Darrell L. Guder (Grand Rapids: Eerdmans, 1981), pp. 177-178.

14 Ibid., p. 68.

the humanity of Christ as the place of the transcendence of God, where God's transcendence is made manifest even in the hiddenness of human flesh.[15]

The implications of the humanity of Christ are certainly endless, but there is one strain in the history of Christian thought which we would like to propose as having particular significance for our question of the reality of salvation. It has been particularly emphasized in dramatic new ways in recent years by the Scottish theologian, Thomas F. Torrance, in his doctrine of the *vicarious* humanity of Christ. In this view, not only is the atonement accomplished by Christ's vicarious death, but also the very essence of salvation includes the vicarious nature of the entire humanity of Christ. This is the humanity which becomes the basis for a renewed and restored humanity. Our proposal is that Torrance's doctrine of the vicarious humanity of Christ develops Bonhoeffer's basic insights into God as the ultimate reality and how God as the ultimate reality relates to the reality of the world. Therefore, we are to look for the reality of salvation in God himself, not God in the abstract, but God in the totality of our humanity, as seen in Jesus Christ. There we find the reality of salvation; there we find our hope in a world of tragedy and sorrow.

Part One of our study examines the problem of the reality of salvation as seen by six contemporary theologians: John B. Cobb, Jr., Leonardo Boff, Jürgen Moltmann, Wolfhart Pannenberg, John Hick and Hans Küng. The problem of their anthropocentric approach for the question of the reality of salvation is then critiqued through Karl Barth's doctrine of the humanity of God, which becomes a bridge leading us into the main body of our study, Part Two, "The Vicarious Humanity of Christ as the External Expression of the Eternal Humanity of God." This part begins with a survey of Torrance's doctrine of the vicarious humanity of Christ with a particular emphasis upon how the doctrine affects the totality of the church's dogmatic task.

The implications of the vicarious humanity of Christ for epistemology and hermeneutics, as seen in the theology of the Scottish theologian John McLeod Campbell, occupies the next

---

[15] Ray S. Anderson, *Historical Transcendence and the Reality of God* (Grand Rapids: Eerdmans, 1975), pp. 139-145.

chapter, followed by a close look at one aspect of the vicarious humanity of Christ, the vicarious *repentance* of Christ, particularly as seen in Campbell, the Anglican theologian R. C. Moberly, and James B. Torrance. Then, the eschatological aspect of the vicarious humanity of Christ is examined in the doctrine of the exalted humanity of Christ found predominantly in the epistle to the Hebrews.

In Part Three, the *locus* of the vicarious humanity of Christ is found in the church, the body of Christ. But this is true only as the church becomes "displaced" by the humanity of "the Judge judged in our place" (Karl Barth) and "restored" as the church becomes "the Community of the last Adam." The character of this community is not found in itself, but in God, through the lordship of the Spirit ("the community of the Spirit") and, then, through the fruit of concrete, often unspectacular, acts of faith, love and hope in the world ("the community of faith, hope, and love"). In all of this, Rashkolnikov's question, the question of every atheist and agnostic, is never far behind: "And what does God do for you?"— the question of the reality of salvation.

THE VICARIOUS HUMANITY OF CHRIST AND THE REALITY OF SALVATION
(An Overview of the Exposition)

PART ONE	PART TWO	PART THREE

THE SOURCE:
The Eternal Humanity of God (as critique of anthropocentric soteriologies)

THE GOAL:
The Exalted Humanity of Christ (the Epistle to the Hebrews)

THE LOCUS:
The Vicarious Humanity of Christ in the Church-
- Humanity Displaced
- Humanity Restored
- The Community of the Last Adam as the Community of Faith, Hope and love

"And What Does God Do For You?"
"Everything!"
(Sonia, in *Crime and Punishment*)

THE SCOPE:
The Vicarious Humanity of Christ as the External Expression of the Eternal Humanity of God

THE DEPTH:
The Vicarious Repentance of Christ

THE PROBLEM of the Reality of Salvation :
"And What Does God Does For You?" (Rashkolnikov, in *Crime and Punishment*)

Figure 1

PART ONE

THE PROBLEM OF THE REALITY OF
SALVATION IN CONTEMPORARY THEOLOGY

The doctrine of salvation in contemporary theology presents many problems which are unique to its own character. At a theological level, the very breadth of the Christian idea of salvation can prove to be very intimidating for the theologian. As Carl Braaten remarks, "When theology and the church address the deepest human questions, they are dealing with the theme of salvation, even though the word is never mentioned."[1] These deep human questions are theological, historical, and existential. Theologically, salvation draws upon so many other theological topics, such as election, the nature of humanity, sin, the person and work of Christ, the role of the Holy Spirit, grace, and faith, to the sacraments, judgment, and glorification.[2]

Historically, the complexities of the doctrine of salvation are also formidable. Braaten's point is apt: "In two thousand years the church never produced a dogma of salvation, as it has done on the Trinity or Christology."[3] This can be understood, Braaten claims, since the whole of theology is developed soteriologically, as we have seen in the preceding paragraph.

---

[1] Carl E. Braaten, "The Christian Doctrine of Salvation," *Interpretation* 35 (April, 1985), p. 118.

[2] David F. Wells, *The Search for Salvation* (Downers Grove, IL: Inter-Varsity Press, 1978), pp. 9-10.

[3] Braaten, p. 117.

The historical situation since the Enlightenment has increased the crisis in soteriology dramatically. Previous to the Enlightenment, theology tended to see salvation as primarily an other worldly eschatological reality, "a radically different world in another time and place."[4] God was "the sole source of salvation."[5] This changed with the Enlightenment focus on human happiness and social welfare. This change was basic and profound. Braaten is again very perceptive:

> The interesting differences in this respect between Voltaire and Rousseau, or between Comte and Darwin, or between Marx and Mao all appear miniscule from a soteriological point of view compared to the difference between a belief in salvation based on human power and one that trusts in the power of God.[6]

But existentially, the doctrine of salvation is also in a crisis as well. This is what we will term the "reality" of salvation. The question is this: Does the Christian preaching of salvation through Christ really make any difference in a world in which sin, evil, and suffering continue to run rampant? Braaten puts it quite bluntly: "Has Christian preaching of salvation noticeably changed the world?"[7] It is this very existential crisis which has been the source of the modern theological shift in the doctrine of salvation from trust in the power of God to salvation as based on human

---

[4] Ibid., p. 121.

[5] Ibid.

[6] Ibid., p. 122. See also the modern problem of linking soteriology to Christology, as ably related by Walter Lowe, "Christ and Salvation," in *Christian Theology: an Introduction to its Traditions and Tasks,* eds. Peter C. Hodgson and Robert H. King (Philadelphia: Fortress Press, 1982), p. 196. Linking soteriology to Christology has appeared presumptuous to many moderns: "After all, it amounts to gathering up the most fundamental of human concerns--the concern with salvation, however defined--and linking it, focusing it, and somehow making it contingent upon a Jewish prophet in a minor Roman dependency some two thousand years ago. The sense of anomaly and tension this creates is often termed 'the scandal of particularity.'"

[7] Braaten, p. 118.

power.[8] This has had very negative results in the life of the church, according to Braaten:

> Is this not why some church groups desperately reach for every modern secular substitute for salvation, whether psychological for the individual person, or more political for the larger collectivities?[9]

As we shall see, we share this negative critique by Braaten. Yet, the question of the reality of salvation must be answered by the church, and particularly by its theological community.

Our premise is that the root problem in the contemporary crisis of the reality of salvation is found in the anthropocentric, experience-oriented approach to salvation particularly characteristic of Christian theology since the Enlightenment. We may even be bold enough to say that in this theology the gift of God has been exchanged for a bowl of anthropological pottage.[10] Yet the question still remains: How can we speak of the reality of salvation in a world which hardly looks like it has been invaded by the kingdom of God? Our proposal is that the teaching on the humanity of God in the thought of Karl Barth and Eberhard Jüngel provides both a critique of anthropocentric soteriologies, and a positive alternative, but only as it is fulfilled in the doctrine of the vicarious humanity of Christ as particularly elaborated by T. F. Torrance. Our goal is to see the humanity of God as a bridge between the contemporary problem of the reality of salvation and its resolution in the reality of the vicarious humanity of Christ.

---

[8] See above, n. 6.

[9] Braaten, p. 118.

[10] Helmut Thielicke's criticism of "Cartesian" theology, a theology which is subordinated to what is experienced by the self is very appropriate here, *The Evangelical Faith*, Vol. 1, trans. and ed. Geoffrey W. Bromiley (Grand Rapids: Eerdmans, 1974), pp. 34ff. It is important to note Thielicke's insistence that this is a more basic division in theology than the terms "modern" and "conservative" (p. 30 f.) As seen in some forms of evangelical, charismatic, and rationalist theologies, the "conservative" can sometimes be the most "Cartesian" in his thinking!

CHAPTER ONE

SALVATION AS IMMANENCE

JOHN B. COBB JR. AND PROCESS THEOLOGY

John B. Cobb Jr. represents the school of process theology in America which originates from the work of the philosopher Alfred North Whitehead.[1] Its theological implications have been further developed by Charles Hartshorne, Cobb's teacher.[2] Cobb's major work on Christology, *Christ in a Pluralistic Age*,[3] makes him a logical representative of the modern school of process theology for our study.

---

[1] Whitehead's major work is *Process and Reality* (New York: Free Press, 1978 (1929)). Other works pertaining to religion include *Religion in the Making* (New York: Macmillan,1926), *Science and the Modern World* (New York: Macmillan, 1925), and *Adventures in Ideas* (Cambridge: Cambridge University Press, 1933).

[2] Hartshorne's seminal theological work is *The Divine Relativity* (New Haven: Yale University Press, 1948). A recent statement is *Omnipotence and Other Theological Mistakes* (Albany: State University of New York Press, 1984).

[3] John B. Cobb Jr., *Christ in a Pluralistic Age* (Philadelphia: Westminster Press, 1975). Other process works on Christology and soteriology include David Griffin, *A Process Christology* (Philadelphia: Westminster Press, 1973) and Norman W. Pittinger, *Christ and Christian Faith* (New York: Round Table Press, 1941), *Christology Reconsidered* (London: SCM Press, 1970), *The Word Incarnate: a Study of the Doctrine of the Person of Christ* (New York: Harper, 1959).

God and the World

Process theology has traditionally had a passion to relate
God and the world. The crucial issue is not God *or* the world but
God *and* the world.[4] Process theology's adversary is the idea of
God as "the unchanging and passsionless absolute" which, in effect, means that God cannot be related to that which is nonabsolute
and finite, namely, the world.[5] To speak of the world means to
speak of its dependence on God. But it would be a mistake to infer
that this means that God is dependent on the world. God is no
longer considered the basis of the status quo. He is not a "cosmic
moralist," and "unchangeable absolute," or a "controlling
power."[6] The notion that what is real is beyond change tends to
disengage God from the world which we experience as "a place of
process, of change, of becoming, of growth and decay."[7] On the
contrary, the Judeo-Christian tradition speaks of a God who
concretely acts in the world and, therefore, changes. This God,
according to Whitehead, is able to redeem evil without removing it
by including it within his very being. "God suffers with us, but
the suffering does not destroy God as it can destroy us."[8]

God as Creative-Responsive Love

The reality of God affecting the world is found by Cobb in
God as "creative-responsive love."[9] Process theology does not see
the world as a manifestation of static order, but rather as an infinite

---

[4] This is the theme of Cobb's book *God and the World* (Philadelphia:
Westminster Press, 1969).

[5] John B. Cobb Jr. and David Ray Griffin, *Process Theology: an Introductory
Exposition* (Philadelphia: Westminster Press, 1976), p. 9. For critiques of
process theology, see Royce G. Gruenler, *The Inexhaustable God: Biblical
Faith and the Challenge of Process Theism* (Grand Rapids: Baker, 1983) and
Colin E. Gunton, *Becoming and Being: the Doctrine of God in Charles
Hartshorne and Karl Barth* (New York: Oxford University Press, 1978).

[6] Cobb and Griffin, p. 9.

[7] Ibid., p. 14.

[8] John B. Cobb, Jr., *Process Theology as Political Theology* (Philadelphia:
Westminster Press, 1982), p. 80.

[9] Ibid., pp. 42-43.

variety of possibilities. "There must be an agency that mediates between abstract forms of pure possibilities and the actual world."[10] This is God.

Hartshorne contrasts traditional theism's unchanging God with the God of "di-polar" theism, who is both unchanging and changing.[11] There is both an "abstract essence of God" and "God's concrete actuality." So there are aspects of God that are eternal and absolute as well as aspects which are temporal and constantly changing. As Cobb says, "In each moment of God's life there are new, unforeseen happenings in the world which only then have become knowable."[12] This changeableness provides the basis for God's creative-responsive love.

The creative love of God in process theology is not a love which is confessed in spite of experiences to the contrary.[13] Rather, "it illuminates our experience."[14] This is because creative love is *persuasive*, promotes *enjoyment*, and is *adventurous*. It is *persuasive* because divine creative activity is based upon "responsiveness to the world."[15] Actuality is essentially self-relatedness, not static being, therefore, God as actuality is essentially related to the world. This relatedness provides an "initial aim" for each worldly actuality.[16] However, this "does not automatically become the subject's own aim."[17] A subjective decision still has to be made by the worldly actuality. Therefore, the action of God in the world involves "risk." Since God is not in complete control of events, he cannot be held accountable for genuine evil. His beneficent *lure* is for all creatures.[18]

---

[10] Ibid.

[11] Ibid., p. 47.

[12] Ibid.

[13] Ibid., p. 51.

[14] Ibid.

[15] Ibid., p. 52.

[16] Ibid., p. 53.

[17] Ibid.

[18] See the biblical process theology of Lewis S. Ford, *The Lure of God: a Biblical Background for Process Theism* (Philadelphia: Fortress Press, 1978).

Creative love also promotes *enjoyment*. Traditionally, Christian theology has seen morality and enjoyment as fundamental opposites.[19] However, according to Cobb and Griffin, morality is in service of enjoyment.While all the subtleties of enjoyment cannot detain us, it suffices to say that promoting enjoyment is to promote the intrinsic goodness of the creature.[20] There is no moral law outside the goodness of the worldly actuality.

Creative love is also *adventurous*. This derives from God's love as a love which takes risks and, therefore, does not know what the outcome will be.[21] This means that God opens himself up to the possibility of discord as well as the beauty involved in finite experiences.[22]

Christ as Creative Transformation

Cobb draws heavily upon Whitehead's sometimes cryptic comments concerning Jesus Christ. In Jesus of Nazareth, Whitehead sees the power of the "absence of force," rather than "over-ruling power."[23] In early Christian theology, Whitehead sees the "mutual immanence of the members of the Trinity," the affirmation of one entity existing in another, as the only fundamental advance in metaphysics since Plato.[24] Cobb builds upon Whitehead through a new form of Logos Christology.[25] The Logos is "the relative givenness of relevant potentiality."[26] It keeps creation from being a confusion of indeterminate potentiality. God as Logos is immanent in all events. "The Logos is truly

---

[19] Cobb and Griffin, p. 57.

[20] Ibid., p. 56.

[21] Ibid., p. 57.

[22] Ibid., p. 61.

[23] Whitehead, *Religion in the Making*, p. 57. Cf. Cobb and Griffin, p. 96.

[24] Whitehead, *Adventures in Ideas*. Cf. Cobb and Griffin, p. 97.

[25] Cobb, *Christ in a Pluralistic Age*. Cf. Wolfhart Pannenberg, "A Liberal Logos Christology: the Christology of John Cobb," trans. David P. Polk, in *John Cobb's Theology in Process*, eds. David Ray Griffin and Thomas J. J. Altizer (Philadelphia: Westminster Press, 1977), pp. 133-150.

[26] Cobb, *Christ in a Pluralistic Age*, p. 75.

incarnate in the world."[27] Christ is the orientation of the Logos to creative transformation.[28] Christ is not in every manifestation of the Logos, although the potentiality is there. Even as the "unrecognized" or "misunderstood" working of the Logos in the world, Christians can name as Christ creative transformation in art, in persons of other faiths, and in the planetary biosphere.[29] Cobb hastens to add, however, that Christ is also the name, in a more certain way, for "the singular figure of a Nazarene carpenter."[30]

In his more recent writing, Cobb has acknowledged that in his earlier Christology Christ the incarnate Logos does not suffer with the world, but only associated God's suffering with the Holy Spirit and the kingdom of God. This he recognizes now as a mistake. The Incarnation should not be excepted from the general activities of the Trinity.

> Let us think instead quite straight-forwardly that it is God who is incarnate in Jesus and that this God is the Trinity in its totality. Then Christ names God in God's relation to the world without limitation. *Christ* names this suffering as much as *Christ* names creative transformation.[31]

However, the extent of the effectiveness of Christ as creative transformation depends upon the creature. "Christ is present to a greater or lesser extent as the creature decides for or against the Logos."[32] This decision is the decision of growth or "novelty," but not just change for change's sake.[33] Creative transformation is involved in all responsive love. "To love another person in this way is to allow that person's feelings to affect oneself."[34] The

---

27 Ibid., p. 77.
28 Ibid., p. 87.
29 Ibid.
30 Ibid., p. 97.
31 John B. Cobb, Jr., "Christ Beyond Creative Transformation," in *Encountering Jesus*, ed. Stephen T. Davis (Atlanta: John Knox Press, 1988), p. 153.
32 Cobb and Griffin, p. 98.
33 Ibid., p. 100.
34 Ibid.

practical outcome of this is the inclusiveness of Christ as creative transformation beyond Jesus of Nazareth.

> Original thinking in science and philosophy, original art in all of its forms, original styles of life and social organizations, all witness to the peculiarly effective presence of Christ.[35]

The result of this is found in the thesis of Cobb's book, *Christ in a Pluralistic Age*:

> Christ is no more bound to any particular system of religious belief and practice than is the creative power of art to any particular style.[36]

Given the contemporary problems of nuclear and political holocaust and political tyranny, "we should not use the symbol *Christ* for anything less than the power that works savingly in this comprehensive way."[37]

Salvation as Process

Cobb's view of salvation is integrally related to the process of creative transformation in the world. The work of God is in "confronting the world with unrealized opportunities" and, therefore, opening up the possibility for freedom and creativity.[38] This is the place of Cobb's insistence on the structure of human existence as the occasion for salvation.[39]

> "Saving faith," the kind of faith that alone can bring wholeness, is primarily a matter of the basic emotions, attitudes, and commitments from which one's behavior follows. That is *faith is fundamentally a mode of*

---

[35] Ibid., p. 101.

[36] Cobb, *Christ in a Pluralistic Age*, p. 33.

[37] Cobb, "Christ Beyond Creative Transformation," in *Encountering Jesus* p. 143.

[38] Cobb and Griffin, p. 98.

[39] Cf. John B. Cobb, Jr., *The Structures of Christian Existence* (Philadelphia: Westminster Press, 1967).

existence [emphasis mine]. Beliefs are important only
to the extent that they support this mode of existence.[40]

The danger is when our conscious beliefs are in conflict with our
experiences. A dualistic life can result. But note Cobb's emphasis
on experience as the epistemological criterion. This will continue
to echo throughout his thought.

The result of salvation includes the expression of
"enjoyment" which Whitehead calls "peace."[41] This is bound in a
special way to one's relationship to God. In contrast to our
"restless egotism," the extent to which our lives are consonant
with God's "initial aim" is the basis for peace.[42] It is "the
harmony of the soul's activities with ideal aims that lie beyond any
personal satisfaction."[43] Whitehead does not suggest a method for
attaining peace, but warns that "the deliberate aim of peace very
easily passes into its bastard substitute, Anaesthesia."[44] The
immanence of deity is the source of peace. It consists of "the zest
of self-forgetful transcendence belonging to Civilization at its
height,"[45] "the removal of the stress of acquisitive feeling arising
from the soul's preoccupation with itself" and a consequent
"surpassing of personality."[46]

The place of human responsibility as a part of salvation is
extremely important to Cobb.This is seen particularly in his emphasis upon a "theology of survival." The danger of a "good, omnipotent God" is seen very dramatically in a consequent devaluation of genuine human responsibility.[47] If God is in control,
where is the need for human action? The results of this are obviously disastrous. Rather the full responsibility for action must be

---

40 Cobb and Griffin, pp. 31-32.
41 Ibid., p. 124.
42 Whitehead, *Adventures in Ideas*, p. 371. Cf. Cobb and Griffin, p. 125.
43 Ibid.
44 Ibid.
45 Ibid., p 381. Cf. Cobb and Griffin, p. 12.
46 Whitehead, *Adventures in Ideas*, p. 367. Cf. Cobb and Griffin, p. 126.
47 Ibid., p. 156.

placed upon human beings.[48] Cobb's desire to be non-dualistic is
very obvious at this point:

> There is no divine action apart from creaturely action,
> but equally the divine action is the principle of hope in
> the creaturely action. Hence we cannot divide up re-
> sponsibility for an action, supposing that the more God
> is responsible for what occurs, the less human beings
> are responsible, or the more human beings are
> responsible, the less God has to do with it. On the
> contrary, it is precisely in the freest and most re-
> sponsible of human actions that the action of God is
> most clearly discerned.[49]

Therefore, the problem of evil is only a "problem if one
considers God to be another agent alongside his creatures."[50] God
acts only in and through his creatures. But this also means that the
future is not determined by self-destruction. There are infinite new
possibilities for survival that are available if we allow God to make
all things new.[51] We trust God, not because whatever happens
will work out for the good, but because God's choice is wise and
good. "To be responsible in this context is not finally to shoulder
an unendurable burden. It is to share in the divine adventure in the
world."[52]

Cobb crystallizes the problem of the reality of salvation in a
cryptic, yet penetrating, way in *Christ in a Pluralistic Age*: "Can
Christ be alive where his image has passed from our basic vision?"[53] He proposes that his book offers an affirmative answer to
that question. The problem arises from two sources: 1) the profane
consciousness of the modern world and 2) the inescapable pluralism of the modern culture.[54] The profane consciousness has

---

48   Ibid., p. 157.
49   Ibid.
50   Ibid.
51   Ibid., p. 158.
52   Ibid.
53   Cobb, *Christ in a Pluralistic Age*, p. 17.
54   Ibid., p. 18.

written off as irrelevant any reference to the sacred Christ. Pluralism has made us realize the integrity and truth of other religions, which have valid contributions to make to our own.

It may be that Christ has disappeared from the modern world in the sense of the importance of the sacred, according to Cobb. He builds upon André Malraux's thesis that universal western art has triumphed over particularistic Christianity, but differs from Malraux in that he believes that Christ is still present in the creative transformation which is art.[55] The implications of this are very profound for Cobb's Christology and soteriology. Cobb claims that he takes the Incarnation of the Logos in Jesus "literally and seriously," but because of the pluralism of structures of existence in human history, one cannot claim that Jesus' existence is the only valid manifestation of the Logos.[56] In fact, "incarnation is seen everywhere because it is seen first and decisively in Jesus life, message, passion, and resurrection."[57] Such an action of creative transformation "warns us against establishing even our relation to that narrative as absolute and... opens us to transformation in the present by the new that comes."[58]

However, this does not mean that Cobb follows the tendency of modernism to reduce Christianity to one common denominator.[59] This is not true pluralism. True pluralism does not study Gautama, Confucius, and Paul from one standpoint, such as Freudian theory, but rather allows them to stand on their own terms.[60] Thus, each structure of existence should be allowed to manifest the Logos, apart from the tyranny of an alleged exclusivity of one over the others.

---

[55] Ibid., p. 31. André Malraux, *The Voices of Silence*, trans. Stuart Gilbert (Garden City, NY: Doubleday, 1953), *The Metamorphosis of the Gods*, trans. Stuart Gilbert (Garden City, NY: Doubleday, 1960).

[56] Cobb, *Christ in a Pluralistic Age*, p. 27.

[57] Cobb, *Process Theology and Political Theology*, p. 140.

[58] Ibid.

[59] Ibid.

[60] Ibid., p. 58. Cf. David Tracy, *The Analogical Imagination: Christian Theology and the Culture of Pluralism* (New York: Crossroad, 1981).

The Pauline theme of "In Christ" describes for Cobb the operation of salvation as "the field of force of Christ."[61] Paul thinks in decidedly non-dualistic ways, according to Cobb. "In Christ" is not to be limited to either an ethical, mystical, or physical sense.

> The real past event of the crucifixion and resurrection of Jesus, involving his total being, has objectively established a sphere of effectiveness or a field of force in which people can enter.[62]

But the question remains whether we can think of the influence of past historical events upon the present.[63] The objectivist believes that the past is wholly determinate upon the present. The subjectivist believes that there is no past apart from the experience in the present. There is truth in both, according to Cobb. But, as Whitehead stated, what is important is not the *location*, but the *pervasion* of event.[64] Events do not exist as substances, but in the midst of the field of force of many events, as they mutually influence each other. The event of Jesus is one event among many which is kept alive by our remembrance of his significance. Thus, it has an important part to play in our experience.[65] Memory is the basis of conformation which is the power of the past upon the present.[66]

The Church

What is the place of the church in Cobb's scheme of salvation? One might think that in such an antiparticularist theology the church and its exclusivistic tendencies would be ignored, or at least devalued. It is true that Cobb sees the church as part of the problem of the reality of salvation. The church is often defined as

---

61 Cobb, *Christ in a Pluralistic Age*, p. 117.
62 Ibid.
63 Ibid., pp. 117-118.
64 Ibid., p. 118.
65 Ibid., p. 121.
66 There is a mild emphasis upon liberation in Cobb's earlier works (see *Christ in a Pluralistic Age*, p. 57), which has become more pronounced in his later writings. See *Process Theology as Political Theology*.

the "body of Christ" or "the extension of the incarnation," or in a process sense, as "a voluntary community of mutual participation" and as "an eschatological community of peace." But how does this reckon with the empirical church?[67] Certainly, creative faces have existed outside the church, which the church has usually not recognized. Furthermore, it must be admitted that the presence of Christ is not restricted to the church, according to Cobb.[68]

However, Cobb does admit that there is a loss where Christ is not acknowledged. There is the tendency to lose a commonality of purpose, as seen in the modern university. The church is not to accept everything in the culture uncritically. The principle of creative transformation becomes the criterion by which the church can discern what is appropriate and what is not.[69] For Cobb, soteriological reality involves any place where "creative transformation" occurs, whether it be Christian or not.

LEONARDO BOFF AND LIBERATION THEOLOGY

Leonardo Boff is one of the foremost advocates today of "liberation theology."[70] A Brazilian priest best known for his re-

---

[67] Cobb and Griffin, p. 178.

[68] Ibid., p. 129.

[69] Ibid., p. 131.

[70] For basic works of liberation theology, see Gustavo Gutiérrez, *A Theology of Liberation*, trans. and ed. Sister Caridad Indu and John Eagleson (Maryknoll, NY: Orbis Books, 1973), José Míguez Bonino, *Doing Theology in a Revolutionary Situation* (Philadelphia: Fortress Press, 1975), Juan Luis Segundo, *Liberation of Theology*, trans. John Drury (Maryknoll, NY: Orbis Books, 1976), Robert McAfee Brown, *Theology in a New Key: Responding to Liberation Themes* (Philadelphia: Westminster Press, 1978); from a feminist perspective, Letty M. Russell, *Human Liberation in a Feminist Perspective-- a Theology* (Philadelphia: Westminster Press, 1974); from a black American perspective, James Cone, *A Black Theology of Liberation* (Philadelphia: Lippincott, 1970). Other Christologies besides Boff include Jon Sobrino, *Christology at the Crossroads: a Latin American Approach* (Maryknoll, NY: Orbis Books, 1978) and *Faces of Jesus: Latin American Christologies*, ed. José Míguez Bonino, trans. Robert R. Barr (Maryknoll NY: Orbis Books, 1983). Critiques of liberation theology include, J. Andrew Kirk, *Liberation Theology: an Evangelical View from the Third World* (Atlanta: John Knox Press, 1979), Michael Novak, *The Spirit of Democratic Capitalism* (New

cent silencing by the Vatican, Boff has penned several important works, the best known being *Jesus Christ Liberator* and, with his brother Clodovis, *Salvation and Liberation*.[71]

Boff sees his understanding of a theology of salvation squarely within the broader concerns of a theology of liberation. Liberation theology emphasizes concerns for economic, political, and educational liberation, as well as spiritual and moral liberation. Boff hastens to stress that there is a genuine "theological" element in liberation theology which can be discerned only by faith.[72] "Only faith enables one to see this element present within the economic, the political, and the educational."[73] Therefore, Boff is anticipating the critics who claim that liberation theology is only a political agenda disguised by theological terminology.

The crucial question at hand that liberation theology must answer, according to Boff, is the question of the relationship between salvation and liberation.

> How is this process [liberation] related to the salvation offered by Jesus Christ? Is there a difference between them? What is the difference? Or are they the same thing? Or have they simply no connection with each other at all? Is there an articulation, a set of connections between them? What is the nature of this articulation?[74]

York: American Enterprise Institute/Simon and Schuster, 1982), pp. 287-297, *Will it Liberate? Questions About Liberation Theology* (New York: Paulist Press, 1986), and *Liberation Theology*, ed. Ronald H. Nash (Milford, MI: Mott Media, 1984).

71 Leonardo Boff, *Jesus Christ Liberator: a Critical Christology for Our Time*, trans. Patrick Hughes (Maryknoll, NY: Orbis Books, 1984). Other works by Boff include *Liberating Grace*, trans. John Drury (Maryknoll, NY: Orbis Books, 1979), *The Lord's Prayer: the Prayer of Integral Liberation*, trans. Theodore Morrow (Maryknoll, NY: Orbis Books, 1983), and *The Church: Charism and Power* trans. John W. Dierksmeier (Maryknoll, NY: Orbis Books, 1984).

72 Leonardo Boff and Clodovis Boff, *Salvation and Liberation*, trans. Robert R. Barr (Maryknoll, NY: Orbis Books, 1984), p. 17.

73 Ibid.

74 Ibid., p. 20.

To prove that there is an integral, yet not identical, relationship is the burden of the Boffs' book, *Salvation and Liberation*. The distinction of liberation theology today, according to Boff, is its development of a theological criterion in the midst of socio-economic liberation.[75] It definitely has a theory of its own; it is not "blind praxis."[76] However, it is theological discernment present within the economic, political, and social realities.[77] Therefore, it must take those realities very seriously.

Religious Experiences: the Foundation

As in John Cobb's theology, we also find the root of Boff's theology in religious experience and, in particular, "the encounter of the poor with the Lord."[78] Boff is very adamant about the foundation of theology in spiritual experience: "A theology—any theology—not based on a spiritual experience is mere panting—religious breathlessness."[79] Yet, Boff is careful in articulating what he means by "spiritual experience." He discerns two ways of "reworking" the same experience, which often result in two different approaches to liberation theology: the "sacramental" and the "socio-analytical."[80]

The "sacramental" articulation of liberation theology proceeds through three steps: 1) "The misery of the poor is perceived," 2) The ethico-religious indignation at the misery is firmly stated, and 3) Solidarity is expressed in the concrete form of active help and action.[81] This is in contrast to the church's traditional role of merely offering "assistance" to the poor, in an indirect sense. Therefore, the church in society is no longer to be defined exclusively by its religious practices, in the strict devotional or liturgical sense. "It has become the matter of holding to religious practices ethical and social ones as well, practices concerned with

---

75 Ibid., p. 45.
76 Ibid., p. 29.
77 Ibid., p. 56.
78 Ibid., p. 2.
79 Ibid.
80 Ibid.
81 Ibid., pp. 2-3.

the promotion and advancement of the whole human being and all human beings."[82]

The "socio-analytical" articulation involves a distinct critique of the sources behind the misery of the poor.[83] This assumes that the misery of the poor can be explained through analyzing the oppressive structures which create and maintain poverty.

These two approaches are based on a general assumption of the ability of humanity to perceive the Transcendent. Boff's theological anthropology affirms that persons are "permanently open to the Transcendent, and giving, from within his or her concrete situation, an answer to God: yes or no."[84] This assumption allows Boff to assert the primacy of religious experience, even in rereading canonical texts. The scriptures are to be reread in light of "a perception of the real situation of the poor."[85] Therefore, biblical narratives are interpreted in such ways as the history of the people of God as they are squeezed between the great powers of the Middle East and Egypt, Jesus of Nazareth as liberator, and the kingdom of God as "total liberation."[86]

Theology as Praxis

"Praxis" has become the code word for liberation theology in its stress upon actual action, rather than simply theorizing about salvation. Boff takes the discussion of praxis one step further: Often "praxis" can itself be mere sloganeering. "The real question is, what praxis will *actually*, and not just seemingly, be of help?"[87] Good intentions are not enough. One must be able to help, not just offer rhetoric.

Therefore, Boff develops the place of the "three mediations" in liberation theology.[88] A "mediation" is a means by which actual

---

82 Ibid., p. 3.
83 Ibid., p. 4. Cf. Puebla 30/128 in *Puebla and Beyond: Documentation and Commentary* (Maryknoll, NY: Orbis Books, 1979).
84 Boff and Boff, p. 18.
85 Ibid., p. 25.
86 Ibid.
87 Ibid., p. 4.
88 Ibid., p. 5.

help is brought to the poor. The three mediations are the process of that help. These are 1) social-analytical mediation: seeing, 2) hermeneutic mediation: judging, and 3) the mediation of pastoral practice: acting.

Social-analytical mediation involves seeing. This is an awareness of reality. It can be done in three ways, two of which are insufficient: 1) *Empiricism* moves from a) the facts to b) a naive awareness, to c) "assistantialism." In this procedure, the facts of poverty and oppression are discerned, but the deeper reasons for the situation are still invisible. 2) *Functionalism* moves from a) socio-economic circumstances, to b) a critical consciousness, to c) "reformism."[89] The facts are seen as a whole, interrelated to the organic social body, yet the real question of why the rich get richer and the poor get poorer is never addressed.[90] 3) *Dialectical structuralism* is the most satisfying alternative. It moves from a) structure, to b) a radical critical awareness, to c) "liberation."[91] Its deep analysis of the reasons behind poverty extends to the "global structure of the system," that is, capitalism, with its absolute right and lack of social obligations.[92] Boff is thus able to define liberation as "an organization of society based on everyone's labor, with everyone sharing in the means and the goods of production as well as in the power."[93]

"Hermeneutic mediation: judging" concerns interpreting the texts of theology by the facts of oppression. "What is God trying to tell us in these social problems, now adequately grasped by scientific reason?"[94] Thus, from the categories of salvation history, through a critique of our faith-tradition itself, a theological reading is made of the situation, with a corresponding judgment upon church and society.[95]

---

[89] Ibid., p. 6.
[90] Ibid., p. 7.
[91] Ibid.
[92] Ibid.
[93] Ibid., p. 8.
[94] Ibid., p. 9.
[95] Ibid., pp. 9-10.

A practical result of this process helps the Christian to discern the right political option for action.[96] Boff is careful to say that Christianity is not exhausted by a particular political practice, or a particular form of society. But Christian faith does help one to choose "a particular instrument of social analysis as being the better way to unmask the mechanisms that are the vehicles of injustice and violence, especially against the poor."[97] Today, "the Christian ideal is closer to socialism than to capitalism."[98] This is not to say that these ideals cannot be realized within a capitalistic system, to some extent.

> But the capitalist system is attended by many contradictions that could be overcome in another system—which for its part will present other contradictions, but lesser ones.[99]

"Mediation of pastoral practice: acting" is realistic action based upon what actually can be done in the particular situation. "As a general rule, we do not do what we wish to; we do what objective conditions of reality permit us to do."[100] This means that the church should not just act symbolically, but "act on the directly political and infra-structural level."[101] However, the goal is always not merely reformist measures, but "a qualitatively new society."[102]

The three mediations must be seen as parts of one movement, in order to avoid the pitfalls of "sociologism," "politicization," "theologism," or "pastoral pragmatism."[103] However, Boff does admit that "the critical point" is mostly in the first movement of social-analytical mediation.[104]

---

[96] Ibid,. p. 10
[97] Ibid.
[98] Ibid.
[99] Ibid., p. 11.
[100] Ibid.
[101] Ibid.
[102] Ibid.
[103] Ibid., pp. 12-13.
[104] Ibid., p. 13.

In other works, Boff is frank to admit that the concrete experience of Latin Americans means that one is

> accustomed to view everything from the perspective of liberation or oppression: the educational system, theology, preaching, the sacraments, political systems, economic opinions—everything. Almost instinctively we come to ask the questions: to what extent is a doctrine liberating us or keeping us enslaved?[105]

Boff proceeds then to comment on the Incarnation and the Trinity based on these questions.

Salvation and Liberation is a carefully conceived book, in which the Boffs seek to anticipate the characteristic objections which many in the Vatican have about liberation theology. In this light, they dialogue with statements of Paul VI and John Paul II on liberation theology. The Boffs commend Paul VI's objection to the reductionisms of the political side, in which the church's mission is reduced to simply a temporal project, and the religious side, in which the church dissociates itself from humanity's temporal problems.[106]

> The church links human liberation and salvation in Jesus Christ, but she never identifies them because she knows through revelation, historical experience, and the reflection of faith that not every notion of liberation is necessarily consistent and compatible with an evangelical vision of man, of things, and of events.[107]

Boff's problem with traditional theology is that often the connection between the two relationships is merely asserted, but not demonstrated.[108]

---

105 Leonardo Boff, *God's Witnesses in the Heart of The World*, trans. and ed. by Robert Fath (Chicago: Claretian Pubs., 1981), p. 35.

106 Paul VI, "Evangelii Nuntiandi," nos. 32 and 34, trans. in *On Evangelization in the Modern World* (Washington, D.C.: USCC, 1976), cited by Boff and Boff, p. 21.

107 Ibid., pp. 21-22.

108 Ibid., p. 23.

John Paul II has also been critical of liberation theology when it becomes a "false theology." By this he means a "politicized" theology, a theology which makes use of systems which are not Christian. "Liberation theology, surely," says John Paul, "but which?"[109] Boff sees no contradiction between this and his statement:

> Liberation in Jesus Christ is not identified *with* political, economic, and social liberation, but it is historically identified *in* political, economic, and social liberation.[110]

The Boffs admit that "social analysis covers only one segment of reality."[111] It must realize its limits. "God is present in the social, to be sure—but God's presence and activity are not reduced to the social area."[112]

Jesus Christ Liberator

Jesus Christ is the basis in Boff's soteriology for his emphasis upon salvation as encompassing all of life. Because God the Son has assumed human nature, the totality of human life, the biological, economic, social, personal, and religious, is "sanctifiable."[113]

Jesus is God's answer to the human condition.[114] The one who has introduced the realities of bringing the Good News to the poor, of proclaiming liberty to the captives (Lk. 4:18-19,21), is the liberator of humanity.[115]

> The word of God assumed not just 'human nature' in general, nor even just any random concrete human nature, but the human nature of a particular human being in an altogether determinate *social* condition: that of a

---

109   Cited by Boff and Boff, p. 31.
110   Boff and Boff, p. 32.
111   Ibid., p. 51.
112   Ibid.
113   Ibid., p. 54.
114   Boff, *Jesus Christ Liberator*, pp. 49-50.
115   Ibid., pp. 52-53.

poor person, a laborer, who preferred the poor, surrounded himself with them, and identified with them.[116]

He is already inaugurating the kingdom of God. The resurrection of Jesus is the place where the yearned for utopias of Plato's Republic, Kant's City of Eternal Peace, and Marx's Proletarian Paradise are realized.[117] "Human hope was realized in Jesus resurrected and is already being realized in each person."[118]

The destiny of each person is seen in the Incarnation. Incarnation is not the starting point of theology, but its destination.[119] We learn what it is to be human from his radical way of being human.[120] This radical humanity was not achieved by affirming the "I" but by surrendering his "I" to others. "The more God existed in Jesus, the more God was humanized."[121] Jesus is the "archetype of the true human being that each of us ought to be but is not as yet."[122] This is based on Boff's assumption that the human being is capable of identifying with the Infinite. "Jesus realized in an absolute and full manner this human capacity to the point of being identified with the Infinite."[123] The resurrection is the realization of human reality, the final step in the evolutionary process. Therefore, in Jesus Christ, humanity is divinized and God is humanized.

More recently, Boff has developed his theology in a more trinitarian vein. "Human society," he declares, "has been eternally willed by God to be the sacrament of trinitarian communion in history." This communion has been thwarted by "social and

---

[116] Leonardo Boff and Clodovis Boff, *Liberation Theology From Dialogue to Confrontation*, trans. Robert R. Barr (San Francisco: Harper and Row, 1986), p. 26.

[117] Ibid., pp. 134-135.

[118] Ibid., p. 135.

[119] Ibid., p. 188.

[120] Ibid., p. 197.

[121] Ibid.

[122] Ibid., p. 203.

[123] Ibid., pp. 209-210.

structural sin."[124] Because of "the lack of cohesion and of
solidarity on the personal and social levels" theologians need "to
stress communion as the first and fundamental principle of God
and in all beings, which are made in the image and likeness of the
relationship inside the Trinity."[125]Since communion is the first
principle, bolstered by the doctrine of the Trinity, such a society
"cannot tolerate class differences, dominations based on power
(economic, sexual or ideological)..."[126]

Christ is the absolute mediator, being both God and human
(I Tim. 2:5) yet this absolute mediation does not rule out "the mediations of his sisters and brothers. Rather it grants them, pen-
etrates them, confers upon them their *raison d' être*."[127] The most
immediate mediation in the light of Christ is that of the Blessed
Virgin Mary. She answers the question "How does the feminine
reveal God? And from the opposite direction, How is God revealed in the feminine?"[128] As the "Mediator of All Graces" the
mediation of Mary has, of course, been prominent in traditional
Catholic theology. But because modernity has chosen to define itself as "logocentric", i.e. "to assign the primacy of the spirit to
rationality and the power of ideas," a profoundly masculinizing
tendency, the feminine has become "marginalized" along with the
distinctive traits of the feminine: "purity, self-sacrifice, and the
protection of the weak and the oppressed."[129] Thus, the mediation
of Mary becomes even more important today. Boff declares, " As
we see it, each new generation finds itself in Mary, projecting its
dreams, its social-cultural ideals upon her."[130] Today's society
finds in Mary its "deliverance from the captivity of a political and
economic system that exploits human work." So Mary is the

---

124 Leonardo Boff, *The Trinity and Society*, trans. Paul Burns (Maryknoll, NY:
Orbis, 1988), p.24.

125 Ibid., p. 78.

126 Ibid., p. 151.

127 Leonardo Boff, *The Maternal Face of God: The Feminine and Its Religious
Experience*, trans. Robert R. Barr and John Diercksmeier (San Francisco:
Harper and Row, 1987), p. 180.

128 Ibid., p. 3.

129 Ibid., p. 182.

130 Ibid., p. 251.

avenger of the weak and oppressed, although this must not be held in tension with the historical Mary, and particularly her humility.[131]

The Presence of the Resurrected Christ Today

The problem of the reality of salvation is particularly addressed by Boff when he discusses the presence of the resurrected Christ today. If one takes seriously the Incarnation, Boff claims, one must see that fact as pointing to the impregnation of all creation with Christ.[132] In words reminiscent of Teilhard de Chardin, Boff sees Christ as the human being who overcame the limitations of space and time, and now lives in the divine sphere as the end result of cosmic evolution.[133] As the end result, Jesus is also the beginning, the origin, and the meaning of all things, the *Logos*.[134]

If everything has been created by and for Christ, then all human beings bear the mark of his image. The human being is "Christ's great sacrament."[135] Therefore, every human being is a brother or sister to Christ.[136] Each human being should remind us of the human being who was Jesus.

> To accept a poor person as poor is to accept the poor Jesus. He hides himself, he is incognito, behind each human face.[137]

The presence of Christ is also seen in "anonymous Christians." Borrowing from Karl Rahner, Boff admits that the Resurrected One is present in all who seek the good and the just and open themselves to "the normative Transcendent." This is because "the cause for which he [the Resurrected One] lived, suffered, was

---

[131] Ibid., pp. 250-251.
[132] Ibid., p. 209.
[133] Ibid., pp. 209-210.
[134] Ibid., pp. 211-212.
[135] Ibid., p. 217.
[136] Ibid., p. 218.
[137] Ibid.

tried and executed is being carried forward."[138] The basis for this is in the "christic structure" which exists within humanity.[139] This is in analogy to God's eternal existence of love as Father, Son, and Holy Spirit.[140] Existing since all eternity, the christic structure received a name with the coming of Jesus Christ.[141] "Jesus lived it so profoundly and absolutely that his surname became Christ."[142] Thus, even in the bare fact of "the transparency of the world," people experience the living God.[143] This can be found in the experience of the human person:

> The person lives in a concrete historical situation in which one is obliged to take a position, make decisions, and affirm oneself as human. By assuming one's historical situation in a radical way, one comes to experience effectively that one is a being-in-the-world, but at the same time is capable of raising oneself infinitely above the world and everyday concrete situations, reasoning and making choices which define one decisively and which signify or express one's salvation or damnation.[144]

Boff immediately adds a caveat, however: still, "the intervention of God is totally unforeseeable. God cannot be 'imprisoned'... in the molds of our sciences."[145]

The presence of Christ is different, however, for avowed Christians and the church. This is a matter of degree of influence. The resurrected Christ is present "in a more profound manner" in those who chose to follow him.[146] The Christ who is present "achieves his highest level of historical concretion" in the

---

138   Ibid., p. 219.
139   Ibid., p. 248.
140   Ibid., p. 257.
141   Ibid., p. 249.
142   Ibid.
143   Boff, *God's Witnesses in the Heart of the World*, pp. 29-30.
144   Ibid., p. 31.
145   Ibid.
146   Ibid., p. 219.

church.[147] The church only differs from other religions in that it is "a special institutional articulation of Christianity."[148] The christic structure extends to all religions. Therefore, there is no such thing as a natural religion. "All have their origin in a reaction to the salvific action of God, which is offered to all without discrimination."[149]

Nonetheless, Boff's emphasis on theology as praxis means that the church should not be spoken of in an idealistic way. This is important because "Christian faith is constantly incarnated in the world in ideas, ideologies, and customs."[150] Christianity is, therefore, impossible without "historical mediation." To him, this is the essence of the Catholic tradition. But the implications of such statements will be the very thing that leads to Boff's celebrated confrontation with the Vatican.

If Christianity must have an historical mediation, Boff contends, it must be found in the church, "the historical-cultural expression and religious objectification of Christianity."[151] But historical entities do not exist without changing. In fact, "syncretion" is theologically desirable because it is founded on "the offer of universal salvation to all through religion," *contra* Barth and Bonhoeffer who see religion as "a human effort aimed at guaranteeing salvation and faith as a free gift from God."[152] All of this is said while maintaining that in the life of Jesus of Nazareth, "this powerless man", early Christianity realized that it was faced with "the total and definitive self-communication of God (incarnation)... revealing God as Father, Son, and Holy Spirit."[153]

The church does not exist in a vacuum. It has an historical context. Therefore, judgments can be made on the historical manifestation of the church. One such contemporary judgment is based on the Marxist analysis that "the organization of a society

---

147 Ibid., p. 222.
148 Ibid., p. 257.
149 Ibid., p. 256.
150 Boff, *Church: Charism and Power*, p. 73.
151 Ibid., p. 92.
152 Ibid., p. 95.
153 Ibid., p. 102.

revolves around its means of production."[154] "Means of production is a way of speaking of the societal organization necessary to produce goods. Such a society always has a dominant class responsible for the growth of the society.

> This dominant class always strives to consolidate, deepen, and widen its power, persuading those who are dominated to accept their domination, conquering them through ideological agreement.[155]

Such a situation exists in the contemporary (Catholic) church, where the hierarchy makes the decisions, guarding the means of production, giving orders to the laity.[156] The solution to this problem is a church for and of the poor in which "the entire community is ministerial, not only some of its members."

It was such an ecclesiology which subsequently incurred the wrath of the Vatican's Sacred Congregation for the Doctrine of Faith, lead by Cardinal Joseph Ratzinger, on Leonardo Boff, leading to his temporary censure.

The heart of the Vatican's concern about liberation is found in two published documents by the Congregation: *Instruction on Certain Aspects of the 'Theology of Liberation'* [157] and *Instruction on Christian Freedom and Liberation.* [158] Ratzinger and the Congregation criticize what they perceive to be the sacrificing of a theological perspective for the sake of Marxist analysis.

---

154 Ibid., p. 110.

155 Ibid., p. 111.

156 Ibid., p. 119.

157 Sacred Congregation for the Doctrine of the Faith, *Instruction on Certain Aspects of the 'Theology of Liberation'*, Publication No. 935 (Washington D.C.: United States Catholic Conference, 1984).

158 Sacred Congregation for the Doctrine of the Faith, *Instruction on Christian Freedom and Liberation*, Publication No. 995 (Washington, D. C.: United States Catholic Conference, 1986). The Vatican's specific criticism of Boff is found in "Doctrinal Congregation Criticizes Brazilian Theologian's Book", *Origins*, NC Documentary Service, vol. 14, no. 42, April 4, 1985, pp. 683, 685-687. Defenses of Boff were made by Robert McAfee Brown, "Leonardo Boff: Theologian for all Christians." *Christian Century*, July 2-9, 1986, pp. 615-617, and Harvey Cox, *The Silencing of Leonardo Boff: The Vatican and the Future of World Christianity* (Oak Park, IL: Meyer- Stone, 1988).

In this new system, every affirmation of faith or of theology is subordinated to a political criterion which in turn depends on the class struggle, the driving force of history.[159]

Such a methodology leads one to deny the "radical newness" of the New Testament, to misunderstand the person of Christ and "the specific character of the salvation he gave us, that is above all liberation from sin, which is the source of all evils."[160] This sets aside "the authoritative interpretation of the Church denounced as classist," robbing one of "an essential theological criterion of interpretation," and thereby welcoming "the most radical theses of rationalist exegesis."[161]

---

[159] Sacred Congregation for the Doctrine of the Faith, *Instruction on Certain Aspects of the 'Theology of Liberation'*, p. 23.

[160] Ibid., p. 27.

[161] Ibid., p. 28.

CHAPTER TWO

SALVATION AS ESCHATOLOGY

JÜRGEN MOLTMANN

Christianity as Eschatology

The immense influence of Jürgen Moltmann's book, *Theology of Hope*, has solidly established eschatology at the forefront of contemporary soteriological discussion.[1] It is Moltmann's contention that the dogma of eschatology as the "doctrine of the last things" has historically led to a devaluation of eschatology in theology.[2] He interprets this as a socio-political development. With the rise of Constantinian Christianity and Roman primacy, the revolutionary impact of eschatology began to be relegated to cult groups. But this goes against the core of Christianity, ac-

---

[1] Jürgen Moltmann, *Theology of Hope*, trans. James W. Leitch (New York: Harper and Row, 1967). Other major works of Moltmann's include *The Crucified God*, trans. R. A. Wilson and John Bowden (New York: Harper and Row, 1973), *The Church in the Power of the Spirit*, trans. Margaret Kohl (New York: Harper and Row, 1977), *The Trinity and the Kingdom*, trans. Margaret Kohl (New York: Harper and Row, 1981), and *God in Creation: A New Theology of Creation and the Spirit of God*, trans. Margaret Kohl (San Francisco: Harper and Row, 1985). Major studies on Moltmann include M. Douglas Meeks, *Origins of the Theology of Hope* (Philadelphia: Fortress Press, 1974), and Christopher Morse, *The Logic of Promise in Moltmann's Theology* (Philadelphia: Fortress Press, 1979),

[2] Moltmann, *Theology of Hope,* p. 15.

cording to Moltmann. "Christianity is eschatology" in its forward-looking, revolutionary nature.[3] Eschatology is not just an aspect of Christianity, but is "the medium of Christian faith as such, the key in which everything in it is set, the glow that suffuses everything here in the dawn of an expected new day."[4] Therefore, theology needs to be constructed with eschatology at the beginning, not at the end.

Moltmann regards the rediscovery of eschatology at the beginning of the twentieth century by Johannes Weiss and Albert Schweitzer as one of the most important movements in recent Protestant theology.[5] The immediate benefit of this was to show that Christianity is always "counter-cultural," not upholding the status quo. Nevertheless, Weiss and Schweitzer did not pursue the implications of eschatology because they viewed Jesus as an apocalyptic fanatic who had little concern for the world.[6]

In Western theology, the great obstacle which stands in the way of realizing the radical implications of eschatology has been "transcendental eschatology," beginning with the Greek philosophers and continuing through Kant. This interpretation of eschatology sees the *Logos* as "the epiphany of the eternal present of being."[7] However, in contrast to this, the real language of Christian theology is not *logos*, but *the promise of God* which has been expressed in his relations with Israel.[8] In transcendental eschatology, revelation is not an invasion into history of God's promise, but rather the manifestation of an eternal present order.[9]

The classical form of transcendental eschatology is found in Kant.[10] Kant's "ethical reduction of eschatology" cuts him off from the eschatological realities and does not allow these realities

---

[3] Ibid., p. 16.
[4] Ibid.
[5] Ibid., p. 37.
[6] Ibid., p. 38.
[7] Ibid., p. 40.
[8] Ibid., p. 41.
[9] Ibid., p. 46.
[10] Ibid., pp. 46-47.

to be experienced in the flow of historical experience.[11] In Kant's thought, history cannot be experienced from an eschatological framework, but only based upon "the eternal conditions of possible experience."[12]

Contemporary theology has reversed the trend of seeing eschatology as the "last article" of the theological encyclopedia, mainly through the new appreciation for *apocalyptic*.[13] This is no longer simply seen as an elaboration of "earlier cosmological schemata found in myth" (G. von Rad), or "the first attempt to provide a sketch of world history on the basis of the prophetic eschatology" (K. Koch and W. Pannenberg), but the serious understanding of the entire world as the arena of God's soteriological activity.[14] "Without apocalyptic a theological eschatology remains bogged down in the ethnic history of men or the existential history of the individual."[15]

But it is not that salvation is the end result of the progression of events in world history. The God of Jesus Christ who abruptly raised him from the dead is also the Creator who created the world *ex nihilo*.[16] He calls into being the things which were not, and brings to nothing the things which are (I Cor. 1:28). Since this kingdom is not of this world, the world causes the sufferings of Christians.[17] But it is this suffering which points to the "this worldly" nature of the kingdom. It cannot and must not be spiritualized. Nevertheless, in the midst of suffering, eschatology teaches the Christian that this is a world of possibilities, of change, not of the status quo. In this world we can "serve the future."[18]

Moltmann contrasts his view of eschatology and history with that of Karl Barth. Barth claims that "God can only be known

---

[11] Ibid., p. 50.
[12] Ibid., p. 47.
[13] Ibid., p. 136.
[14] Ibid., p. 137.
[15] Ibid.
[16] Ibid., p. 221.
[17] Ibid., p. 222.
[18] Ibid., p. 338.

through God" and that revelation can only be God's self-revelation. But this kind of language seriously devaluates history, in Moltmann's opinion.[19] Barth's "self-revelation" of God and his doctrine of the Trinity are based on God's eternity, not his historical interactions with humanity. Barth explicitly bases his doctrine of the Trinity on the lordship of God. What seems more important to Barth than understanding the Trinitarian life of God is seeing the Trinity as the revelation of a more basic, eternally present, lordship of God.[20]

Moltmann claims that "God can only be known through God" is not necessarily a Christian statement, but rather has sources in neoplatonic gnosticism, medieval mysticism, and Hegel's philosophy of religion.[21] Without any elaboration, this statement speaks of a God who as the Absolute simply reflects upon himself. This kind of God could not possibly be related to "that bundle of historical reports" concerning Jesus of Nazareth which is the basis of the Christian faith, but rather to an "esoteric gnosis."[22] In addition, Barth's emphasis upon the immanent doctrine of the Trinity is always in danger of leaving out the "eschatological character of the Holy Spirit, who is the Spirit of the resurrection of the dead."[23]

Although Barth later saw the importance of a "real end" to eschatology, he refused to allow it to influence his understanding of revelation. The "self-revelation" of God for Barth means that the "pure presence of God" is an "eternal presence of God in time," a "present without any future."[24] The result of this is that the resurrection of Christ is entirely "realized" eschatology. It does not point to something anticipated and awaited.

---

[19] Ibid., pp. 54-55.

[20] Ibid., p. 56.

[21] Ibid., p. 57.

[22] Ibid.

[23] Ibid.

[24] Karl Barth, *Church Dogmatics*, eds. G. W. Bromiley and T. F. Torrance (cited afterward as *CD*), I/2 (Edinburgh: T. & T. Clark, 1956), p. 114. Cf. Moltmann, *Theology of Hope*, pp. 57-58.

Promise and the Present

As we have seen, the language of Christianity is not *logos* but *promise*, according to Moltmann. Promise is the language centered in the reality of the resurrected Jesus. It is in the resurrected Jesus that God reveals himself in both *identity* with himself and in *differentiation* from himself.[25] In the crucifixion, the revelation of God is God in identity with himself. But the resurrection is the revelation of God in differentiation from himself, God as he will be in the future. "Through hope the life of believers is hidden with him in God—yet in a hiddenness that is made for future unveiling, and aims at it, and presses toward it."[26]

The nature of promise as the language of salvation is particularly seen in Israel.[27] The promise to Israel points to a reality which did not exist, providing a sense of history in which the power and faithfulness of God would be made manifest, despite evidences to the contrary in the life of Israel (e.g., the Babylonian captivity). The promised word, therefore, created a tension between the existing circumstances and the promised reality of the salvation of God.[28] This meant that a sphere of freedom was created in which Israel could obey or disobey God. But what was at stake in the promised word?

That which was at stake in the Old Testament concept of promises was also true in the New Testament: the dependability of God. The faithfulness of God is in his essence, not in his absoluteness.[29] This is what was at issue in Paul's discussion with the Galatians on promise versus law.[30] If promise was bound to the fulfillments of the law, then the promise would be invalidated (Gal. 3). The law would become the institutional form of unbelief, of not trusting in the dependability of God. The Christ event is "the validation of the promise" to Paul.[31]

---

25 Ibid., p. 87.
26 Ibid.
27 Ibid., p. 103.
28 Ibid., p. 104.
29 Ibid., p. 143.
30 Ibid., p. 145.
31 Ibid., p. 147.

It is crucial to see that Moltmann stresses the effect of the promised word upon the present. Through the promise, "the hidden future already announces itself and exerts its influence on the present through the hope it awakens."[32] However, as we have seen, the proclamations of promise are contrary to present experiences in a world of evil. "They do not result from experiences, but are the conditions for the possibility of new experiences."[33] Therefore, the imperative of the Pauline call to new life is not "merely... a summons to demonstrate the indicative of the new being in Christ," but it also has a definite eschatological aspect: "Hence it ought not to be rendered merely by the saying: 'become what you are!' but emphatically also by saying 'become what you shall be'"[34]

"The Risen Christ is and Remains the Crucified Christ"

What does it mean for the Christ event to be "the validation of the promise?" For Moltmann, it is Jesus Christ and his future who distinguishes eschatology from utopia.[35] Christian theology does not speak of the future as an abstract principle apart from the reality of Jesus Christ and his future.

Two propositions distinguish genuine Christology, according to Moltmann:[36] 1) The God who raised Jesus from the dead was *Yahweh*, the God of Abraham, Isaac, and Jacob, the God of promise. He is not to be confused with Parmenides' "eternal present" of Being, nor Plato's highest Idea, nor the Unmoved Mover of Aristotle. He is thoroughly eschatological and historical. 2) As a part of his context in eschatology and history, it mist be confessed unambiguously that Jesus was a Jew, with all the history and promises of the Old Testament standing behind him. Moltmann continues to emphasize his antipathy to the Greek static view of the being of God and his dedication to the Old Testament matrix of promise as the context for the Incarnation. For

---

32 Ibid., p. 18.
33 Ibid.
34 Ibid., p. 162.
35 Ibid., p. 17.
36 Ibid., pp. 141-142.

history to lose its eschatological dimension is for Moltmann a retreat from the real world in which humanity suffers and hopes.[37]
Therefore, when one speaks of the risen Christ, one must
automatically see his continuity with the crucified Christ. "The
risen Christ is and remains the crucified Christ."[38] In the cross
God experiences "the negation of himself." Therefore, it is quite
proper to speak of the God of the resurrection as an "a-theistic"
God. This is what Bonhoeffer meant when he said that God allows himself to be pushed out of the world, to be weak and powerless in the world, for that is the only way he can help us.[39] The
risen Christ is not simply clothed in "eternalized... heavenly
glory," but in "the foreglow of the coming, promised glory of
God."[40] The purpose of the Easter appearances was to give us a
glimpse of the eschatological Christ event, and therefore cause us
to seek the future revelation of this event.[41] The Spirit is born out
of the event of the resurrection as a pledge of the future of
Christ.[42] As a pledge, the Spirit provides the power for Christians
so that they might participate in the sufferings of Christ.[43]

The Crucified God

Moltmann, of course, elaborates much more on the place of
the cross in the sufferings of Christ in his book *The Crucified
God*. The crucial issue in this work is the question of the
impassivity of God. Moltmann presents a penetrating critique of
this doctrine. He sees its roots in Plato's description of the eternal
perfection of God as *apatheia*.[44] In Judaism and Christianity,
apatheia became the "higher divine sphere" of the Logos, unaf-

---

[37] Ibid., p. 158.

[38] Ibid., p. 171.

[39] Dietrich Bonhoeffer, *Letters and Papers from Prison*, the enlarged edition, trans. Reginald Fuller et al., ed. Eberhard Bethge (New York: Macmillan, 1971), pp. 360-361.

[40] Moltmann, *Theology of Hope*, p. 201.

[41] Ibid., p. 203.

[42] Ibid., p. 211.

[43] Ibid., p. 212.

[44] Moltmann, *The Crucified God*. p. 268.

fected by lower drives and compulsions.[45] But, building upon Abraham Heschel's study on the Hebrew prophets, Moltmann argues for the importance of the *pathos* of God.[46] The pathos of God in the prophets was God identifying with the situation of the people and, therefore, allowing himself to be affected by people and events. "The history of God cannot therefore be separated from the history of his people."[47] For Christians, this takes on a decidedly trinitarian color.[48] It is Christ who reveals the fatherhood of God and the power of the Spirit. "Through Christ, God himself creates the conditions of entering into that relationship of *pathos* and *sympatheia*."[49] Salvation means that God takes upon himself "the eternal death of the godless and the godforsaken," and they are therefore lifted up into life with Christ.[50] This makes it possible to accept life whole, including suffering and death.[51] This is the basis for Moltmann's claim that there would have been no "theology after Auschwitz," that is, retrospective sorrow and the recognition of guilt, apart from a "theology *in* Auschwitz."

> God in Auschwitz and Auschwitz in the crucified God—that is the basis for a real hope which both embraces and overcomes the world, and the ground for a love which is stronger than death and can sustain death.[52]

The Trinity as the Foundation for Human Freedom

One of Karl Barth's main comments on *Theology of Hope* was his opinion that it lacked a doctrine of the immanent Trinity. Barth complained that Moltmann subsumed all theology under the

---

45 Ibid., p. 269.
46 Ibid., p. 270.
47 Ibid.
48 Ibid., p. 275.
49 Ibid.
50 Ibid., p. 276.
51 Ibid., p. 277.
52 Ibid., p. 278.

principle of eschatology. This seems to create a truncated doctrine of God. As he put it to Moltmann personally in his usual inimitable way, "If you will pardon me, your God seems to me to be rather a pauper."[53] It does not seem too much to say that Barth's pointed criticism has led Moltmann to pursue the trinitarian dimensions of the theology, first, with *The Crucified God*, and then culminating with his work, *The Trinity and the Kingdom*.

As we have seen, Moltmann criticizes Barth's doctrine of the Trinity for being more concerned with maintaining the lordship of God than with working out the trinitarian development of God's self-revelation.[54] Such an immanent doctrine of the Trinity, in Moltmann's opinion, is always in danger of obscuring "the historical and eschatological character of the Holy Spirit, who is the Spirit of the resurrection of the dead."[55] Moltmann continues this line of thinking in *The Trinity and the Kingdom* when he claims that an immanent Trinity "in which God is simply by himself, and without the love which communicates salvation," denies the Christian concept of God.[56] Doxology teaches us that the immanent Trinity cannot be thought of apart from the economic Trinity. The workings of the Triune God are found within the praise and worship of the church: "Glory be to the Father and to the Son and to the Holy Ghost!"[57] Therefore, one must not develop a doctrine of God apart from knowledge of his saving works, nor to speak of salvation apart from its foundation in God.[58] So, creation in the Spirit can become a critique of a monarchial lordship of the Trinity "which corresponds best to the ecological doctrine of creation which we are looking for and need

---

[53] Karl Barth, *Letters, 1961-1968*, ed. Jürgen Fangmeier and Hinrich Stoevesandt; trans. and ed. Geoffrey W. Bromiley (Grand Rapids: Eerdmans, 1980), pp. 175-176.

[54] Moltmann, *Theology of Hope*, p. 56.

[55] Ibid., p. 57.

[56] Moltmann, *The Trinity and the Kingdom*, p. 151.

[57] Ibid., p. 152.

[58] Ibid., p. 153.

today," rejecting the mechanistic chauvinistic domination of God as Father.[59]

The Trinity sharply defines salvation as the process of drawing creation into the eternal life of God "with all the fullness of its relationships."[60] Unity with the Triune God is not to be found in God as "one, single, homogeneous divine essence (*substantia*). or in the one identical, absolute subject," but in the fullness of life seen in the eternal *perichoresis* of the Trinity. This means nothing less than the Trinity's self-openness to the unification of all creation. Therefore, creation is not to be simply distinguished from the creator. "Creation is also the differentiated presence of God the Spirit, the presence of the One *in* the Many."[61] God is the creator of the world, not the cause of it. We know this because of the Spirit whose relationship to creation should be viewed as "an intricate web of unilateral, reciprocal, and many-sided relationships."[62]

What does this trinitarian salvation look like? For Moltmann, it means that a community is created in which true human freedom is realized. The fellowship of the Father, the Son and the Holy Spirit does not correspond to "the solitary human subject in his relationship to himself," nor a human individual lording over the world. The true correspondence is found in a human fellowship which forsakes its privileges and hierarchies, and loves one another with open-mindedness. In fact, one may say that the more openminded a people are with one another, the more it can be said that they are one with the Triune God (Jn. 17:21).[63] In contrast to the "religiously motivated monotheism" of history, which has been used to legitimate oppression, the doctrine of the Trinity is the basis for true human freedom expressed as "a community of men and women without supremacy and without subjection."[64]

---

[59] Jürgen Moltmann, *God in Creation: A New Theology of Creation and the Spirit of God,* trans. Margaret Kohl (San Francisco: Harper and Row, 1985), p. 12.

[60] Ibid., p. 157.

[61] Moltmann, *God in Creation*, p. 14.

[62] Ibid.

[63] Ibid., p. 158.

[64] Ibid., p. 192.

Personality and sociality are harmonized without sacrificing one for the other.[65]

The Church and the "Trinitarian History of God's Dealings with the World"

Moltmann firmly grounds the nature of the church on its foundation in Christ.[66] As Christ's church, it must proclaim the tradition of "messianic liberation" and "eschatological renewal of the world," yet as a tradition which is always open to change.[67] As Christ's church, it must not surrender to a purely sociological or historical analysis, but must find its moorings in a theological concept of the church.[68] This will find the foundation of the church in the "trinitarian history of God's dealings with the world."[69] Therefore, a theological criterion is established to judge the church's actions, not merely to justify them.

It is on the subject of the church that Moltmann deals most directly with the problem of the reality of salvation. This is traditionally seen in ecclesiology as the tension between faith and experience, the church as an ideal and the church in practice.[70] Three possible solutions are perennially raised: 1) "paradoxical identity," 2) "the anticipation of hope," and 3) "sacramental identification," in each of which Moltmann finds partial, yet incomplete, truth.

1) "Paradoxical identity": This line of argument is analogous to the Lutheran doctrine of justification. The church is "at the same time" an eschatological and historical reality, just as the individual Christian is *simul justus, simul peccator*.[71] Therefore, what is

---

[65] Ibid., p. 199.
[66] Moltmann, *The Church in the Power of the Spirit*, xiv.
[67] Ibid., p. 3.
[68] Ibid., p. 4.
[69] Ibid., p. 5.
[70] Ibid., p. 20.
[71] Ibid., p. 22.

meant by the church's unity, holiness, and catholicity is not an analysis of what is, but a statement about what will be.[72]

2) "The anticipation of hope": The church is also the object of both hope and experience.[73] This is closely related to Jesus' theology of the kingdom of God. "Christ made the church at the same time possible and impossible."[74] The church is possible because of Jesus' gracious offer of the kingdom. It is impossible because "the people presses on beyond itself to this all-fulfilling kingdom."[75] Therefore, the church has a temporary nature, dependent upon both the inauguration and fulfillment of the kingdom of God.

3) "Sacramental identification": Sacramental identification links together the redemptive events of the past with the present existence of the church. The church can only understand itself, not on a phenomenological basis, but on the basis of the preached human word which is the Word of God, the presence of the eschatological Christ in the bread and the wine, and the coming of the Spirit in baptism.[76] But how can this sacramental efficacy be understood? How can the common bread, the common wine, relate to the "bundle of historical reports" concerning Jesus of Nazareth? It is at this point that one sees the partial truth of all of these answers: The sacramental event cannot be "created" or "calculated," in order to explain the problem of faith and experience. The solution has to be found in *pneumatology*.[77] It is only through the "perception," the "awareness" and the "fellowship" of the Holy Spirit that we know the "history" of Christ.

Moltmann understands the Spirit of fellowship and freedom from sin to be the same Spirit which is the "creative urge" embracing all of history.[78] The church needs to understand itself as a part of this history of the Spirit, existing in the tension between

---

[72] Ibid., p. 23.
[73] Ibid., p. 24.
[74] Ibid.
[75] Ibid.
[76] Ibid., p. 26.
[77] Ibid., p. 27.
[78] Ibid., p. 34.

faith and experience, but nonetheless, it is still "the concrete form in which men experience the history of Christ" and, in a long term sense, it is the entrance into the kingdom of God.[79] Nevertheless, it is imperative to see the church as standing in the midst of the Triune God's dealings with the world, but not as its fulcrum.[80] The Spirit is over the church because of his eternal procession from the Father and the Son. An experience of the Spirit is an experience of God, the God who makes himself open to humanity in history. "In the sending of the Son and the Spirit, the Trinity does not only manifest what it is in itself; it also opens itself for history and experience of history."[81]

WOLFHART PANNENBERG

The Knowledge and Idea of God

Pannenberg, who sees salvation from an eschatological perspective, has both great similarities and dissimilarities with the other prominent eschatological theologian, Jürgen Moltmann.[82] He is particularly concerned with the modern world's lack of need for, or lack of recognition of, the idea of God. "The idea of God is no longer the absolute and indispensable foundation of our life and

---

[79] Ibid., p. 35.

[80] Ibid., pp. 52-53.

[81] Ibid., p. 56.

[82] The primary source for Pannenberg on the reality of salvation is *Faith and Reality*, trans. John Maxwell (Philadelphia: Westminster Press, 1977); other major works by Pannenberg include *Revelation as History* (ed.) trans. David Granskou (New York: Macmillan, 1968); *Basic Questions in Theology*, 2 vols., trans. George H. Kehm (London: SCM Press, 1970); *Jesus — God and Man,* trans. Lewis L. Wilkins and Duane A. Priebe (Philadelphia: Westminster Press, 1968); *Theology and the Philosophy of Science,* trans. Francis McDonagle (London: Darton, Longman, and Todd, 1976); *Ethics*, trans. Keith Crim (Philadelphia: Westminster Press, 1981); *The Church*, trans. Keith Crim (Philadelphia: Westminster Press, 1983); *Anthropology in Theological Perspective*, trans. Matthew J. O'Connell (Philadelphia: Westminster Press, 1985). Standard studies on Pannenberg include E. Frank Tupper, *The Theology of Wolfhart Pannenberg* (Philadelphia: Westminster Press, 1973), and Carl Braaten and Philip Clayton, eds., *The Theology of Wolfhart Pannenberg* (Minneapolis: Augsburg, 1988).

behavior in the world."[83] Although our tendency is to retreat and
to jealously guard our traditions, that is only a temporary victory.
Perhaps the problem is not so much the idea of God, but the *traditional* idea of God.[84] Perhaps the reality of God is something quite
different than the sense of One who is the first cause of the world.

The primary place of humanity over nature, life, and history
has supplanted the place of God in modern thinking.[85] The result
of these human investigations has left behind "the essential reality
that applies to life in general: namely, that individual life can be
fulfilled only if it transcends itself in time and in space."[86]
Humanity must become conscious of the "miracle" of nature, life,
and history.

Reality and History

Pannenberg argues that "reality" must not be simply restricted to the mere presence of things, but to that which is definitely essential and that concerns life as a whole, "the highest degree of reality is found at the level of which there is a complete
unity of all reality that can be experienced by us."[87]

Although the biblical concept of reality changed in details
throughout the different canonical books, one can still say that
there is continuity found in "the history of God and his dealings
with men."[88] In fact, Pannenberg claims that history is a legacy
from the biblical tradition. History means that Israel was to be always open to Yahweh, open to future possibilities, not held captive to a Greek concept of "order." Modern views of progress are
based upon the Israelite view of the unity of history as dependent
upon God.[89]

---

83 Pannenberg, *Faith and Reality*, p. 1.

84 Ibid., p. 2.

85 Ibid.

86 Ibid., p. 6.

87 Ibid., p. 7.

88 Ibid., p. 8.

89 Ibid., pp. 9-10.

Pannenberg faces the problem of the hiddenness of God very frankly.[90] Although humanity cannot cease to ask questions about God, it is evident that this is because God is quite unlike anything we know. Certainly the Old Testament was aware of this: "No one can see God and live" (Ex. 33:20). Therefore, one should not say that revelation is to be equated with theophanies. "If a human being meets us, it does not necessarily mean that he discloses his very self to us."[91] Revelation to Israel was an indirect proceeding. Yahweh does not restrict revelation to a few chosen persons.[92] Indeed, revelation is known only at the *completion* of the events:

> And Israel saw the great work which the Lord did against the Egyptians, and the people feared the Lord; and they believed in the Lord and in his servant Moses (Ex. 14:31).

But has not history continued its course since the time of Jesus? This is the place of Jesus as a man of Jewish apocalyptic, according to Pannenberg. The end times spoken of in apocalyptic literature have already taken place in a human being, by his resurrection from the dead.[93] This is the definitive self-disclosure of God and the meaning of the Trinity for Pannenberg. The Spirit reveals the oneness between the Father and the Son, i.e. the being of God, through the resurrection of Jesus.[94]

But the working of God should not be restricted to a special sense of "salvation history," according to Pannenberg. God uses "pagan" instruments such as the Enlightenment and science and technology to promote his goal of "spiritual unity." We should be looking for new forms of the unification of humanity, beginning with the job of unifying a disunited church.[95]

---

[90] Ibid., p. 16.
[91] Ibid., p. 50.
[92] Ibid., p. 51.
[93] Ibid., p. 231.
[94] Ibid., p. 232.
[95] Ibid., p. 60.

Thus, God is certainly different from the world, but not out-side it.[96] But when God does reveal himself, it happens in the world. "History is God acting in his creation. Therefore history cannot be fully understood without God."[97] This continuum be-tween salvation history and world history has great implications for both ethics and spirituality. Christians can act in their own particular situation without two sets of ethical principles, one secular and one religious.[98] If Jesus' resurrection is the fulfillment of the world, then Christian spirituality will be motivated to trans-form every aspect of the present in light of this reality.[99] "God is not seen as acting in competition with man in history, but through human action, both in its success and failure."[100]

Since God works in the context of "ordinary" not "salvation history, "the historical method and its results are of utmost impor-tance for theology. Christianity is not simply for the credulous. It must be able to stand up to verification, verification not just of a narrow personal experience, but of a wide public criterion.[101] The modern thinking person has no other choice. We live in a world transformed by historical thinking, transformed from the old ways of authoritarian ways of thought.[102] As an outgrowth of the rise of modern science and the discovery of the Newtonian mechanistic universe of cause and effect relationships, a new sense of the unity of truth was uncovered. So, for the modern person, since there is a "unity of the reality in which we live," truth can only be one.[103] The historical method affirms that oneness of truth as it examines the contingent facts of existence, acknowledging that what was once considered to be an immutable truth is now known to be a

---

96   Ibid., pp. 85-86.

97   Ibid., p. 87.

98   Ibid.

99   Ibid., p. 89.

100   Ibid., p. 129.

101   Wolfhart Pannenberg, *The Apostles' Creed in the Light of Today's Questions,* trans. Margaret Kohl (Philadelphia: Westminster Press, 1972), p. 35.

102   Herbert Neie, *The Doctrine of the Atonement in the Theology of Wolfhart Pannenberg* (Berlin, New York: De Gruyter, 1978), pp. 90-91.

103   Pannenberg, *Basic Questions in Theology,* vol. 2, pp. 1ff.

natural effect of a natural cause. No longer can one simply understand the Reformation, for example, as an act of God (or, the
devil!), but as an historical movement naturally explained by historical forces in the late Middle Ages. Pannenberg argues, one
must face up to this world and its way of thinking. This is true in
at least three crucial theological concerns: 1) anthropology , 2)
Israel and Christology, and 3) salvation.

Anthropology must go beyond the study of simply human
salvation. This is one of the great limitations of Karl Barth. Barth
certainly saw the danger of theologians who are only concerned
with themselves and not God, the true subject of theology. Yet can
the historically minded theologian begin theological reflection
without an understanding of the fundamental anthropological concensus in non-theological studies?[104] Otherwise, the theologian is
simply playing into the hands of the atheistic critics' arguments
about belief in God as pure subjectivity. If a criterion of "universal
validity" does not exist, all the theological talk about "the Godness
of God" is useless and even counterproductive.

So also, when a theologian turns to biblical religion, to Israel
and Jesus Christ, such a concern for universal validity must be
maintained. This is the place of the historical method and its hard
work of sifting contingent evidence in order to lead to the truth
concerning God's revelation to Israel, and then in Christ. This is
what one finds woven within the theology of the Hebrew Bible
(Ex. 14:31). Thus it was "the evidence of historical facts that
brought about salvation and revealed Jehovah's deity and
power,"[105] an "indirect revelation" of Yahweh's deity through his
acts.[106] A similar concern, *mutatis mutandis,* exists in
Pannenberg's approach to Christology. Well known for his advo-
cacy of a Christology from "below," Pannenberg gives three reasons for rejecting a Christology from "above," the traditional approach of the ecumenical creeds:[107] 1) Such a view presupposes
the divinity of Jesus. This is not something to be assumed but ob-

---

[104] Pannenberg, *Anthropology in Theological Perspective,* pp. 15ff.

[105] Pannenberg, "Dogmatic Theses on the Doctrine of Revelation," in
Revelation as History, p. 126.

[106] Ibid., p. 128.

[107] Pannenberg, *Jesus-God and Man,* pp. 34-35.

viously needs to be proven, if such an astounding claim is true. 2)
The Jewishness of Jesus is underestimated in such a Christology;
and 3) A Christology from "above" assumes that one can stand in
the position of God himself. Rather, the only human perspective is
the perspective from "below," from historical existence.
Therefore, one must begin with the "historical singularity" of the
man Jesus. Beginning with historical questions about the man
Jesus postpones any concern with soteriology, as is frequently
found in the history of theology. To do otherwise would be to expose oneself to a great danger:

> Has one really spoken then about Jesus himself at all?
> Does it perhaps rather involve projections onto Jesus'
> figure of the human desire for salvation and deifica-
> tion, of human striving after similarity to God, of the
> human duty to bring satisfaction for sins committed, of
> human experience of bondage in failure, in the knowl-
> edge of one's own guilt. And most clearly in neo-
> protestantism, projection of the idea of perfect reli-
> giousity, of perfect morality, of pure personality radi-
> cal trust?[108]

What needs to be established first, by historical investigation, is
the possibility of the unity of Jesus with God.[109] This is validated
by the resurrection of Jesus from the dead. But, the resurrection of
Jesus not only is the unity between Jesus and God established, but
so also does the power of the future come into the present, when
"the end of history is experienced in advance as anticipation."[110]
The meaning of Jesus is only known "retroactively," from the
perspective of the end of his life, the resurrection. Meaning lies
only in the future vindication. Yet, it is not without meaning for
the present because of its "retroactive" power. Therefore, we
know that Jesus has always been one with God.[111]

---

[108] Ibid., p. 47.

[109] Ibid., pp. 38ff.

[110] Pannenberg, "Dogmatic Theses on the Doctrine of Revelation," in
Revelation as History, p. 134.

[111] Pannenberg, *Jesus-God and Man* p. 136.

The power of the future and its implications for the meaning of Jesus reflect Pannenberg's ontology, based on anthropological observations. Ideas are not based on a speculative, timeless view of the essential in a thing (Aristotle). The future is, rather, unpredictable and open.

> Then the essence of a man, of a situation, or even of the world in general is not yet to be perceived from what is nonvisible. Only the future will decide it.[112]

Not only does the future affect the meaning of Jesus, but God himself is also known in terms of the future then, because of the resurrection of Jesus. Since the resurrected Christ is also the historical Jesus from "below," his message of the kingdom of God helps define one's doctrine of God. As Pannenberg states, this is "to believe that one power dominates all."[113] If this is true, then

> in a restricted but important sense God does not yet exist. Since his rule and his being are inseparable, God's being is still in process of coming to be. Consider this, God should not be mistaken for an objectified being presently existing in its fullness.[114]

Or, as Pannenberg states it elsewhere, "He is God only in the execution of his lordship and this full accomplishment of his lordship is determined as something future."[115]

All of this, however, must be understood in terms of Pannenberg's belief in the "retroactive" power of the future. This does not mean that God is only in the future. "Quite the contrary, as the power of the future he dominates the remotest past."[116] "Only in the future of his kingdom come will the statement 'God exists'

---

[112] Ibid.

[113] Pannenberg, *Theology and the Kingdom of God* (Philadelphia: Westminster Press, 1969), p. 55.

[114] Ibid., p. 112.

[115] Pannenberg, *Basic Questions in Theology,* Vol. 2, p. 240.

[116] Pannenberg, *Theology and the Kingdom of God,* p. 62.

prove to be definitely true. But then it will be clear. Thus the statement will always be true."[117]

The path, then, is cleared for Pannenberg to speak of the nature of salvation and atonement. The implications of Jesus' death on the cross must also pass the test of Pannenberg's historical method. And the criterion of meaning is completely in terms of whether of not the cross is compatible with the contemporary *Wirklichkeit-Verstandhis*. Does the cross of Christ make a difference to reality?[118]

Such a meaning in the context of reality can be found in the Jewish understanding of the just man who suffers for his people, based on the Hebrew view of the interwovenness of the individual into the whole fabric of society.[119] This is buttressed by the teaching of modern anthropology on the interconnectedness of human beings. "Substitution is a universal phenomenon."[120]

Pannenberg's startling statement that "in a restricted sense, God does not yet exist" is not softened or explained away by his caveat that "the power of the future" has a "retroactive" force. One wonders whether the "future" has been elevated to a Hegelian pedestal as a principle controlling the doctrine of God. For Pannenberg, there is no place for the *a priori* humanity of God, the Triune God, to act in grace, both epistemologically and soteriologically. Pannenberg's God is already defined in terms of absolute power, not in terms of his self-revelation as a triune unity and relationship of eternal love, the humanity of God as the basis for the humanity of man.[121] Without a *prior* God, can there be any hope of a *future* God, not to mention *present* God? The latter becomes obviously important when we seek to ask the question of the reality of salvation today. When Pannenberg does use trinitarian concepts it is in terms of a "clarification" of "the creative arrival

---

117 Ibid.
118 Neie, *The Doctrine of the Atonement in the Theology of Wolfhart Pannenberg*, pp. 129-130.
119 Pannenberg, *Jesus- God and Man*, p. 268.
120 Ibid.
121 Pannenberg, *Theology and the Kingdom of God*, p. 112.

of this powerful future in the event of love."[122] It seems almost anti-climactic when Pannenberg says, "The trinitarian idea of God is congruous with historical process, when the notion of a supreme entity speaks of a 'divine thing' outside man's history."[123] Certainly, the humanity of God is a problem if it remains simply *Deus absconditus,* but, as we shall argue, that is the reason for the vicarious humanity of Christ as the "external expression" of the "eternal" humanity of God.

"The Spirit of Life"

The Spirit has been traditionally viewed in a soteriological sense as the principle of the new life in faith. Pannenberg seeks to revive its place in the creative order (Gen. 2:7; I Cor. 15:45).[124]In the history of theology, the Spirit has increasingly been restricted to personal piety (Pietism).[125] Paul Tillich and Pierre Teilhard de Chardin have revived the idea of the Spirit as "the amazing power of all life" and Pannenberg accepts this with some modification.[126] The distinctiveness of the human being is the advanced stage he represents with his reflective mind.[127] This is human self-transcendence as "a new stage of participation in the power of the Spirit."[128] The experience of the Spirit is not an independent experience apart from the totality of world history.[129] Such an experience is not needed in order to come to know God in Jesus. In fact, it is the other way around; "the Spirit is present when anyone recognizes Jesus' life-history as a revelation of God."[130]

---

[122] Ibid., p. 70.
[123] Ibid., p. 71.
[124] Pannenberg, *Faith and Reality,* p. 134.
[125] Ibid., pp. 20-22.
[126] Ibid., p. 25.
[127] Ibid., p. 27.
[128] Ibid., p. 36.
[129] Ibid.
[130] Ibid., p. 65.

CHAPTER THREE .

SALVATION AS UNIVERSALISM:
JOHN HICK

One outstanding exponent in recent years of a Christian theology based on sensitivity to and dialogue between Christianity
and other religions has been John Hick.[1] Hick represents a kind of

---

[1] Hick's most concise statement on Christianity and world religions is *God Has
Many Names* (Philadelphia: Westminster Press, 1983), which we will look at in
detail. He has also discussed the issue in *God and the Universe of Faiths*
(London: Macmillan, 1973); *Death and Eternal Life* (London: Collins, 1976);
Evil and the God of Love (London: Macmillan, 1966); "Jesus and the World
Religions," in *The Myth of God Incarnate,* ed. John Hick (London: SCM Press,
1977); *Truth and Dialogue on World Religions: Conflicting Truth Claims,*
(editor) (Philadelphia: Westminster Press, 1974); *Christianity and Other
Religions,* eds. John Hick and Brian Hebblethwaite (Philadelphia: Fortress
Press, 1981); *Why Believe in God?* (with Michael Goulder) (London: SCM
Press, 1983); "Only One Way to God?," *Theology* 86 (March, 1983), pp. 128-
129; "Christianity in an Age of Religious Pluralism," *Journal of Theology for
South Africa* 35 (June, 1981), pp. 4-9; "Is There Only One Way to God?"
Theology 85 (January 1982), pp. 4-7; "On Grading Religions," *Religious
Studies* 17 (December, 1981), pp. 451-467; "Pluralism and the Reality of the
Transcendent: How My Mind Has Changed," *Christian Century* 98 (January 21,
1981), pp. 45-48; "Learning From Other Faiths IX: The Christian View of Other
Faiths," *The Expository Times* 84 (November 1972), pp. 36-39; and "The
Philosophy of World Religions," *Scottish Journal of Theology* 37, no. 2
(1984), pp. 229-236; and, most recently, *An Interpretation of Religion: Human
Responses to the Transcendent,* (New Haven: Yale University Press, 1989).
Hick has been critiqued by Philip L. Aland, "John Hick's "Copernican
Theology," *Theology* 86 (January 1983), pp. 36-41; Peter D. Byrne, "John
Hick's Philosophy of World Religions: *Scottish Journal of Theology* 35, no. 4

soteriology which is actually a strong polemic against the exclusive claims of traditional Christianity. Grounded in the validity of universal religious experiences, regardless of the particular religion, Hick's soteriology is a theology of tolerance above everything else.

RELIGIOUS EXPERIENCE: THE CONTEXT OF SALVATION

Hick frankly admits that it was his experience with other religions and appreciation of their experiences which has determined the form and content of his theology of salvation. As he began to attend the worship services of other faiths in the cultural melting pot of Birmingham, England, it became evident to him that "essentially the same kind of thing" was occurring in their religious experiences as in the Christianity which he knew.[2] This same experience consisted of "human beings opening their minds to a higher divine Reality, known as personal and good and as demanding righteousness and love between man and man."[3] This creates a major crisis for Christianity, in his opinion. If Christianity alone is true among all other religions, that means that other faiths are false. This would mean that the majority of humanity are walking in darkness. This is untenable for Hick.[4]

The issue of religious experience is the center of Hick's soteriology. The basic issue in the philosophy of religion is simply

---

(1982), pp. 289-301; J. Lipner, "Christians and the Uniqueness of Christ," *Scottish Journal of Theology* 28, no. 4 (1975), pp. 359-368; Duncan B. Forrester "Professor Hick and The Universe of Faiths," *Scottish Journal of Theology* 29, no. 1 (1976), pp. 65-72; Julius Lipner, "Truth Claims and Interreligious Dialogue," *Religious Studies* 12 (June, 1976), pp. 217-230; Max Warren, "Uniqueness of Christ," *Modern Churchman* 18 (Winter, 1974), pp. 55-66; Chester Gillis, *A Question of Final Belief: John Hick's Pluralistic Theory of Salvation* (New York: St. Martin's Press), 1988; Roger Trigg, "Religion and the Threat of Relativism," *Religious Studies* 19, (1983), pp. 297-310, and Gavin D'Costa, *John Hick's Theology of Religions: A Critical Evaluation* (Lanham, MD: University Press of America, 1987).

[2] Hick, *God Has Many Names,* p. 18.
[3] Ibid.
[4] Ibid., pp. 79-80.

the question of the meaning of religious experience.[5] Is religious experience merely a "modification" of human consciousness, generated by purely natural reasons, or does it arise from contact with "supramundane reality" and have implications for ultimate meaning?[6]

Hick responds to this challenge by stressing 1) the structural continuity of religious experience with other spheres of reality. and 2) an openness to experimental confirmation.[7] "Meaning" is the key concept which links religious and mundane experience. "Meaning" for Hick is seen in the difference which a particular conscious act makes for an individual. This, of course, is relative to any particular individual.[8] Verification of this experience is eschatological because of the universal belief in all religions that the universe is in a process leading toward a state of perfection.[9]

The epistemological basis for such an approach is found in the philosophy of Immanuel Kant. Hick's soteriology is based on "Kant's broad theme, recognizing the mind's own positive contribution to the character of its perceived environment," which "has been massively confirmed as an empirical thesis by modern work in cognition and social psychology and in the sociology of knowledge."[10] The Kantian phenomena in this case are the varied experiences of religion. All have their obvious limitations in finite humanity, so none are absolutely true.

In contrast to Kant, however, Hick believes that the "noumenal" world is reached by the "phenomenal" world of religious experience. "The Eternal One" is "the divine noumenon" experienced in many different "phenomena." So the divine can be experienced, but only under certain limitations faced by the phenomenal world.[11] Many appropriate responses can be made to "the divine noumenon." But these responses are as many as the

---

[5] Ibid.
[6] Ibid., p. 80.
[7] Ibid.
[8] Ibid.
[9] Ibid., p. 82.
[10] Hick, *An Interpretation of Religion,* p. 240.
[11] Hick, *God Has Many Names,* p. 84.

different cultures and personalities which represent the world in which we live.[12] Similar to Wittgenstein's epistemology of "seeing-as," Hick sees a continuity between ordinary experience and religious experience which he calls "experiencing-as".[13]

The goal of all these religious experiences is the same, Hick contends: "the transformation of human existence from self-centeredness to Reality-centeredness."[14] This transformation cannot be restated to any one tradition.[15]

> When I meet a devout Jew, or Muslim, or Sikh, or Hindu, or Buddhist in whom the fruits of openness to the divine Reality are gloriously evident, I cannot realistically regard the Christian experience of the divine as authentic and their non-Christian experiences as inauthentic.[16]

RELIGIOUS EXPERIENCES OF WORLD RELIGIONS: THE BREADTH OF SALVATION

If religious experience is the context of salvation for Hick, then the religious experiences of world religions manifest the breadth of salvation for him. Hick maintains that there are three traditional approaches to the relationship between Christianity and other faiths: 1) "The phase of total rejection." In the Catholic tradition, this has meant consigning all non-Catholics to hell, as seen in the papal pronouncement of Boniface VIII in 1302, who says "that to submit to the Roman Pontiff is, for every human creature, an utter necessity of salvation."[17] The Protestant Karl Barth is equally as strong when he says that Christianity

---

12 Hick, *An Interpretation of Religion,* p. 248.
13 John Hick, *Faith and Knowledge,* second edition (Glasgow: Collins, 1978), p. 142.
14 Ibid., p. 36.
15 Hick, *Problems of Religious Pluralism*, p. 32.
16 Ibid., p. 91.
17 Denzinger, H., *The Sources of Catholic Dogma,* trans. Roy J. Deferarri (St. Louis: B. Herder, 1957), no. 468. Cited by Hick, *God Has Many Names,* p. 8.

alone has the commission and the authority to be a missionary religion, i.e. to confront the world of religions as the one true religion, with absolute self-confidence to invite and challenge it to abandon its ways and to start on the Christian way.[18]

2) "The phase of the early epicycles." This phase still believes that only Catholics can be saved, but it allows clemency for those who for reasons of circumstances were never exposed to Catholicism. In analogy to the doctrine of transubstantiation, they are not Catholics, according to human observation, as the bread and the wine of the Mass are ordinary bread and ordinary wine, but in their metaphysical substance they are Catholics without knowing it.[19]

3) In "the phase of the later epicycles," as long as one experiences liberation, renewal, new creation, or authentic human existence, then they can be called "anonymous Christians" (Karl Rahner).[20] One form of this later epicycle does not have a "this-life" restriction: It may be that in the next life all people will accept Christ as Savior and Lord, if they have not done so already.[21] Although this is attractive to Hick, it still denies the presence of salvation outside of Christianity.[22] It is Hick's contention that the breadth of salvation must include all major religious faiths, since all point to the same "higher divine Reality," which demands righteousness and love between human beings.[23]

This does not mean that the particularities of religions must be abolished. The scriptures, the liturgies, creedal belief, stories of saints and heroes, all provide the "life" and "power" which nourishes the faiths.[24] But it must be recognized that the other religious traditions can enrich our own. It is this mutual enrichment which is at the heart of Hick's soteriology. It is true that Hick hastens to

---

18 Barth, CD I/2, p. 357. Cited by Hick, *God Has Many Names*, p. 8.
19 Ibid,. pp. 31-32.
20 Ibid., pp. 33-34.
21 Ibid., p. 35.
22 Ibid., pp.35-36.
23 Ibid., p. 18.
24 Ibid., p. 21.

add that some religious traditions are "more adequate" than others.[25] He would admit that some primitive expressions are "eccentric, repulsive, horrible, or destructive."[26]

GOD: THE CENTER OF SALVATION

Hick proposes a "Copernican revolution" in the Christian understanding of other faiths. No longer should we consider religions from a "Christianity-centered" paradigm, but rather from a "God-centered" paradigm.[27] In the universe of faiths, we find differing responses to the same Reality. The Reality remains the same, but the various religions show us that there can be varied responses to the same Reality. This is the basic weakness of the traditional theologies of religions: their doctrine of God.[28] To say that the majority of humanity is bound for hell is contrary to the Christian doctrine of God as loving and benevolent. The other more modern alternatives are certainly better, but lack a certain respect for the particularity of each religion and the mutual enrichment which they can experience among each other.

In his most recent writings, Hick favors calling the transcendental reality "the Real," which he prefers even to "the Divine" or "the Eternal One." The latter are "perhaps too theistically coloured."[29]. This allows the question of the personal or non-personal nature of the Real to remain open. Hick anticipates the problem of the great gap between a personal and impersonal God, such as the personal God of Christianity and the impersonal God of Hinduism. This he sees in terms of the Hindu distinction between Nirguna Brahman, the God who is "the eternal self-existent divine reality" and Saguna Brahman, the God who is "God in relation to his creator," who possesses such "communicable attributes" as personality and goodness. Both can exist.[30]

---

25 Ibid., pp. 25-26.
26 Ibid.
27 Ibid., pp. 18-19. Cf. Hick, *God and the Universe of Faiths.*
28 Hick, *God Has Many Names,* p. 31.
29 Hick, *An Interpretation of Religion,* pp. 10-11.
30 Hick, *God and the Universe of Faiths,* p. 144.

Given the influence of Kant, epistemological issues concerning God have always been a concern of Hick's. Thus, early in his career, he suggested a response to the challenge of the linguistic analysis school of philosophy, and their concerns for verification, which he titled "eschatological verification." Verification should be taken seriously, Hick agrees, but the greatest and most appropriate verification for an experience of God is to participate in the fulfillment of the knowledge of God in the afterlife, which most religions promise.[31] Christianity, at least, cannot be falsifiable because its fulfillment lies in the future.[32] This is at the heart of Hick's well known "Irenaean" theology, based on the faith that good will triumph in the end. In the consummation, sin and evil will be seen as vital to the "soul-making" program of God. This also gives some credence to belief in reincarnation as part of this gradual and often difficult pilgrimage of "soul-making." All of this will be vindicated in the afterlife.[33] Verification of divine truth will always be asymmetrical. As long as the divine purpose remains unfulfilled, we cannot fulfill it. It may well be fulfilled in the future.[34]

INCARNATION AS METAPHOR: THE CHRISTIAN MANIFESTATION OF SALVATION

What, then, is the place of Christology in Hick's soteriology? For Hick, the reinterpretation of the Incarnation is central. He puts it frankly: If Jesus was God Incarnate, "it is then very hard to escape from the traditional view that all mankind must be converted to the Christian faith."[35] But the Incarnation can still have a place in Hick's universalistic soteriology if one considers

---

[31] Hick, *An Interpretation of Religion*, pp. 177ff.

[32] John Hick, *The Center of Christianity*, (San Francisco: Harper and Row 1978), pp. 97-103.

[33] Ibid., p. 83, 85, 116.

[34] John Hick, "Theology and Verification," *Theology Today*, 17 (1960), pp. 12-31, reprinted in *The Logic of God: Theology and Verification*, ed. Malcolm L. Diamond and Thomas V. Litzenburg (Indianapolis: Bobbs-Merrill, 1971), p. 204.

[35] Ibid., p. 19.

the Incarnation "metaphorically rather than literally, as an essentially poetic expression of the Christian's devotion to his Lord."[36]
Two facts necessitate this need for a new doctrine of the Incarnation:[37] 1) It is "most certain" that the historical Jesus did not consider himself to be God, and 2) the insoluble problem which Christian theologians have had over the years concerning how the infinite God can partake of finite humanity. The "metaphorical" interpretation of the Incarnation is something we are thoroughly familiar with: Jesus is "God Incarnate" in the sense that he "incarnated in human life the selfless acts of love which made manifest his full openness to God." Therefore, Incarnation does not have to mean sharing the same substance or being as God. "Agape is incarnated in human life whenever someone acts in selfless love; and this occurred in the life of Jesus to a startling and epoch-making degree."[38] The specific purpose of God is the promotion of *agape*. Christians see the *agape* of God in one sense, in Jesus.[39] True to his foundation on religious experience, Hick sees the knowledge of God from deeds, not an abstract view of divine substance. The "historicization" of God in Jesus Christ is more apt than "incarnation."[40] "Let us proclaim *homoagape* rather than *homoousia!*" cries Hick. For while we know what is meant by love, "substance" is incomprehensible and irrelevant.[41] Such an interaction between the divine and the human is the real meaning of Christology. Following Donald Baillie and G. Lampe, Hick claims that, in Jesus Christ, both divine initiative and human response came together. But such a "paradox" is not unique to Jesus. It can occur in any human being, and does, in differing degrees.[42]

---

36 Ibid. Cf. Hick, "Jesus and the World Religions," in *The Myth of God Incarnate.*

37 Hick, *God Has Many Names*, p. 28.

38 Ibid.

39 Hick, *God and the Universe of Faiths*, p. 152.

40 John Hick, "Christology at the Crossroads," in *Prospects for Theology*, ed. F. Healey (London: James Nesbit, 1966), p. 153.

41 Ibid., p. 16.

42 John Hick, "An Inspiration Christology for a Religiously Plural World, " in Stephen T. Davis, ed. *Encountering Jesus*, pp. 5-21.

CHAPTER FOUR

SALVATION AS HUMANIZATION:
HANS KÜNG

CHRISTIANITY AS RADICAL HUMANISM

Hans Küng, noted for his censure as a Roman Catholic theologian, presents a soteriology which is very much a social critique as well as a search for common ground with the modern world.[1] It is at the point of humanism that Küng finds such a

---

[1] Küng's most detailed statement on his soteriology is found in *On Being A Christian*, trans. Edward Quinn (Garden City, NY: Doubleday, 1976). Küng first came to notoriety with his study of Karl Barth and the Council of Trent, *Justification: the Doctrine of Karl Barth and a Catholic Reflection*, trans. Thomas Collins, Edward E. Tolk, and David Granskou (Philadelphia: Westminster Press, 1981 (1964)). The Vatican's eyebrows were raised by *Infallible? An Inquiry*, trans. Edward Quinn (Garden City, NY: Doubleday, 1971) and *The Church*, trans. Ray and Rosaleen Ockenda (Garden City, NY: Doubleday, 1967). In recent years Küng has turned to the question of the existence of God in *Does God Exist? An Answer for Today*, trans. Edward Quinn (Garden City NY: Doubleday, 1980) and eschatology in *Eternal Life? Life After Death as a Medical, Philosophical and Theological Problem*, trans. Edward Quinn (Garden City NY: Doubleday, 1984). The major studies on Küng include Herman Haring and Kari-Josef Kusched, eds., *Hans Küng, His Work and His Way* (Garden City NY: Image Books, 1979); Robert Newell, *A Passion for Truth: Hans Küng and His Theology* (New York: Crossroad, 1984); and John Kiwiet, *Hans Küng* (Waco, TX: Word Books, 1985). Küng's controversy with the Vatican has been chronicled in *The Küng Diaglogue* (Washington, DC: United States Catholic Conference, 1980); Leonard Swidler, ed., *Küng in Conflict* (Garden City NY: Doubleday, 1981); and Peter Hebblethwaite, *The New*

common ground. Küng sees a connection between what he perceives as "the poverty of Christianity" and "the poverty of humanism" in the modern era.[2] Christians have the tendency to cover up the very human traits of Christianity, whereas secularists often refuse to admit the great influence of Christianity upon their values.[3] It is for this reason that Küng says that Christianity and humanism are not opposites. In fact, he will argue that the essence of true Christianity is "radical humanism."[4]

Küng is quick to point out that the critique of a "radical humanism" should be addressed to both the church and the secular culture. Certainly there is a need for the church to be made more human, although, Küng hastens to add, without selling out the Christian substance.[5]

But secular humanism is not without its own disappointments—Copernicus, Marx, Darwin, Freud, existentialism, fascism, Nazism, etc. A certain skepticism has settled into secular humanism which has resulted in the emphasis upon the natural sciences in order to establish the positive data (Positivism) and the formal structures (Structuralism) without regard to meaning. The quest for the meaning of the whole has been surrendered to individual projects of "measuring, calculating, controlling, programming, and prognosticating the individual sequences."[6]

Both the ideology of the "technical revolution" and the ideology of a "politico-social revolution" have been shattered. The increasing demands for "growth" have created more of a sense of insecurity than freedom.[7] Technology has not been able to engineer a social state of complete equality by manipulating the envi-

---

Inquisition? The Case of Edward Schillebeeckx and Hans Küng (San Francisco: Harper and Row, 1980).

[2] Küng, *On Being a Christian*, p. 30.

[3] Ibid., p. 31.

[4] Ibid.

[5] Ibid., p. 37. Küng adds wryly, "Theologians have been denigrating the world for so long that it would be surprising if they did not now feel the temptation to make amends for everything at once."

[6] Ibid., p. 38.

[7] Ibid., pp. 39-40.

ronment of the individual (The "Great Society" under L.B. Johnson), because it wrongly assumed that the individual is good if only his environment is good.

So also the "ideology of a politico-social revolution," leading naturally to humanity has been found to be wanting.[8] The weaknesses of Marx's theory of history and society as a total explanation are obviously seen if one lives in a society where freedom of criticism exists, a rare commodity in a Marxist society.[9] Marx's basic assumption has been proven wrong: it *is* possible to improve the lot of the proletariat without revolution. The sad empirical reality of Marxist "classless" society is the promotion of the "overwhelming power of the state," in which the state has been identified with society.[10] Marxism in the end betrays its own ideals: The use of force brings violence and oppression which is *dehumanizing* to humanity, rather than humanizing.[11]

The response to this should not be nostalgia or reformism, but concrete judgments and concrete actions, based on "an unromantic, serious meditation on the past," which aims at a change in humanity itself.[12] This can be done, Küng suggests, if we look dispassionately at the human situation and "judge it in the light of human existence with all its depths."[13] Only thus can humanity be delivered from the bondage to efficiency and achievements, the modern forms of what Paul calls "the curse of the law."[14] At this point one is brought to what is truly decisive: faith, faith in God, regardless of one's weaknesses or achievements.[15]

THEOLOGICAL METHOD: FROM "BELOW"

Küng has a distinct theological method by which he will seek to discover Christianity as "radical humanism." For Küng,

---

[8]   Ibid., p. 43.
[9]   Ibid., p. 45.
[10]   Ibid., p. 45.
[11]   Ibid., p. 49.
[12]   Ibid., pp. 53-55.
[13]   Ibid., p. 56.
[14]   Ibid., pp. 584-587.
[15]   Ibid., pp. 587-588.

one begins with the contingent nature of reality in order to deduce the existence of God. Reality itself makes a demand upon us, but in the sense of its "primal reason, primal support, and primal goal."[16] This is a theological method which starts out from "below, from man's questions, from human experience."[17] Küng is quick to add that this does not mean any "highhandedness" on humanity's part as a way in which humanity can control God, but rather a way to be "open to reality."[18] Küng admits that apologetics is one of the reasons for this method. This is the way to relate the knowledge of God to the modern person "where he is actually living."[19]

JESUS AS THE ARCHETYPE OF THE NEW HUMANITY

Despite his emphasis upon starting with human experience, Christology has an indispensable place in Küng's soteriology. In answer to the question, "What is special to Christianity?" Küng answers unhesitatingly, "Jesus Christ."[20] It is the Jesus who as "ultimately, decisive, definitive, archetypal, for man's relations with God," who is nonetheless a "dangerous memory," as he unsettles the rigid structures of every society.[21] Jesus as the distinctive center of Christianity runs counter to the de facto practice of abstract axioms, concepts, principles, and ideas as the center of the faith.[22] This is a Christianity which naively assumes that it knows who Jesus is.

How do we know the true Jesus, then, according to Küng? Like Pannenberg, Küng stresses the importance of the historical method, first of all.[23] In fact, his confidence in the historical

---

[16] Ibid., p.73.

[17] Ibid., p. 83.

[18] Küng, *On Being a Christian*, p. 84.

[19] Ibid.

[20] Ibid., p. 123.

[21] Ibid., pp. 120, 123-124. Cf. the discussion of J. B. Metz's concept of the "dangerous memory" of Jesus in David Tracy, *The Analogical Imagination* (New York: Crossroad, 1981), pp. 425-427.

[22] Küng, *On Being a Christian*, p. 124.

[23] Ibid., p. 156.

method is so great that he believes that it has made it possible to get back to the historical Jesus in a way not possible ever before. The historical method helps us to see the importance of Jesus as a Jewish man of Palestine.[24] If one is to object that this is simply a modernist tool, Küng is quick to point out that the disciples themselves had to start out this way, considering Jesus of Nazareth as a man and a Jew first, and not as the Messiah, much less as the Son of God.

What does the historical method discover about the historical Jesus, according to Küng? It is the uniqueness of Jesus which is paramount to Küng.

> He [Jesus] is on a different plane; apparently closer than priests to God, freer than ascetics in regard to the world, more moral than the moralists, more revolutionary than the revolutionaries.[25]

The Gospels are replete with incidents in which both Jesus' friends and enemies fail to understand him. Whatever parallels there are in detail to other religious teachers, "the historical Jesus in his wholeness turns out to be completely unique—in his own time and ours."[26]

SALVATION AS HUMANIZATION

The uniqueness of Jesus points to a fundamental change in humanity which needs to be made: humanization.[27] It is not made through right thinking (Socrates) or through the education of the fundamentally good person (Confucius), but through the surrender of the individual to God's will. But what is God's will? God's will is "man's well-being." [28] It is a liberating, healing, saving will, which brings great happiness to both the individual and humanity as a whole. "God's cause" is not law nor cult, but human-

---

24 Ibid., p. 174.
25 Ibid., p. 212.
26 Ibid.
27 Ibid., p. 247.
28 Ibid., p. 251.

ity.[29] God's will is not an absolute legal system, nor a liturgy, nor an   institution, nor dogmatism. This is not meant to idolize humanity. That would be no less de-humanizing, according to Küng. [30] Humanity's will does not replace God's will. "But God's will is made concrete in the light of the concrete situation of man and his fellow men."[31] Moreover, service of humanity does not replace service of God. However, service of humanity is what proves the genuineness of the service of God.

Jesus is the archetype of what it means to serve humanity, according to Küng, but he must be seen on his own terms. The uniqueness of Jesus is particularly seen in relation to politics. The charge made against Jesus during his lifetime was that he sought political power and saw himself as a political messiah. That was patently false, of course.[32] Jesus did not have a "highly political" gospel, according to Küng, but it was not "unpolitical."[33] Jesus had a "thoroughgoing 'religious' message and mission, which of course later had incisive 'political' implications and consequences."[34] Therefore, it could be said that Jesus' message and mission was "indirectly political."[35]

Küng relativizes politics because of his emphasis upon the importance of the "encounter" between the individual and the reality of God.[36] This is the only way in which life will gain any meaning. It is "the crucified and yet living Jesus" who is "the final judge, the reliable, permanent, ultimate, definitive standard... the model of human existence."[37]

---

29 Ibid., p. 253.
30 Ibid., p. 252.
31 Ibid., p. 253.
32 Ibid., p. 337.
33 Ibid., p. 338.
34 Ibid.
35 Ibid. Küng says that both the left and the right fail to "see the true political relevance of the Christian message, from which it is impossible directly to deduce particular policy and particular detailed solutions for questions of law and constitution, for economic, social, cultural and foreign policy."
36 Ibid., p. 394.
37 Ibid., p. 395.

True human existence has suffered under traditional theories of the atonement, according to Küng, and must now be promoted by new theories. In Anselm's theory, "satisfaction" for the honor of God became a "purely external" atonement. The redeemed are not really changed.[38] A modern theory of the atonement must include 1) "connection with the proclamation and activity of the historical Jesus," 2) "with the living presence of the risen Christ," and 3) "with modern man's horizon of experience."[39] This is the basis for true transformation of both the individual and the world.

Küng is careful when he defines the aspects of salvation. For instance, "redemption" is not to be confused with "emancipation."[40] Küng includes both as parts of "liberation," but "emancipation" is something that happens between human beings, whereas "redemption" is "liberation of man by God."[41] It is possibly only by redemption for humanity to be liberated from its guilt before God. It is this alone which brings an awareness of being accepted for all time and eternity, and thus, gives the new person impetus to work for his fallen fellow human beings.

But where do we "encounter" God in Christ? Christ is encountered in the meaninglessness of suffering and death that obtains meaning when seen in light of our encounter with "the perfect suffering and dying of this One."[42] In Küng's opinion, it was a major setback when the early church followed Irenaeus and emphasized incarnational theology rather than an "exaltation Christology."[43] An "exaltation Christology" starts with a human Messiah, who was subsequently exalted to be the Son of God.[44] The Irenaean emphasis makes the Christian message considerably more difficult to understand today. Rather than starting from "below" with the human Jesus, we ask the world to start from ideas of pre-existence and incarnation, a difficult height to leap.

---

38 Ibid., p. 423.
39 Ibid., p. 426.
40 Ibid., p. 430.
41 Ibid., p. 430.
42 Ibid., p. 433.
43 Ibid., p. 422.
44 Ibid.

The emphasis in this model is on "deification," as found in Eastern Christian theologies, rather than on "humanization."[45] The cross is supplanted by the Incarnation and concern for becoming "godly" supercedes "the transformation of the world and society."[46] As Küng states, "Our problem today is not the deification but the humanization of Jesus."[47]

WORLD RELIGIONS AND HUMANIZATION

Like other contemporary theologians, Küng is also sensitive to the "challenge of world religions."[48] Küng is impressed with the devotion and effort which people of different religions exercise. Is it not true, he asks, that all major world religions start from "the same perennial questions" as Christianity?[49] Küng lauds the post-Vatican II attitude toward a state of salvation for all of humanity because of the eternal covenant which God has made with them.[50]

But this does not mean that all religions are equally true, in contrast to Hick. "They will be saved, not because of, but in spite of, all untruth and superstition."[51] Thus, the world religions can only be called "ways of salvation" in a "relative" sense.[52]

Küng is critical of both the "dogmatic repression of the problem of religion" by Barth and the liberal "agnostic-relativistic indifferentism" which approves of religions indiscriminately.[53] The attitudes of Christianity toward world religions should be a "dialectical unity of recognition and rejection."[54] In turn, Christianity can claim uniqueness. but not exclusiveness. In the end, the question of humanization, of course, is paramount. It is

---

45 Ibid.
46 Ibid., p. 442.
47 Ibid.
48 Ibid., pp. 89ff.
49 Ibid., p. 92.
50 Ibid., pp. 90-91.
51 Ibid., p. 104.
52 Ibid.
53 Ibid., pp. 111-112.
54 Ibid., p. 112.

not simply an issue of concepts, ideas, and doctrines, but of living human beings with genuine religious experiences. Therefore, they must be taken seriously.[55]

---

[55] Ibid., p. 115.

CHAPTER FIVE

THE HUMANITY OF GOD AS CRITIQUE OF
ANTHROPOCENTRIC THEOLOGIES

Karl Barth's teaching on the "humanity of God" has raised
not a few eyebrows since his essay of the same name was published in the 1950's.[1] Despite its own apparently paradoxical
meaning, our proposal is that the humanity of God as expounded
by Karl Barth provides a telling critique of the dangers of the anthropocentric tendencies in modern theology, and particularly
concerning the question of the reality of salvation. The humanity
of God provides a "bridge" for us between the problem of the reality of salvation in this present world and our proposed solution
in the doctrine of the vicarious humanity of Christ.

KARL BARTH ON THE HUMANITY OF GOD

Christopher Kaiser has helpfully outlined three meanings of
the humanity of God in the theology of Barth.[2] The first meaning
involves the historical acts of God, the second, God's communion
with humanity, and the third, and most important for our purpose,

---

[1] Karl Barth, *The Humanity of God*, trans. John Newton Thomas and Thomas
Wieser (Atlanta: John Knox Press, 1960).

[2] Christopher B. Kaiser, *The Doctrine of God* (Westminster, IL: Crossway Books,
1982), pp. 116-118. John Thompson sees election and time as the focal points
of Barth's theology of the humanity of God in "The Humanity of God in the
Theology of Karl Barth," *Scottish Journal of Theology* 29, no. 3 (1976),
p. 251. We are more comfortable with Kaiser's outline, and would see election
as under God's communion with humanity and time under the historical acts of
God's being.

is the foundation of true humanity in the eternal humanity of God, existing as the Trinity, and reflected in the Incarnation. Our exposition of Barth will be followed by a look at critiques of Barth on the humanity of God. We will then look at how the doctrine of the humanity of God provides a critique of modern soteriologies, as represented by John B. Cobb, Jr., Leonardo Boff, Jürgen Moltmann, Wolfhart Pannenberg, John Hick and Hans Küng.

Barth's first meaning of the humanity of God, according to Kaiser, is a compensation on Barth's part for what he admits was an overemphasis in the earlier stages of his theology.[3] The early Barth, of course, boldly proclaimed the otherness of God against humanity, God as "Wholly Other." Barth does not now discount this. In fact he intends to "derive the knowledge of the humanity of God from the knowledge of His deity."[4] Barth can see now that he and his compatriots did not rightly perceive the radical consequences of their doctrine of the deity of God.[5] The God of the dialectical theologians is not the God of the philosophers, but the God of Abraham, Isaac, and Jacob. Thus, he is the God who is involved in acts of history with humanity. The humanity of God means that God acts in this history with humanity.

Kaiser discerns a second meaning of the humanity of God in Barth, but it would be just as proper to see it as part of his first meaning. Since God is the God of Abraham, Isaac, and Jacob, the God of salvation history, he is also the God who seeks to be in community with humanity. God acts because of his desire to be a partner with humanity "though of course as the absolutely superior partner."[6] This is an expression of God's freedom, for he is under no compulsion to be in communion with humanity. And this freedom defines the essence of God's deity. "It is precisely God's *deity* which, rightly understood, includes his humanity."[7] How is this known? This is known only through Jesus Christ, in whom God is not isolated from humanity, nor humanity from God. Jesus

---

[3] Barth, *The Humanity of God*, pp. 37-38.

[4] Ibid., p. 45.

[5] Ibid., p. 46.

[6] Ibid., p. 45.

[7] Ibid., p. 46.

Christ as the Mediator and Reconciler comes forward as human being in behalf of God and to God on behalf of humanity. [8]

If Jesus Christ is the only place where both true deity and true humanity are found, then this leads us to another meaning of the humanity of God, according to Kaiser: God himself in Jesus is the foundation of true humanity. That which is hinted at in Barth's essay "The Humanity of God" is developed further in the *Church Dogmatics*. God himself is antecedently *human*, in a way which becomes the foundation for created humanity. This is made explicit in the section "Jesus, Man for Other Men" in *Church Dogmatics* III/2.[9] In the midst of discussing the nature of the covenant between God and humanity, Barth observes that its origin is in God himself. The covenant is not an afterthought, but is ontological. It becomes "revealed and effective in time in the humanity of Jesus," but he hastens to add that this is something which "we might almost say [is] appropriate and natural to Him."[10] In the covenant, God makes a "copy" of himself. "Even in His divine being there is relationship" as Father, Son, and Holy Spirit.[11]

> He is Himself the One who loves eternally, the One who is eternally loved, and eternal love; and in this tri-unity He is the original source of every I and Thou, of the I which is eternally from and to the Thou and therefore supremely I.[12]

However, Barth does not want to deny that Jesus' incarnate humanity was creaturely humanity. Since Jesus belongs to this creaturely world, his humanity is like our humanity.[13] This is not an analogy of being, therefore, but an analogy of relationship.[14] The relationship between the being of God and that of humanity, and the relationship in the being of God himself as Father, Son,

---

[8]   Ibid., p. 47.
[9]   Barth, *CD* III/2, pp. 218-220.
[10]   Ibid., p. 218.
[11]   Ibid.
[12]   Ibid.
[13]   Ibid., p. 219.
[14]   Ibid., p. 220.

and Holy Spirit is an *analogia relationis*. Barth puts this in the context of God's freedom. God is free to posit himself in relation as Father, Son, and Holy Spirit from all eternity. So, also, he is free to create humanity in his own "image." Therefore, we need not look for the meaning of true humanity elsewhere than in the humanity of Jesus Christ. We shall see that this can be the basis for a decisive critique of contemporary soteriologies.

CRITICISMS OF BARTH

Apart from the sometimes arbitrary judgments on the doctrinal use of the Fourth Gospel by Barth from some New Testament scholars, criticism of Barth's doctrine of the humanity of God have centered on the two issues:1) the problem of anthropomorphism, and 2) the Incarnation as an event in history.[15]

The most obvious objection to the doctrine of the humanity of God is its anthropomorphic language. Is it not a contradiction in terms to associate "humanity" with "God," the finite with the infinite, or the creaturely with the uncreated?

Anthropomorphisms become a particular problem for theology, but a problem which only the nature of one's theology can solve. Kornelis Miskotte considers anthropomorphisms in the Old Testament, where God has hands, a nose, etc., only to be a problem if one has a natural theology which disdains the "strangeness" of specific, special revelation and instead opts for the universal

---

[15] See the cavalier dismissal of the Fourth Gospel as a source for contemporary theology because of its alleged historical unreliability and "mythic" teaching in Anthony Tyrrell Hanson, The *Image of the Invisible God* (London: SCM Press, 1982), p. 94. This kind of dualistic thinking in some historical critics is answered by T. F. Torrance, in the chapter "Theological Questions to Biblical Scholars," in *Reality and Evangelical Theology* (Philadelphia: Westminster Press, 1982), pp. 52-83. Of related interest is the question of the pre-existence of Christ in the New Testament. Some scholars find abundant evidence throughout the N.T., and even the critical James D. G. Dunn admits that a full blown doctrine of pre-existence is present in the Fourth Gospel. See *Christology in the Making: a New Testament Inquiry into the Origins of the Doctrine of the Incarnation* (Philadelphia: Westminster Press, 1980), pp. 213 ff.

lowest common denominator of general revelation.[16] Ray
Anderson stresses that it is one's theological perspective on the
relationship between the Being and Act of God which is at
stake.[17] Anthropomorphisms are culturally based means of expressing that which otherwise would be hidden by a purely cogni-
tive approach. This is true with the humanity of God, as it is true
with the nature and event of love and the meaning of art.[18] To
seek to "demythologize" the anthropomorphisms would sever the
relationship between God and the concrete world of the creaturely.[19] Anderson himself relates this to the humanity of God:

> If we allow our minds to be conformed to the in-
> escapable fact of the humanity of God in his self-com-
> munication, a fact that presses upon us the inner
> coherence of Word and deed, we can begin to under-
> stand that God's being-with and being-one-with hu-
> man life is not alien to the nature of God.[20]

But does not "the humanity of God" necessitate an understanding of humanity as creaturely, something we cannot ascribe
to God in his eternal being? This is where the importance of one's
theological anthropology comes into play. What, indeed, do we
mean by "humanity"? Barth and Anderson are helpful here as
well. Barth makes it plain that while creatureliness is a fact of humanity, it does not reveal the inner logic of what it means to be
human.[21] As Anderson puts it, "Creatureliness is an undifferenti-
ated field upon which the occasion of the human occurs."[22] There
is a "continuum of creaturely life" shared between human beings

---

16 Kornelis Miskotte, *When the Gods are Silent*, trans. John W. Doberstein (New
York: Harper and Row, 1967), p. 129.

17 Anderson, *Historical Transcendence and the Reality of God*, p. 113.

18 Ibid., p. 116.

19 Ibid., p. 113.

20 Ibid., p. 117. Anderson, however, differs from Barth and associates the
humanity of God with God's transcendence, not immanence. Ibid., p. 118, n.
32.

21 Barth, *CD* III/2, p. 249.

22 Ray S. Anderson, *On Being Human* (Grand Rapids: Eerdmans, 1982), p. 21.

and all creatures.[23] But human beings are, in Anderson's terms, creatures of the "seventh day." While they must pass through the sixth day, the day of physical creation, they are not determined by the sixth day, but by the "seventh day," the day in which God rested, the day which belongs to God. So also the meaning of humanity is not mere creatureliness but has its origin in the determination by the Word of God.[24] Therefore, one is free to say that the humanity of God is God's self-determination within his eternal trinitarian life. It manifests itself in the occasion of the Incarnation, but its ultimate source and determination is God's eternal being as Father, Son, and Holy Spirit.

Some have criticized Barth on the grounds that a pre-incarnate humanity of God negates, or at least overshadows, the event of the Incarnation. Colin Brown argues that Barth projects the Incarnation "back into the being of God before the event took place."[25] There is no exegetical basis for such an interpretation as this, according to Brown. H. Zahrnt claims that Barth's doctrine denigrates the genuine dialogue between God and humanity which took place in the Incarnation in favor of a "monologue in heaven" between the persons of the Trinity.[26] Emil Brunner agrees: "If the eternal pre-existence of the God-man were fact, then the Incarnation would not be an event at all; no longer would it be the great miracle of Christmas."[27]

However, it seems that this criticism does not reckon with the fact that, in the Incarnation, we are face to face with the being of God, not in a modalistic sense, but in the sense of an actual knowledge of God. As Barth is famous for saying, in the man Jesus of Nazareth we have actual knowledge of God. As John Thompson puts it, "In the light of the Incarnation, we cannot think

---

23 Ibid., p. 23.

24 Ibid., pp. 24, 28, 33ff.

25 Colin Brown, *Karl Barth and the Christian Message* (London: Tyndale Press, 1967), pp. 109-110.

26 H. Zahrnt, *The Question of God, Protestant Theology in the Twentieth Century*, cited by Thompson, p. 264.

27 Emil Brunner, *The Christian Doctrine of God*, trans. Olive Wyon (Philadelphia: Westminster Press, 1950), p. 347. Cited by Thompson, p. 263.

of God at all apart from man."[28] Indeed, it seems puzzling how someone can consider the Incarnation in Barth's thought not to be an event. First, he states that the eternal covenant between God and humanity is "revealed and effective" in time in the humanity of Jesus.[29] It happens in time in order for it to be made efficacious. Secondly, the Who, the How, and the What of revelation cannot be separated if there is a genuine revelation of God.[30] The uniqueness of the revelation of God in Jesus Christ demands this. If the "Who" is the action of the self-revealed God, the "How" comes "through" God himself, by his own means, and the "What" is the result, a genuine knowledge of God himself. *"God* reveals Himself. He reveals Himself *through Himself.* He reveals *Himself."*[31] The difficulty which modern theologians seem to have is in accepting the fact that God is involved not only as an object of revelation, but as *subject,* and therefore he also is intimately involved in the *means* of revelation. This is what Barth means by the identity of God's *Act* in his *Being* and, therefore, with its effect.[32] The Incarnation can be taken seriously because it is an event with roots in God's own being, not external to it. This points us squarely in the direction of our critique of the problem of salvation in contemporary soteriology: The reality of salvation is to be found in God himself, not in the phenomena of world process or experience. A detailed look at how the humanity of God provides a critique of the problem is now in order.[33]

---

28   Ibid., p. 262.

29   Barth, *CD* III/2, p. 218.

30   Ibid., I/1, pp. 295-296.

31   Ibid., p. 296.

32   Ibid.

33   Ibid. At the root of this problem seems to be the failure to identify the *economic* Trinity with the *immanent* Trinity. See Karl Rahner, *The Trinity,* trans. Joseph Donceel (New York: Herder and Herder, 1970) and T. F. Torrance, "Towards an Ecumenical Consensus on the Trinity," *Theologische Zeitschrift* 31 (1975), pp. 335-350.

THE DEITY OF GOD AND SALVATION

Barth states that God's deity does not exclude, but includes his humanity.[34] Thus, the humanity of God first of all has radical consequences for a doctrine of God. As we have seen, contemporary soteriology is aware of the implications of the doctrine of God for a theology of salvation. Process theology's doctrine of God is one example. But it is the understanding of the deity of God as reflected in his humanity which provides a telling critique of the anthropocentricity in contemporary soteriology.

In his exposition of the Nicene Creed, Barth understands the confession of the "only-begotten" Son as an emphasis upon the uniqueness and exclusiveness of the revelation of God in Christ.[35] There is no other Son of God besides this Son; no other revelation exists in which God's Being is communicated in a particular Act. This is because the Son is who God is "antecedently in Himself."[36] To know the Son is to know the humanity of God.

Eberhard Jüngel states that "begotten, not made" maintains a tension in confessing not only that "God comes from God," but also, "God comes to God."[37] God's origin is always himself, but he does not choose to be without us. That is one sense of the humanity of God. But it is equally true that "God comes to God" cannot be said apart from "God comes from God." God's eternal being is already expressed in the eternal Son. The result of this is that God cannot be spoken of *per se,* but only in this relationship between the Father and the Son through the Spirit.[38] In contrast, the "di-polar" theism of John Cobb and process theology, with its distinction between God in his essence and God in his actuality, seems to wrench God apart in an ontological dualism. There is differentiation in process theology, but no unity, and what is most important, no eternal foundation of humanity in God himself. The one pole of essence in di-polar theism means that God still has an

---

34 Barth, *The Humanity of God*, p. 49.

35 Barth *CD* I/1, p. 424.

36 Ibid., p. 425.

37 Eberhard Jüngel, *God as the Mystery of the World*, trans. Darrell L. Guder (Grand Rapids: Eerdmans, 1983), pp. 37, 384.

38 Ibid., p. 384.

"unchangeable part" in a process doctrine of God, which is the very criticism which process theologians lodge against classical theology.

Jüngel defines the material content of the humanity of God as self-relatedness which is made manifest in the selflessness of the Incarnation of God.[39] As a part of the trinitarian life of God, this event is not outside his being. Thus, "the Crucified One belongs to the concept of God."[40] "In him, the love of God has appeared (I Jn.4:9), because that love has happened in him."[41] By contrast, although he affirms the identity between the economic and immanent Trinity, the cross in Jürgen Moltmann's theology has only a "retroactive" effect on the being of God.[42] There is not an "eternal cross" so to speak, in God's heart, for Moltmann.

Why is this so for Moltmann? Perhaps we have a clue when we study his statement on the relationship between the Trinity and human love. Moltmann can define "the history of salvation" as "the history of the eternally, triune God who draws us into and includes us in his eternal triune life...," but this is not a movement which originates from God to humanity.[43] In contrast to Jüngel, Moltmann confuses the order of the Trinity and human love. For him it is not the Trinity which creates the capacity for love in us, but it is the phenomenon of "open-mindedness" toward others which creates oneness with the Father, the Son, and the Holy Spirit.[44] God "draws us" into "his eternal triune life," but he does so, according to Moltmann, on the basis of our "open-mind-

---

[39] Ibid., p. 372.

[40] Ibid.

[41] Ibid.

[42] Moltmann, *The Trinity and the Kingdom* p. 160. This is recognized by Leonardo Boff in his criticism of Moltmann. For Boff, Moltmann's crucified God leads to atheism because "God appears as Pain and Death," the Father causing the death of the Son. *Passion of Christ, Passion of the World: The Facts, Their Interpretation and their Meaning Yesterday and Today* trans. Robert R. Barr, (Maryknoll, NY: Orbis, 1987), pp. 111-114. *Contra* Boff, for Moltmann, pain and suffering is something that God chooses to enter into by his grace.

[43] Ibid., p. 157.

[44] Ibid., p. 158.

edness" towards others, not out of his grace. Indeed, there is also a question in Boff's use of the Trinity primarily as communion, almost to the exclusion of the distinction between the persons of the Godhead, whether this is simply constructing a doctrine based on a perceived need and thereby not allowing Boff to listen to the truth and implications of God as Trinity.

Such an abstract, albeit admirable moral principle as "open-mindedness" is symptomatic of the sources of Moltmann's problem with Barth's doctrine of the Trinity. Moltmann's egalitarian principles run counter to Barth's view of a dynamic, living relationship between distinctive persons of the Trinity, which Scripture expresses as, for example, the sending by the Father and the obedience of the Son (Jn. 17:3-4). For Moltmann, this unfortunate interpretation of the Trinity reflects Barth's doctrine of sovereignty and lordship, so that all analogously "antithetical relationships" are seen from this standpoint: " God and the world, heaven and earth; soul and body and, not least, man and woman, too."[45] This runs counter to the triune God as "the mutuality and the reciprocity of love."

But is such a doctrine of the Trinity as Moltmann's less a reflection of the dynamic, personal relationship between the Father and the Son which one finds in Scripture, and more beholden to abstract anthropocentric principles such as "open-mindedness" and "equality" which carry their own loaded definitions, supplied from non-theological contexts? Does the reality of salvation defined *a priori* by Moltmann, based upon western liberal values, admirable in their own right, undermine the distinctive reality of God as Trinity, and, therefore, fail to give the *hope* which Moltmann so desperately desires?

In a similar way, the other eschatological theologian, Wolfhart Pannenberg, contends that "the sole meaning of the doctrine of the Trinity is to express the being of God revealed in Jesus' resurrection."[46] Since Pannenberg starts from "below," from an historical-critical stand point, he is able to see the validity of the Trinity only as an expression of an event in history, the resurrection. What is missing is the eternal origin and source of that event

---

45   Moltmann, *God and Creation,* pp. 16-17.
46   Pannenberg, *Faith and Reality,* p. 60.

in the eternal love of God. The problem of the reality of salvation
is left to whatever bits may be gleaned from the historical-critical
method, rather than from looking for the reality of salvation in
God himself. Reality is restricted to an anthropocentric center, obviously bending with the changing whims of human ideas, regardless of their truth and therefore, demanding room for "a new
experience of God,"[47] bound by the straight jacket of the demands
of "universal validity."[48].

John Hick's doctrine of God can also be criticized as a retreat from God as the One who loves in an eternal relationship of
love (Trinity) into a reductionistic doctrine of God as "the Eternal
One." In his obviously sincere desire to create a unity between
people of all faiths, he draws a distinction between "the Eternal
One" and the various perceptions of him as seen in the differing
religious faiths.[49] But is not this idea of an "Eternal One" who lies
behind all religions simply another human perception, liable to a
culturally relative situation as any other? By contrast, the humanity
of God speaks of the God who has revealed himself uniquely in a
manifestation of his eternal being of love. A God who is merely
"the Transcendent" in an abstract and impersonal sense cannot be
said to be love. But the One who makes known his being as eternally love in the Father, the Son, and the Holy Spirit provides the
basis for viewing the consistency between God's being and the
salvation of humanity.[50] In his One we can find the reality of salvation in a world of turmoil and tragedy.[51]

A more detailed look at aspects of the deity of God involves
a closer look at what is meant by the self-revelation of God, and
"the Way of the Son of God into the Far Country," that is, the in-

---

[47] Ibid., *The Apostles Creed in the Light of Today's Questions,* p. 25.

[48] Ibid., *Anthropology in Theological Perspective,* p. 16.

[49] Hick, *God Has Many Names,* p. 24.

[50] Hick admits the problem of the "less adequate" religions, but does not offer
any solution. It seems that this is Hick's Achilles heel. As Conrad Hyers
states, the problem with a world theology such as Hick's is not diversity in
religions, but genuine contradiction. Review of *God Has Many Names* by John
Hick, *Theology Today* 40 (April, 1983), p. 71.

[51] Barth, *CD* I/1, p. 295.

tegral relationship of the lowliness and humiliation of the Son to
the being of God.

The Self-Revelation of God

The humanity of God involves the self-revelation of God.
Barth sees very clearly the significance of God's *self*-revelation
for the doctrine of revelation. God is the origin and source of revelation. As the only source of revelation, God's revelation must be
understood in its uniqueness, according to Scripture. "But this
means that it [revelation] insists absolutely on being understood in
terms of its subject, God."[52] If this is true for revelation, how
much more is it true for salvation? We have come to an absolutely
crucial point in our understanding of the reality of salvation. Salvation cannot be separated from revelation, if salvation truly has
its origin in God. If revelation is to be understood only in terms of
God as the Who? How? and What? it necessarily follows that we
must look to this God as the *reality* of salvation, as well as its *origin*. "*God* reveals Himself. He reveals Himself *through Himself*.
He reveals *Himself*."[53] Salvation is of God. As such, God
himself is the reality of salvation, the God whose being is identical
with his act. Barth states, "Revelation is indeed God's predicate,
but in such a way that this predicate is in every way identical with
God Himself."[54] So we could also say the reality of salvation is
God's predicate, but in such a way that it is identical with God
himself. This is why much of modern soteriology is unsatisfactory
in its answers to the problem of the reality of salvation. Trapped
within an anthropocentric framework, it is unable to see the
"predication" of salvation in God himself, and turns in despair to
the ambiguities of world process, history, and religious
experience.

This problem is seen in Pannenberg's soteriology. Pannenberg is careful to separate God from the world. God is "quite different" from it.[55]

---

52   Ibid., p. 296.
53   Ibid.
54   Ibid., p. 299.
55   Pannenberg, *Faith and Reality*, p. 87.

> But insofar as he reveals himself, he is in the world.
> That, in fact, is history: that God makes himself mani-
> fest in the world. History is God acting in its creation.
> Therefore history cannot be understood without
> God.[56]

Pannenberg, in effect, tends to identify the revelation of God with all of world history. Considering the course of folly in world history, this is not very flattering to God! In addition, he effectively robs the created order of its own rationality.[57] This "resacralization" of the world recreates the lack of respect for the "world come of age," and becomes vulnerable to Bonhoeffer's well-known criticisms.[58]

Moltmann has a similar problem when he sees the humanity of God in the humanity of every person.[59] Barth sees definitely the universal implications of the humanity of God. Because of the humanity of God, we have to think of "every human being, even the oddest, most villainous or miserable, as one to whom Jesus Christ is Brother and God is Father."[60] But this is a knowledge which comes from knowing the humanity of God, God's self-revelation. For Moltmann, human experience in all of its ambiguity and sin somehow points to the humanity of God, a tenuous position to hold at best.

In fact, is S. Paul Schilling right in his review of *Theology of Hope*, that there is no revelation of God in the present for Moltmann?[61] We might put it this way: Does Moltmann neglect the *Being* of God for the sake of emphasizing the *Act* of God in the future, in contrast to Barth's more integrated approach? It is true that Moltmann does not ignore the present, but there seems to

---

[56] Ibid.

[57] The rationality of the created order is related to God's contingent relationship to the world by T. F. Torrance, *Divine and Contingent Order* (cited afterwards as *DCO*) (Oxford: Oxford University Press, 1981), pp. 71-72.

[58] Bonhoeffer, *Letters and Papers from Prison*, p. 326.

[59] Moltmann, *The Crucified God*, pp. 276-277.

[60] Barth, *The Humanity of God*, p. 53.

[61] S. Paul Schilling, Review of *Theology of Hope* by Jürgen Moltmann, *Interpretation* 22 (October, 1968), p. 483.

be a revelation of God for him only *indirectly*, as the future impinges upon the present. Schilling argues convincingly that the past and the present must always be seen as the context for the future, in order to avoid viewing the future as merely a romantic hope.[62]

Nevertheless, we must view Moltmann's eschatological soteriology somewhat ambivalently. The strength of Moltmann's position is the rightful importance he gives to the future. He is right that in some ways only the future can still speak of the reality of God, whereas the past and the present have already spoken. Events and people from the past and the present can influence us, but only God can affect us from the vantage point of the future.[63]

The weakness of Moltmann's approach is that he reduces all too quickly the Being and Act of God exclusively to the future. Does not the humanity of God speak of God and his salvation in the past, the present, and the future? In fact, it would seem that Barth's doctrine of the humanity of God would logically drive him to emphasize a "future" eschatology, and might well have, if he had lived to complete the *Church Dogmatics* volumes on eschatology. To speak of an eternal humanity of God is to speak of the past, the present, and the future. Moltmann's anthropocentric methodology is less than adequate at this point.

"The Way of the Son of God into the Far Country"

In *Church Dogmatics* IV/1 Barth uses the parable of the Prodigal Son to illustrate a crucial point concerning the humanity of God. The journey of the Son of God into the "far country" is the journey of the Incarnation. This is the way of obedience to the Father, to tread the path of sinners.[64] But this act of obedience is not extrinsic to the being of God. In fact, Barth states strongly, "This is the first and inner moment of the mystery of the deity of Christ."[65] In other words, the humanity of God is at the heart of the deity of God.

---

62 Ibid.
63 Moltmann *Theology of Hope*, p. 57.
64 Barth, *CD* IV/1, p. 192.
65 Ibid.

What does the obedience of the Son tell us about the deity of God? It reveals to us that for God it is just as natural "to be lowly as it is to be high, to be near as to be far, to be little as to be great, to be abroad as to be home."[66] The action of God in Jesus Christ is entirely proper to who God is in himself. In Jesus Christ "He exists and speaks and acts as the One He was from all eternity and will be to all eternity."[67] The significance of this reality is profound. God can demand obedience from human beings because obedience is not an alien element to him. Indeed, the saving event in Christ "can demand obedience because it is not itself an arbitrary decision but a decision of obedience." [68]

True, as Barth admits, it is "difficult" or even "elusive" to speak of an obedience within God himself.[69] Implicit in this is that there is both a superior and a subordinate aspect of God's being. Does this mean that there are two divine beings who are not equally divine? Subordinationism in the history of Christian thought has surrendered to this view. "It has solved the mystery of the deity of Christ by dissolving it."[70] The deity of Christ becomes separated from the act of humility. The other alternative, modalism, leaves the same result. Since modalism views the Incarnation as only "economic" for the sake of identification with

---

[66] Ibid., p. 193.

[67] Ibid. Berkouwer's criticism is startling until one remembers how common is his misconception: "When Barth speaks of the suffering of God and even of an 'obedience of God,' and this is not as a bold manner of speaking but as an *essential* element in the being of God over against the God-concept of natural theology, he exceeds the boundaries of the *revelation* which we have in Christ," G. C. Berkouwer, *The Triumph of Grace in the Theology of Karl Barth*, trans. Harry R. Boer (Grand Rapids: Eerdmans, 1956), p. 304. Cf. Klaus Runia, "Karl Barth's Christology," in *Christ the Lord: Studies in Christology Presented to Donald Guthrie*, ed. Harold H. Rowdon (Leicester: InterVarsity Press, 1982), pp. 306-307. One needs only to ask Berkouwer and Runia: Who is this "revealed" God if not the Triune God revealed in Scripture, the God in whose being exists an "obedience," unless they confess a modalistic interpretation of the Trinity? The tragedy of such practical anti-trinitarianism occurs all too often in the history of Christian thought, as J. Moltmann often points out.

[68] Barth, CD IV/1, p. 195.

[69] Ibid.

[70] Ibid., p. 196.

the world, it succeeds in cutting off the Incarnation from "the true and properly non-worldly being of God."[71]

But even T. F. Torrance sees a kind of subordinationism in Barth's doctrine of the humanity of God. He views this as "leftover" from Latin theology, reflecting a diversion from the Alexandrian tradition of the deity of Christ in Athanasius and Cyril of Alexandria.[72] For Athanasius the Son is everything the Father is, but "Father" (*Contra Arianos 3.4*).[73] In the *Church Dogmatics* IV/3, Torrance claims, Barth seems to present the humanity of Christ as "swallowed up" after the resurrection, replaced by "the humanity of God," rather than the emphasis of the Epistle to the Hebrews on the *priestly* ministry of the ascended Christ.[74]

It might be said that there is a danger of reading our *own* ideas of "obedience" into the obedience of the Son to the Father. But this danger exists in all anthropomorphisms used for God in Scripture, and, indeed, all human language about God! The answer to this dilemma, however, is not to empty the persons of the Trinity of all *content* except the bare fact of "Father", "Son", or "Holy Spirit" (see the above citation of Athanasius by Torrance). Scripture will not allow us to do so. The Gospel of John may be taken as case in point. The Father "loves" the Son (3:35; 5:20), he has "sent" the Son (6:57; 8:16,18); the Son "glorifies" the Father, accomplishing the work which he gave the Son to do (17:1,4). There is a dynamic relationship between the Father and in the Spirit which overflows from the pages of the Gospels (e.g. the baptism of Jesus: "This is my beloved Son"- Mt. 3:17, par.), ultimately vindicated by the resurrection of the Son from the dead. Torrance, himself, stresses the importance of equating the economic Trinity (how God appears in human phenomena) with the

---

71 Ibid.

72 T. F. Torrance, "My Interaction with Karl Barth," in *How Karl Barth Changed My Mind,* ed. Donald McKim (Grand Rapids: Eerdmans, 1986), pp. 60-61; cf. "Karl Barth and Patristic Theology," in *Theology Beyond Christemdom: essays on the Centenary of the Birth of Karl Barth, May 10, 1886,* ed. John Thompson (Allison Park, PA: Pickwick Publications, 1986), p. 223.

73 T. F. Torrance, *The Trinitarian Faith: The Evangelical Theology of the Ancient Catholic Church* (Edinburgh: T. & T. Clark, 1988), p. 124.

74 Torrance, "My Interaction with Karl Barth," p. 62.

immanent Trinity (who God is in himself).[75] In fact, Torrance cites his admiration for Barth's doctrine of the Trinity as the Being of God in his Act and the Act of God in his Being.[76] If the Being of God, God's essence, can only be known in his Act of grace in Jesus Christ, then the *context* of that Being must be found in the incarnate life of God's Act, found in the dynamics of the relationship of sending and obedience between the Father and the Son: the mirror of the eternal humanity of God. In fact, the aforementioned danger of reading our ideas into the "obedience" of the Son is relieved when we understand that obedience is *defined* for us by the Incarnation itself, the Being of God in his Act. Indeed, such a definition of obedience becomes a critique of our sinful and imperfect ideas of both authority and obedience, which we often divorce from self-sacrificial love. This is not so in the eternal humanity of God.

Barth maintains that three presuppositions have to be affirmed in order to have a proper understanding of the obedience of God: 1) The proper acting subject in salvation is God himself. Salvation is not delegated to anyone else. "When we have to do with Jesus Christ, we have to do with God."[77] Therefore, subordinationism is unsatisfactory. 2) Atonement is an event which is not external, but internal, in relation to the world. Modalism fails to see this connection, and thus fails to offer a real reconciliation in the world. The third point is the most important. 3) God is so much the subject of this event which reaches so deeply into the world that one cannot separate his Being from this Act of lowliness and obedience in the man Jesus of Nazareth.[78] The implications of such a separation are great. Both modalism and subordinationism evade the cross of Christ "because they start from the assumption that it cannot be accepted as true."[79]

---

[75] T. F. Torrance, "Toward an Ecumenical Concensus on the Trinity," *Theologische Zeitschrift* 31(1975), pp. 335-350.

[76] T. F. Torrance, "Karl Barth and Patristic Theology," in *Theology Beyond Christendom,* ed. John Thompson, pp. 223-224.

[77] Ibid., p. 198.

[78] Ibid., p. 199.

[79] Ibid., pp. 199-200.

Barth claims that we need to free ourselves from two kinds
of thinking if we are to accept the truth of the obedience of God.[80]
The first is a definition of "unity" which sees it as solitary and en-
closed rather than free and open in relation to itself. Unity is not a
prison but a freedom to have more than one mode of being, for
One to be in relation to Another. The second is that obedience
necessarily implies inferiority, and therefore it is unworthy and
improper for God. But this reveals our tendency toward anthropocentric thinking. What is the measure by which we are judging?
God himself has to be the defining agent in understanding the implications of obedience in his innermost being, not our poor
earthly analogies.

The anthropocentric methodology of John Cobb seems to
restrict the truth and action of God to the creaturely realm: "There
is no divine action apart from creaturely action," although he hastens to add, "but equally the divine action is the principle of hope
in the creaturely action."[81] The motive here is to encourage human
responsibility, a worthy goal certainly. However, is it not better to
see the origin of human responsibility as an integral part of the
being of God, rather than simply a "principle of hope"?

This problem in Cobb's thought is grounded in his Whiteheadian doctrine of God. In tune with the great tradition of western philosophy and theology, Whitehead's doctrine of God proceeds from the need to explain order in the world. But, for Whitehead, this order is not the order of a complex machine. As modern
physics has taught us, reality is much more complex than that. But
such a doctrine of the mechanistic universe has influenced theology so that it leads to a doctrine of God as a creator who stands
outside and aloof from his creation. However, Whitehead insists
that God is not the exception to metaphysical rules, to be brought
in *Deus ex machina* as the "answer" to "questions" which are
unanswerable. Rather, he is the essence of those metaphysical
rules himself.[82] Cobb's commentary is telling:

> That there *is* something which we may properly call
> God is sufficiently indicated by the kind of order that is

---

80 Ibid., p. 202.
81 Cobb and Griffin, *Process Theology: an Introductory Exposition*, p. 157.
82 Whitehead, *Process and Reality*, p. 521.

visible to all. But what that 'something' is, where it is, how it functions; these questions can be reflectively considered only in the light of the categories in terms of which the world is understood.[83]

Process thought's strength is, obviously, in its desire to see a relationship between God and the world, rather than a dualistic chasm. But the critical question needs to be asked: Is such an idea already doomed to frustration if God is known "only in the light of the categories in terms of which the world is understood"? Does not this leave the question of the reality of salvation extremely vulnerable to frustration and nihilism, if there is no help from "above", from transcendence? Does one end up purchasing the freedom of humanity at the expense of the freedom of God, a freedom to reveal himself, to express himself, on his own terms?

Cobb's separation of the historical Jesus from the exalted Christ is equally counterproductive. For Cobb, Christ is not bound to any particular religion, but is the power of creative transformation in them all.[84] Leonardo Boff also does not restrict the manifestation of God to the man Jesus of Nazareth, but extends it to all human beings. "The human being can be an articulation of God's history. This was the case at least in Jesus of Nazareth."[85] The humanity of God in Barth's theology is a critique of such anthropocentric theologies because Barth already perceives the basis for the Incarnation in God himself and therefore the unity between God's Being and Act.

Boff, also, can speak of the humanity of God found in the "total complete humanity of Jesus."[86] Such a new view of God is "spiritually Christian, unmistakable and unique," in contrast with our common images of God, which owe too much to pagan and Old Testament (!) religious experience. This does not mean, however, that the humanity of God expressed in Jesus is based on the

---

83 John B. Cobb, Jr., *A Christian Natural Theology Based on the Thought of Alfred North Whitehead* (Philadelphia: Westminster Press, 1965), p. 173.

84 Cobb, *Christ in a Pluralistic Age*, p. 33.

85 Boff, *Jesus Christ Liberator*, p. 244.

86 Boff, *Passion of Christ, Passion of the World: The Facts, Their Interpretation and Their Meaning Yesterday and Today*, xii .

inner being of God himself, as in Barth. Rather, human salvation is in human beings "becoming more and more themselves."[87] Salvation, for Boff, is completely immanent, the actualization of what is already there. No radical transformation is needed. Christ is "the individual to whom God granted the measure of openness to the absolute that enabled him to identify with that absolute."[88] In fact, Christ ends up being used for the sake of an *a priori* view of humanity.

Since Boff and Cobb do not have a ground for human responsibility in God himself, they are forced to consider the reality of salvation in terms of the obedience of human beings; a highly tenuous and unpredictable situation! To seek the reality of salvation in all human beings as in Cobb's and Boff's soteriologies is to end in frustration. The obedience of Jesus Christ points us to God's being itself, and therefore provides an anchor on which to have hope in the midst of a tragic and ambiguous world.

THE TRUE KNOWLEDGE OF GOD AND THE TRUE KNOWLEDGE OF HUMANITY

Contemporary soteriology, as seen in Boff and Cobb, is right to emphasize that salvation must deal with humanity as we now know it. It is no longer adequate to restrict salvation to simply a future existence. Nor is it possible to be satisfied with a theory of the atonement which operates externally to the reality of humanity. Humanity must be regarded in the most realistic and serious sense. The humanity of God in Barth's theology represents an attempt to take humanity seriously, but also to see humanity in all its history, that is, including its origin and source in the being of God himself. The problem of the reality of salvation must deal seriously with humanity. But the humanity of God points us beyond the frailty of human experience into that which is not vulnerable to the sin of humanity and the ambiguities of world history, the eternal being of God.

Jesus Christ does not receive his divine authority from outside of himself, according to Barth. He already possesses it

---

[87] Ibid., p. 98.
[88] Ibid.

"antecedently in Himself."[89] It is also true that the humanity of Christ is not determined by abstract human nature. He does not derive the authority for his humanity from the existential questions or possibilities of humanity. It is rather the opposite.

> As the nature of Jesus, human nature with all its possibilities is not a presupposition which is valid for Him too and controls and explains Him, but His being as man is as such that which posits and therefore reveals and explains human nature with all its possibilities.[90]

Our tendency is to see in Jesus the fulfillment of human hopes and possibilities. The Incarnation, however, teaches us that we must be converted in our thinking concerning what is true humanity. Jesus reveals that true humanity consists of "doing the work of God to the exclusion of all other works."[91] The fact that it is the eternal Son of God who has become human means that human life is included in "the circle of the inner life of the Godhead."[92] "Real man" is known in the reality of the Son of God becoming human and living a life of obedience to the Father.[93] The self-sufficiency of the Son of God means that he is able to be the source of "overflowing being," to use Jüngel's phrase, that is, the source of true humanity.[94] As Boff comments, the sociology of knowledge reminds us that we read our own world view into the meaning we give to the world.[95] But this gives even more reason to view the humanity of God revealed in

---

[89] Barth, *CD* I/1, p. 444.

[90] Ibid., III/2, p. 59.

[91] Ibid., p. 63.

[92] Ibid., p. 64.

[93] Ibid.

[94] Jüngel, p. 384. In an interesting way, Eberhard Jüngel unites both Barth on the humanity of God and Bonhoeffer on the "death" of God (God allows himself to be pushed out of the world on the cross) by affirming the death of God not as the displacement of God by humanity but rather as the humanity of God. Ibid., p. 299.

[95] Leonardo Boff, *Faith on the Edge: Religion and Marginalized Existence*, trans. Robert R. Barr (San Francisco: Harper and Row, 1989), p. 49.

Jesus Christ as the *critique* of our world views and perceptions, a critique which is efficacious because the power of the grace of God is behind it.

Salvation as "humanization" as presented in Hans Küng's theology can sound very attractive. More than any other contemporary theologian, Küng addresses this contemporary need. But it is instructive to note how he plays off *humanization* against *deification*, the great soteriological tradition in the Eastern church and the early Fathers. Küng believes that this tradition from Irenaeus results in a neglect of the cross of Christ, and, most importantly, a supplanting of humanization by a concern for the heavenly destiny. This will not do in the contemporary world, according to Küng. "Our problem is not the deification but the *humanization of man*."[96] That is, the question which modern humanity asks is about humanization, not deification. It is obvious how much Küng is indebted to an anthropocentric methodology which, similar to the existential theologians of a generation past, is determined by the questions of the modern world.

A theological methodology shaped by human questions, however, Küng contends, is not unique to the modern world. Christianity in its earliest manifestations was inescapably "time-bound." In the Synoptics, in Paulinism, in Johannism, we find different ways of thinking, imagining, interpreting based on their distinctive social and cultural background.

> They give us pictorial and conceptual articulation and models from a totally different world of experience, which no longer speak to us directly but must be mediated afresh today.[97]

This statement expresses Küng's profound concern for a "mediating" theology, a theology that does not confuse its time-bound phenomenon with the Christian reality of salvation. This is what occurred with the church Fathers, whose Platonic ideas of timelessness, and therefore omnipresence and incomprehensibil-

---

[96] Küng, *On Being a Christian*, p. 442.

[97] Hans Küng, *Theology and the Third Millenium: An Ecumenical View,* trans. Peter Heinegg (New York: Doubleday, 1988), p. 110.

ity, de-emphasized God's acting in the world and in history.[98] This is not to deny that some cultural translation was needed from the Hebrew world of scriptural times to the Greek world of the Fathers.

> Such a remolding was requisite if full verbal expression was to be given to the God of the Bible who lives in history, and not simply to an intrinsically ambiguous primal ground of all existent reality deduced by logical reference.[99]

But is not the fact of true "timeboundness" of Christianity an argument against viewing salvation as first of all from "below," against Küng's Christology? What becomes of the *criterion* for the "remolding" of the Christian message in a new culture and time, as Küng admits is necessary? Does not the danger exist of the absolutization of our questions as *the* salvific questions, rather than an openness to being questioned by God? So, Küng joins Hegel in his criticism of "the naive and anthropomorphic idea" of One who dwells in a literal or spatial sense 'above' the world, from whom the Son of God 'descends', and to where he 'ascends', and rather encourages a view of God in which "the world is not without God nor God without the world."[100] Thus soteriology must proceed from the historical method and the "historical reality" of Jesus.[101] Humanization may be a worthy goal of salvation, but is it the *only* goal, and is it to be left up to our own definition of what is truly human?

Jesus as the "archetype of true humanity" is Küng's response to the goal of salvation. We should not start out with concepts of God which are "assumed to be obvious." Thus, we must "try to see in the concrete Christ what man is theologically and what God is theologically."[102]

---

[98] Ibid., p. 440.

[99] Hans Küng, *The Incarnation of God: An Introduction to Hegel's Theological Thought as a Prolegomena to a Future Christology*, trans. J. R. Stephenson (New York: Crossroad, 1987), p. 442.

[100] Ibid., p. 461.

[101] Ibid., p. 469.

[102] Ibid., p. 529.

Is Küng, then, closer to the critique of anthropocentric sote-riology which we see in Barth's doctrine of the humanity of God than we thought at first? "The concrete Christ" is the Christ known only from "below," from historical method, and, in fact, as the answer to humanity's questions and as a model of humanity's best responses to those questions. In suffering, doubting, and de-spairing, humanity finds its incapacity, thus leading to "an abso-lute, undeserved trust in the incomprehensible God."[103] In Jesus, God does go to humanity, but only to become the "model" of trusting God.

> If I trustingly rely consistently on this model, it enables
> me to discover and realize the meaning of my being
> human and of my freedom in existing and involving
> myself for my fellow man.[104]

But what is lost when we surrender the traditional doctrine of deification? The humanity of God would suggest that what we lose is the divine origin and destiny of true humanity. Küng ap-pears to be stuck in a quandary. If salvation is humanization, how are we to determine the nature of authentic, as opposed to unau-thentic, humanity? Although he claims that Jesus is the "archetype" of true humanity, this is inconsistent with a theologi-cal methodology which admittedly starts from "below," with the existential questions of humanity. Those questions certainly deal with a mirror of our own fallen humanity, not with that of Jesus. The humanity of God reminds us that God comes to question us.[105]

---

[103] Küng, *Does God Exist?* pp. 623-624.

[104] Ibid., p. 688.

[105] T. F. Torrance, "Questioning in Christ," in *Theology in Reconstruction* (Grand Rapids: Eerdmans, 1965), pp. 117-127. For this reason, Donald Bloesch characterizes Küng's work as more "anthropology" than "theology." Review of *On Being a Christian* by Hans Küng, *Christianity Today* 21 (May 6, 1977), p. 51.

"LOOKING TO JESUS ..." (HEB. 12:2) AS "THEOLOGICAL CULTURE"

Barth states that one of the great implications of the humanity of God is for "theological culture," that is, the world in which the theologian lives, speaks, and acts is informed radically neither by God nor humanity in themselves, but by "the man-encountering God and the God-encountering man."[106] Therefore, theology cannot "introduce" Jesus Christ.[107] It can speak only as it looks to him. In other words, it must follow the exhortation of the Epistle to the Hebrews: "...and let us run with perseverance the race that is set before us, looking to Jesus the pioneer and perfecter of our faith" (Heb. 12:1-2).

The tendency of modern soteriology to "introduce" Jesus only after preliminary considerations of religious, socio-political, or world experience is all too real. The humanity of God keeps us focused on the revelation of God in Jesus Christ only, and therefore, the focus on the problem of salvation is seen in the context of God's own Being and Act. The integral relationship between revelation and reconciliation is particularly important here. In the Vatican's critique of Leonardo Boff there is such a concern for a specific theological criterion. But it is highly doubtful that simply "the authoritative interpretation of the church" can function as that "essential theological criterion" apart from a desire to be criticized itself by the humanity of God revealed in Jesus.[108] Otherwise, it can all too easily absolutize its interpretation, and "introduce" Jesus for the sake of an ulterior agenda.

One must wonder about the Vatican's real motivation in silencing Boff. Could it be, most of all, because he is criticizing the hierarchy? Given the positive advances of Vatican II and ecumenical discussion between Protestants and Catholics, one would hope not. But such statements like this seem to argue otherwise:

> Prophetic denunciation in the church must always remain at the service of the church itself. Not only must

---

[106] Barth, *The Humanity of God*, p. 55.
[107] Ibid.
[108] Sacred Congregation for the Doctrine of the Faith, *Instruction on Certain Aspects of 'The Theology of Liberation'*, pp. 27-28, cf. pp. 19, 23.

it accept the hierarchy and the institution, but it must
also cooperate positively in the consolidation of the
church's internal communication. Furthermore, *the
supreme criterion* [emphasis mine] for judging not only
its ordinary exercise but also its genuineness pertains
to the hierarchy.[109]

Religious Experience

The lack of a means to critique religious experience is very
evident in much of contemporary soteriology. John Cobb and
David Griffin state boldly that some experiences cannot be denied
even if one wishes to deny them.[110] But is not this strange to say
in an age in which Kant has taught us to question our perceptions
of our experiences? The problem here is particularly seen in regard
to Cobb's preference for "enjoyment" over morality. Process theology regards the fundamental goal of God to be the promotion of
the creature's own enjoyment, that is, "that which the creatures
experience as intrinsically good."[111] But what do they mean by
the "intrinsically good"? Is there any objective criterion within
human experience which allows us to discern the "intrinsically
good"? This is extremely doubtful.

For Leonardo Boff, the appearance of grace is not a
"supernatural action", but an "experience of human historicity"
signifying "gift giving, gratuitiousness, benevolence, favor,
beauty."[112] "Experience" is our way of relating to the world, and
in this case, to God.[113] This grace is expressed in our natural desire to love God.

> The natural desire to love God is not a symptom of
> humanity's unbridled egotism or its desire to expropri-
> ate God; nor is it a merely human exigency. It was

---

109 "Doctrinal Congregation Criticizes Brazilian's Book," *Origins*, NC
     Documentary Service, 14. No. 42 (April 4, 1985), p. 687.
110 Cobb and Griffin, pp. 30-32.
111 Ibid., p. 56.
112 Leonardo Boff, *Liberating Grace,* trans. John Drury (Maryknoll, NY: Orbis,
     1979), pp. 37, 45.
113 Ibid., p. 38.

God himself who structured human beings in such a
way that they are permanently open to hearing the
voice of God as it comes to them through things,
through their own conscience, other human mediation,
and God himself.[114]

But is such a confidence in humanity's ability to interpret its experience as the virtue of the "natural desire to know God" warranted?
The classical Protestant polemic against the medieval *gratia sup-
posit naturum* (which Boff gladly endorses[115]) is not irrelevant
here. Both Barth's famous "Nein!" to natural theology and
Calvin's doctrine of the noetic effects of sin provide an important
critique unanswered by Boff.[116] Such an approach negates the
particularity of the Incarnation. Instead of the Incarnation as the
revelation of God to humanity, based on God's initiative of grace,
it is for Boff, rather "the prime expression" of "the mutual opening
up of God and human beings," in which "not only does God come
to encounter humanity but humanity goes out continually to search
for God."[117] However, Boff hastens to add, "the human search
for God is the effect of God's search for humanity."[118] But Boff
still ignores the effect of sin on that search: "God created human
beings in such a way that they are always looking for the absolute."[119] One can only wonder who is the human person Boff is
speaking about, since the only concrete, particular human beings
we know of are *sinful* human beings, certainly created to know
God, but, at the present time, still in the bondage of sin, a
bondage which affects every part of the human being, even our
noblest efforts, including our religious desires (Rom. 1:19-21).
    Such an optimism about the virtue of religious experience
extends for Boff to the church. This is especially true of the

---

114 Ibid., p. 44.
115 Ibid., p. 63.
116 Karl Barth, "No!," in Karl Barth and Emil Brunner, *Natural Theology*
(London: G. Bles, 1975), and T. F. Torrance, *Calvin's Doctrine of Man*
(Westport, CT: Greenwood Press 1977 (1957)), pp. 116-127.
117 Boff, *Liberating Grace*, p. 181.
118 Ibid.
119 Ibid.

church "base communities," small groups of the poor. "The church springs from the people," rather than the traditional, hierarchical church.[120] But is it truly to be compassionate to the poor to burden them with a "reinvention" of the church, expecting the church to "spring up" out of them? Is the reality of salvation to be found in the religious experience of any people? Does such a theology simply cast their burdens back upon themselves?

This same lack of criticism of religious experience is seen in John Hick's soteriology. Hick admits readily that his theology is grounded on deductions made from his observations of the liturgical practices of differing religions.[121] In this straightforward statement it seems that we have a key to the dilemma of an anthropocentric soteriology. Is Hick *able* to "look to Jesus, the pioneer and perfecter of our faith," if his epistemological and soteriological eyes are fixed solely upon differing religious phenomena, and, indeed, if he then allows the religious phenomena, or rather, his *interpretation* of the religious phenomena, to determine his attitude toward Jesus? In effect, as Chester Gillis comments, Hick *expects* to find agreement between religions, particularly about the nature of the Real as love, compassion, and grace. "Could it not be that the religions are indeed saying different things, or making different claims, about the nature of the Real, salvation, ethical conduct, and the fate of the dead?"[122] Thus, any picture of Jesus has the tendency to be more a picture of *me* than the objective person of Christ. Such an approach can lead to atheism and nihilism, claims Roger Trigg, in a most perceptive critique of Hick.[123] Why even bother with religion, not to mention Jesus, if one can move from "self-centeredness" to "Reality-centeredness" in another way? Or why even prefer selflessness to selfishness? Our upbringing undoubtedly has influenced us here as well. Since Jesus as the Son of God does not express any metaphysical status,

---

120 Leonardo Boff, *Ecclesiogenesis: the Base Communities Reinvent the Church*, trans. Robert R. Barr (Maryknoll, NY: Orbis, 1986), p. 7.

121 Hick, *God Has Many Names*, p. 17.

122 Chester Gillis, *A Question of Final Belief: John Hick's Pluralistic Theory of Salvation* (New York: St. Martins Press, 1988), p. 163.

123 Roger Trigg, "Religion and the Threat of Relativism," *Religious Studies*, 19 (1983), pp. 298-299.

but is rather a "mythological" expression of the immense significance of our encounter "with the Real,"[124] then why believe in God or even in objective knowledge? "In other words," Trigg comments, "the emphasis is moved from a question about reality to one about our response to that reality."[125] Hick has effectively cut himself off from any objective non-dualist knowledge of Jesus Christ.[126]

If Hick separates himself from knowledge of Jesus *an sich,* then what implications will that have for knowledge of God and his character? T. F. Torrance relates the moving story of his battlefield experience as a chaplain, when a dying young soldier asked, "Is God really like Jesus?" Such a doubt, Torrance comments, is part of the "insidious damage done to people's faith by dualist habits of thought which drive a wedge between Jesus and God."[127] As Trigg concludes

> If God is not as a particular scheme describes him but is the referent or 'target' of radically different schemes *the question remains as to what he really is like* [emphasis mine].[128]

Implications of this way of thinking are also found in Hick's attempt to accept such contrary views of God, particularly the distinction between God as personal and God as impersonal. He criticizes incarnational Christology for its failure to succeed at the bar of logic:

> How one person can be both eternal and yet born in time; omnipotent and yet with the limited capacity of a human body; omniscient and yet with finite knowledge; omnipresent and yet confined to one region of space at a time: how, in short, the same person can

---

124 Hick, "Jesus and the World Religions," in *The Myth of God Incarnate,* p. 182.

125 Trigg, p. 301.

126 See the problem of dualistic thinking in theology which separates Christ from Israel, and Christ from God, as critiqued by T. F. Torrance, *The Mediation of Christ* (Grand Rapids: Eerdmans, 1983), pp. 11-82.

127 Ibid., p. 70.

128 Trigg, p. 303.

> have the full attributes of both God and men... seems
> indeed to be an a par with the statement that a figure
> drawn on paper has the attributes of both a circle and a
> square.[129]

But is Hick willing to extend the same logic to an even more
problematic issue, how God could be both personal and impersonal? In regard to the Incarnation, the limit of reason as it
"collides" with the paradox of the Incarnation, an insight from
Kierkegaard's thought, should be remembered.[130] Also, T. F.
Torrance's suggestion that "each object, and especially God," has
its own "inner logic," which "goes beyond simple conventionalist
logic," is pertinent here. Such a logic develops out of the integrity
of the object as it discloses itself to the observer, rather than to remain victim to an *a priori,* "external" logic.[131] Hick's only
response to the problem of God is to suggest that the "ultimate" is
personal, but not *an sich.* It is only personal in its interactions with
human beings.[132] God's personhood in the end becomes
dependent on experiences of human personhood. The *Ding an sich*
of Kant remains unknown. The end result is that the problem of
the reality of salvation remains for Hick a question which he
cannot answer. In this case, the ambiguity and tragedy of human
experience speaks all too loudly against any claim of salvation.

Socio-Political Experience

A similar criticism may be leveled at Leonardo Boff's version of liberation theology and its emphasis upon "the socioana-
lytical 'text' of reality" as "theological criteria."[133] Socio-political
history is the occasion for the revelation of God, according to

---

129   Hick, *The Center of Christianity,* p. 31.
130   Søren Kierkegaard, *Philosophical Fragments/ Johannes Climacus,* ed. and
trans. by Howard V. Hong and Edna H. Hong (Princeton: Princeton
University Press, 1985).
131   T. F. Torrance, *Theological Science* (Oxford: Oxford University Press, 1969),
pp. 203-280.
132   John Hick, "Is God Personal?," in *God: The Contemporary Discussion,* eds.
F. Sontag and M. D. Bryant (New York: Rose of Sharon Press, 1982), p. 174.
133   Boff and Boff, *Salvation and Liberation,* p. 9.

Boff. The proper question to ask is, "What is God trying to tell us in these social problems, now adequately grasped by scientific reason?"[134]

But is this an adequate approach for discerning the will of God? Surely every Christian must be empathetic with the plight of the poor and the oppressed, but is there not here a temptation to equate the socio-political situation with the revelation of God, and thus fall snare to another version of an anthropocentric theology? Such a theology still runs the risk of reducing human existence to the political process. Yes, the political nature of humanity is real and is addressed by the lordship of Christ. As Barth wryly states, Pontius Pilate does intrude into the Apostles' Creed, and rather "coarsely and bitingly," like "a dog into a nice room"![135] Again, we must listen to Barth: "Faith without this tendency to public life, faith that avoids this difficulty, has become in itself unbelief, wrong belief, superstition," for Christian proclamation is a proclamation to the world. [136] Yet this does not mean a surrender to the analysis of political ideology, Marxist or otherwise. This results in a reduction of the human being to simply a political animal. The Vatican's observation is astute:

> One needs to be on guard against *the politicization of existence* [emphasis mine] which, misunderstanding the entire meaning of the kingdom of God and the transcendence of the person, begins to sacralize politics and betray the religion of the people in favor of the projects of the revolution.[137]

Is "praxis" itself really an unambiguous concept? Can it be twisted and used for the sake of an ideological agenda, uninformed by the revelation of the Triune God in Christ? As the critics of Boff have stated, "praxis neither replaces nor produces the truth but remains

---

134 Ibid.
135 Karl Barth, *Dogmatics in Outline*, trans. G. T. Thomson (New York: Philosophical Library, 1949), p. 108.
136 Ibid., p. 29.
137 Sacred Congregation for the Doctrine of the Faith, *Instruction on Certain Aspects of 'The Theology of Liberation'* , p. 34.

at the service of the truth consigned to us by the Lord."[138] Certainly theology which is devoid of praxis is a form of "disconnected love" (Ray Anderson) and reflects a non-incarnational theology. But this does not mean that an abstract principle of praxis, virtually a surrender to pragmatism, should be adopted. "Ministry precedes theology and produces theology, not the reverse," as Ray Anderson is fond of saying.[139] But what Anderson means by "ministry" is not simply the church slavishly answering the demands of society fulfilling a religious niche, making the world safe from theological criticism. Rather, he means God's own ministry, revealed in Jesus Christ, his act of revelation on behalf of a needy world.[140] Thus, even praxis itself is under the judging light of the revelation of God in Christ.

John Paul II's critique of liberation theology has yet to be answered: It is in danger of becoming a false theology because it uses "systems or means of analysis" that are not Christian.[141] For Boff, the socio-political is determined by "scientific reason," an unquestioned Marxist analysis of class struggle. While it appears courageous (and necessary) to speak "for the poor" and against the "oppressors," does Boff really accomplish much more than rhetoric? Boff is notoriously ambiguous on what the context is for the church's participation in destroying or building up socio-economic and political structures. The ballot? Violent revolution? Civil disobedience? Terrorism? Despite his disavowal, the utopian element remains in Boff's theology. As Cardinal Ratzinger and the

---

138 "Doctrinal Congregation Criticizes Brazilian Theologians Book," *Origins*, p. 685.

139 Ray S. Anderson, "A Theology for Ministry," in *Theological Foundations for Ministry*, ed., Ray S. Anderson (Grand Rapids and Edinburgh: Eerdmans and T. & T. Clark, 1979), p. 7.

140 See the discussion in my article, "The Atonement as the Life of God in the Ministry of the Church," in *Incarnational Ministry: the Presence of Christ in Church, Society, and Family, Essays in Honor of Ray S. Anderson*, eds. Christian D. Kettler and Todd H. Speidell (Colorado Springs: Helmers and Howard, 1990), p. 58.

141 Cited by Boff and Boff, p. 31. Carl Braaten considers *praxis* to be a "Trojan horse" to theology, similar to other attempts at adapting philosophic principles to Christianity, such as the Stoic *logos*, the Hegelian *Geist*, Heideggerian *Existenz*, and Whiteheadian *process*, p. 128.

Vatican have observed, utopian hopes have given birth to some of the cruelest movements in history.

> Millions of our contemporaries legitimately learn to re-cover their basic freedoms, of which they were de-prived by totalitarian and atheistic regimes which came to power by violent and revolutionary means, precisely in the name of the liberation of the people. This shame of our time cannot be ignored: while claiming to bring them freedom, these regimes keep whole nations in conditions of servitude which are unworthy of mankind.[142]

These sad consequences, which we are all too familiar with in the twentieth century, reveal the intellectual shallowness of utopian ideals through their refusal to consider the *alternatives* to the status quo or the *consequences* of their alternatives, if they have any. As Michael Novak puts it incisively, the *practical* question must be asked:

> Which sorts of economic institutions, in fact, do lift up the poor?... What institutions will it [liberation theol-ogy] put in place, *after* the revolution to protect human rights? Through which institutions, will it open its economy to the initiative, intelligence and creativity of the poorest of its citizens?[143]

The utopian element in liberation theology should be at odds with the concern for praxis, for concrete political and social experience. But this is not so, ironically. As Novak comments,

> One of the most disappointing features of liberation theology is its abstractness and generality. Far from being descriptive, concrete and practical, it is intricately speculative, ideological and academic.[144]

---

142 Sacred Congregation for the Doctrine of the Faith, *Instruction on Certain Aspects of 'The Theology of Libera*tion', p. 32.

143 Novak, *Will it Liberate? Questions About Liberation Theology*, p. 6.

144 Ibid., p. 113, cf. Joseph Ratzinger, with Vittorio Messori, *The Ratzinger Report: An Exclusive Interview on the State of the Church*, trans. Salvatori Attanasio and Graham Harrison (San Francisco: Ignatius Press, 1986) p. 189.

The result of Boff's utopian tendencies is that Boff attempts to "introduce" Jesus at the right time as the proponent of his Marxist class analysis, instead of possessing an openness to the Jesus who is the critic of all ideology, political or religious. Despite the dubious reasons which the Vatican has for defending supremacy of the hierarchy, it is highly questionable that Boff strengthens his criticism of the hierarchy's power when he uses the Marxist analysis of "means of production" in regard to the distribution of the sacraments. The temptation to reductionism, reducing the sacraments to "a mere sociological phenomenon" is too great, as his critics are quick to respond.[145] The sacraments can certainly be used as "weapons" of power, but such a Marxist analysis lends itself to the common criticism of all Marxist thought: is the desire for economic power the exclusive hermeneutic for human experience? Other human desires such as love, creativity, and the ability to transcend (Rahner) argue otherwise. Such a use of Marxist analysis can easily result in "a naive view of the state" and its potential for social change, as Novak comments.[146]

World Experience

A particular concern of modern soteriology is the desire to see more continuity between salvation history and secular history. The concern is certainly legitimate. Theology should not lock itself into a ghetto. The Word became flesh, and that means the flesh of all humanity. What kind of relevant word can the church speak if it does not acknowledge the relevance of the movement of world history? Is not God interested in this?

In that spirit, Moltmann sees the work of the Holy Spirit as the creative Spirit which "embraces human history and natural history" and that has been understood by secular philosophers and historians as "the movement," "the urge," "the spirit of life," "the

---

[145] "Doctrinal Congregation Criticizes Brazilian Theologians Book," *Origins*, p. 686.

[146] Novak, *Will it Liberate? Questions About Liberation Theology*, p. 28.

tension," and "the torment"(!).[147] The church is a part of the history of this creative Spirit.[148]

In a similar way, Pannenberg's view of salvation identifies salvation history with universal history.[149] God is integrally involved in the intellectual and spiritual development of the West:

> God pursued his aim of a universal Christian mission through the West and it is from Europe particularly in modern times that the world has grown into a unity; not however through the spread of the Christian faith, but indirectly by way of Western science and technology, which themselves emerged from the intellectual background of Christianity.[150]

The mission of the church is to look continually for and participate in "new forms of the unification of mankind."[151]

Whether these new forms will ever be fulfilled is left open in the indeterminacy of both process thought and Moltmann. Although Cobb criticizes Moltmann for not making it clear whether or not the promise will actually be fulfilled in the future, process thought is also vulnerable because of its passionate opposition to any charge that God is omnipotent, and therefore, in its estimation, coercive.[152]

Not only is the world experience of history used by anthropocentric theology, but broad categories of human experience are also developed as the conveyors of divine revelation. For Boff, the basic experience of the feminine, as expressed in the Virgin Mary, is a much needed corrective to the domineering force of the masculine in rationalistic modern society. But, does Boff express

---

[147] Moltmann, *The Church in the Power of the Spirit,* p. 34.
[148] Ibid., p. 35.
[149] See Pannenberg, ed., *Revelation as History.*
[150] Pannenberg, *Faith and Reality,* p. 85.
[151] Ibid., p. 86.
[152] Cobb, *Process Theology as Political Theology,* p. 69. See Langdon Gilkey's comment: If God envisions the unlimited possibilities not yet realized in process "then the future God faces is also open, undecided." *Message and Existence: An Introduction to Christian Theology* (Minneapolis: The Seabury Press, 1979), p. 93.

any sensitivity to our warped and inadequate views of human existence, including our ideas of what is feminine and what is masculine? Does not our broad view of what it means to be human need to be criticized by the humanity of God's eternal being as Trinity, revealed by the Incarnation of the Son which at the same time both relativizes our sexuality (the Word took upon the flesh of *all* people, male and female) and establishes our sexual distinctions, yet without stereotypes (the Word took upon the flesh of a particular, individual, Jewish male, not a mythic "androgynous" human being)?

The problem with these attempts is the same as the problem with anthropocentric theologies built upon religious and socio-political experiences. Where are the criteria to discern what is a genuine movement of the Spirit and what is a movement of the devil? Boff can speak of the "humanity of God," but as the ability of the human spirit to soar above contingent limitations— the humanity of God from "below," if you will.[153] But is this really God, then? In this view does the word of judgment from on high exist to call humanity to accountability? Does this view fall victim to the Feuerbachian critique of religion as simply the expression of humanity's highest value?[154] In effect, is the grace of God handcuffed, imprisoned by human sin, disabling sin that refuses to recognize the grace of God's initiative, expressed in a specific act? This is the imperative of the humanity of God from "above." The humanity of God as seen in Barth and Jüngel's theology is a critique of such attempts to bring forth a natural theology which is not dependent upon a specific *Act* of the *Being* of God. Such universal soteriologies tend to "introduce" Jesus as a participant in a universal movement of history, rather than as the revolutionary Jesus of the Gospels who not only refuses to be identified with the *Zeitgeist* of first century Judaism and Rome, but, in fact, was crucified because of this refusal.

---

[153] Boff, *Faith on the Edge*, pp. 49-50, 162.

[154] Ludwig Feuerbach, *The Essence of Christianity*, trans. George Eliot (New York: Harper and Row, 1957), pp. 12ff.

THE VICARIOUS HUMANITY OF CHRIST AS THE EXTERNAL EXPRESSION OF THE ETERNAL HUMANITY OF GOD

A constant theme runs through the variety of the modern soteriologies which we have surveyed: They are all children of the Enlightenment. The this-worldly concerns of post-Enlightenment theology, despite the genuine contribution of a concern for humanization, have created the dominance of anthropocentric methodology in Christian theologies of salvation.

But how are we to view anthropocentric methodology in regard to the question of the reality of salvation? Does not this methodology lead ultimately to despair, as humanity is cast back upon its own resources? Are not religious experience, sociopolitical experience, and world experience all too ambiguous to say anything concerning the reality of salvation? We must look to God. In God himself is the only anchor, rock, and refuge for salvation as the Psalms never tire in proclaiming (Ps. 3:8; 9:14; 13:5; 18:35, 46; 20:5; 21:1; 24:5; 25:5; 27:1,9; 38:22; 50:23; 51:14; 62:2,7). Our discussion has discovered that what might be a truism for some has yet to be learned in all of its radicalness by contemporary theology. Still, we must learn from modern theology that one cannot speak of God apart from humanity. To do so would be cruel and idealistic. We must also look to humanity.

The humanity of God speaks of the origin and source of humanity in God's eternal relationship between the Father and the Son through the Spirit. Humanity is not something alien to God. Created humanity is the *analogia relationis* of the eternal relationship of love between the Father and the Son through the Spirit.

But that humanity has now been expressed in space and time in the Incarnation. Still, we must be careful to see not only the *identification* of the Word with our flesh, but also the imperative for us to *participate* in his eternal humanity. The implications of this are profound. As T.F. Torrance has proposed, the vicarious *atonement* of Christ must be understood as the vicarious *humanity* of Christ. What does this mean? In *scope*, it means that nothing is left unaffected by the vicarious humanity of Christ: knowledge of God, creation, salvation, the church, or eschatology. At every point, Christ, and Christ as the basis for our humanity, takes his rightful place, and does not surrender to our creaturely frailties. In *depth*, this means that even to the point of our *repentance*, Christ has gone before us. He does not intend us to stand in the folly of our self-sufficiency. As a *goal*, it means that God intends to bring us to himself as sons and daughters because of the exalted eschatological humanity of the Son, who is as his right hand. The *locus* of the reality of salvation in the world today, then, is the community of the Last Adam, the community of the Spirit, the community of imperfect, yet concrete, acts of faith, hope, and love, the church. But this is not a community which has any rights of origin in itself. It has been displaced by the vicarious humanity of Christ, and is restored only when that community, finding its new being in Christ, allows the Spirit of Christ to break through in concrete, albeit sometimes meager, acts of faith, hope, and love. This is the reality of salvation which we are to enter into and strive towards. This is the reality of salvation which is based on God alone. This is the vicarious humanity of Christ, to which we turn next.

PART TWO

THE VICARIOUS HUMANITY OF CHRIST
AS THE EXTERNAL EXPRESSION
OF THE ETERNAL HUMANITY OF GOD

CHAPTER SIX

VICARIOUS HUMANITY AS THEOLOGICAL REALITY:
T. F. TORRANCE

Thomas F. Torrance is one contemporary theologian who has repeatedly in his writings brought up the significance of the *vicarious* humanity of Christ for salvation.[1] This is a humanity which becomes the basis for a renewed and restored humanity. Certainly such an approach holds promise to help us in our search for "the reality of salvation."

Let us begin by outlining Torrance's ideas on the place of the humanity of Christ in Christology and soteriology. We will follow this with a look at its implications for the reality of salvation, as seen in the doctrine, life, and ministry of the church.

CHRISTOLOGY AND SOTERIOLOGY: THE LIFE OF GOD AS RECONCILIATION

St. Athanasius has been one of the great influences on Torrance's theology of the vicarious humanity of Christ. This is

---

[1] Biographical studies of Torrance are found in R. F. Kernohan. "Tom Torrance: The Man and the Reputation," *Life and Work,* 32, No 5 (May, 1976), pp. 14-16 and I. John Hesselink, "An Interview with Thomas F. Torrance," *Reformed Review* 38, No. 1, (Autumn, 1984), pp. 47-64. Significant studies of Torrance include Robert J. Palma, "Thomas F. Torrance's Reformed Theology," Ibid., pp. 2-45, and W. Jim Neidhardt, "Key Themes in Thomas F. Torrance's 'Integration of Judeo-Christian Theology and Natural Science'," introduction to Thomas F. Torrance, *The Christian Frame of Mind: Reason, Order, and Openness in Theology and Natural Science* (Colorado Springs: Helmers and Howard, 1989), xi-xliv. Cf. Iain R. Torrance, "A Bibliography of the Writings of Thomas F. Torrance 1941-1989," *Scottish Journal of Theology* 43 (no. 2, 1990), pp. 225-262.

particularly interesting when we remember that Athanasius is usually remembered as the great champion of the deity of Christ. But instead of overreacting to the Arians' emphasis on the human aspects of the incarnate Christ, Athanasius turned the tables by stressing the high priestly ministry of Christ. Christ not only ministered the things of God to man, but also ministered the things of humanity to God.[2] But for Torrance it is entirely logical for Athanasius to move from the deity of Christ to his humanity. This is true because the humanity of Christ is so inseparable from "the Creator Son," "the Word of God," that we are able to be "humanized" through union with him in the Spirit.[3] It is this "double movement" of Christ as the way of God to humanity and as the way of humanity to God which the Fathers used to critique the twin heresies of Docetism and Ebionitism. Docetism started with an abstract concept of God and therefore eliminated any need for the humanity of Christ. Ebionitism was a false way of trying to see Christology "inductively," by beginning with the humanity of Jesus, but ending up with an idealizing of humanity.[4]

A common problem of Docetism and Ebionitism, along with Apollinarianism and Nestorianism, was their difficulty in conceiving of the possibility of the unchangeable, eternal God taking upon human flesh, with its contingency and passion.[5] The patristic emphasis was one of God coming as a human being, not simply in a human being. The former is a participation of divine Being in human existence; the latter is only a human being who is "divinized" and empowered by divine Being.[6] God coming as a human being rejects any kind of "deistic disjunction" between God and creation. It creates a new understanding of the possibility of the interaction of the living God with space and time. As Cyril of Alexandria wrote, "The Logos became man and did not just enter into man."[7] That is the significance of the emphasis in the Epistle to the Hebrews on Christ as our High Priest. Since the Logos be-

---

2   T. F. Torrance, *Theology in Reconciliation* (cited afterwards as *Theol. in Reconcil.*) (Grand Rapids: Eerdmans, 1975), p. 228.
3   Ibid., p. 210.
4   *Theological Science* (cited afterwards as TS) (Oxford: Oxford University Press), pp. 45-46.
5   *Theol. in Reconcil.* p. 202.
6   Ibid., pp. 135-146.
7   Cited by Torrance, Ibid., p. 157.

came human, Christ is able to be the mediator through his obedience and sacrifice.[8] This contrasts with the Catholic Tridentine priest who provides the mediation between God and humanity by reenacting the sacrifice of Christ. It was impossible for the Reformers to agree with this concept of priesthood because of their theology of the vicarious humanity of Christ. Calvinism sought to extend the reality of the humanity of Christ to include both heaven and earth through its teaching on the so-called *extra Calvinisticum* ("Calvinist extra"). By doing so, they denied that the humanity of Christ was bound by spatial or temporal limitation.[9] Torrance believes that the Lutheran principle of *finitum capax infiniti* (finitude may contain infinity), in contrast to the Calvinist rejoinder, *finitum non capax infiniti*, paved the way for the eighteenth and nineteenth century liberal doctrine of the capacity of the human spirit.[10] Calvinists maintained that the humanity of Christ and his obedience provides the capacity for an obedient response to God, not any latent ability within humanity. Furthermore, the lack of a doctrine of the vicarious humanity of Christ in liberal thought made Christ only "a special and exemplary instance of man's own capacity for the divine."[11]

Since the Logos became human and did not just enter into humanity, one must take the nature of the divine Logos seriously. This is the importance of the doctrine of the *homoousion* with the Father. If the Logos is of the "same essence" as the Father, this means that the very life of God is communicated into human flesh in the Incarnation.[12] The true humanity, as well as the true divinity of Christ, falls within the life of God. It was the theme of atonement as Christ communicating the life of God which was so dear to John McLeod Campbell, the nineteenth century theologian to whom Torrance is much in debt. In the doctrine of the *homoousion* we are dealing not just with a facade or a mask, but with the very life of divine Being himself.

---

8 *Conflict and Agreement in the Church,* Vol. 2 (London: Lutterworth Press, 1959-60), p. 137 (cited afterwards as CAC).

9 *Space, Time, and Incarnation* (cited afterwards as STI) (Oxford: Oxford University Press, 1969), pp. 31-32.

10 Ibid., p. 41.

11 Ibid.

12 T. F. Torrance, "Toward an Ecumenical Consensus on the Trinity," *Theologische Zeitschrift* 31 (1975), p. 339.

The life of God communicated to us in Jesus Christ is of vital importance for the doctrine of the atonement. For this to be understood, according to Torrance, we must take another suggestion from the Greek Fathers, and see the inseparable reality of the humanity of Christ and the atonement. The famous saying of Cyril encapsulates this concern: "For what has not been taken up has not been saved."[13] According to Athanasius, salvation is not simply Christ's external relations with sinners, based on a purely forensic model, which has been so dominant in the West. Salvation is based on the incarnate life of the Mediator:

> The Saviour having in very truth become man, the salvation of the *whole* man [Torrance emphasis] was brought about....Truly our salvation is not merely apparent, nor does it extend to the body only, but the whole body and soul alike, has truly obtained salvation in the Word himself.[14]

Therefore, atonement is not simply a secondary issue, but the center of our understanding of Christology. We must understand that reconciliation takes place in the human flesh of Jesus which grew in wisdom and obedience, confronting our darkness and actually "bending" the will of humanity.[15] This all can take place because he has assumed human nature. Christ is not simply the agent of our salvation, "but its very matter and substance."[16]

For Christ to assume our human nature means that a "correlation" and "correspondence" is established between our flesh and his flesh.[17] This is the heart of the mediation between Christ and humanity which provides a middle ground between the

---

13 *In Ioannis Evangelium*, cited in *Theol, in Reconcil.*, p. 167. Cp. the contemporary discussion about Christology and soteriology in Wolfhart Pannenberg, *Jesus—God and Man*, pp. 47-52; Walter Lowe, "Christ and Salvation," in *Christian Theology: An Introduction to its Traditions and Tasks*, eds. Peter C. Hodgson and Robert H. King, pp. 196ff.; Colin E. Gunton, *Yesterday and Today: A Study of Continuities in Christology*, pp. 24ff.

14 *Ad Epictetum* 7, cited in *Theol. in Reconcil.*, p. 230.

15 *Theology in Reconstruction* (cited afterwards as *Theol. in Recons.*) (Grand Rapids: Eerdmans, 1965), p. 132.

16 *Theol. in Reconcil.* p. 94.

17 *God and Rationality* (cited afterwards as GR) (Oxford: Oxford University Press, 1971), pp. 144-145.

self-giving of God and the reception by humanity, but a middle ground which exists in an "inner determination" of life. In Jesus Christ, a "reciprocity" has been created between God and created being which in turn creates a "wholeness" and "integrity" within the structures of creation.[18] Whether this makes any sense in the real, present world of sin, pain, and death is a question which Torrance must undoubtedly face. It suffices to say that Torrance takes very seriously the power of the holy and righteous life of Jesus as it encounters in his human nature the "contradiction" of our sinful human nature. This confrontation results in a victory for the sinless human nature of Christ and a healing, sanctifying, and renewing of our sinful human nature.[19]

The inner logic behind salvation through assumed and sanctified human nature, for Torrance, is the reality of substitution and incorporation. Athanasius can speak seriously of Christ being "made sin" and "made a curse" for us, and taking upon himself the inheritance of divine judgment upon us.[20] But atonement also means our incorporation into Christ through union with him. It is important for Christ's substitutionary work to be concerned with our human nature. This makes all the difference in how we interpret the death of Christ. Not only is his death substitutionary, but it is also an act of uniting himself with us, even in "our death."[21]

The inseparability of substitution and incorporation is particularly seen if we look at the implications of the *anhypostasia* and *enhypostasia* in the person of Christ.[22] *Anhypostasia* implies that it is only in God's act that the saving person of the human Jesus could have existed. *Enhypostasia* implies that only through the individual human being, Jesus of Nazareth, is salvation a reality. If only *anhypostasia* is applied to the atonement, as in Aulén's *Christus Victor*, that would signify a purely naked act of God upon the person, not really affecting one's humanity, because there is no incorporation into that humanity. However, a sole *enhypostasia* emphasis would mean that atonement is simply a human, Pelagian deed which placates God with a sacrifice. It is im-

---

18 GR, pp. 162-163.
19 *Theol. in Reconcil.,* p. 149. Cf. p. 143. Cf. *DCO,* pp. 137-140. For a fuller description of Torrance's theodicy, see pp. 85-142.
20 Ibid., p. 153.
21 Ibid., p. 148.
22 CAC, vol. 1, p. 244.

portant to note that for all his emphasis on the humanity of Christ, Torrance is able to see it balanced in the light of the *anhypostasia* doctrine. Thus, substitution and incorporation find an integral place within the twin Christological realities of *anhypostasia* and *enhypostasia*: Atonement is still an act of God, but it is an "act of God *done into our humanity, wrought out in our place, and as our act.*"[23]

The humanity of Christ is integrally related to salvation history in Torrance's thought. The emphasis in modern theology on the historical perspective inherent in the mighty acts of God in Israel provides a welcome foundation for a theology of the vicarious humanity of Christ.[24] The reality of God acting in human history gives more credence to a Nicene/Chalcedonian Christology which emphasizes the Incarnation, rather than in opposition to it, contrary to modern opinion. The circumcision of Abraham is the beginning of a covenant relationship between Yahweh and humanity, which is always concrete and historical, as indicated by the circumcision of *the flesh*.[25] This circumcision was fulfilled in the flesh of Jesus Christ. Through his circumcised flesh, his humanity, the New Covenant was inaugurated for all of humanity.

The "consummation" of salvation history as God taking on human flesh is seen in the resurrection and the ascension. In the ascension, humanity is taken up into the glory, presence, and life of God, and thus exalted by God precisely because our humanity is gathered into the humanity of the risen Christ. This is "the goal of the Incarnation."[26] This does not mean that humanity is swallowed up into "the infinite ocean of the divine Being." This is guaranteed by the fact that Christ shares in our humanity as we share in his. Therefore, we are able to share in his glory. The vicarious risen humanity also warns us not to consider the resurrected state as a transformation into another nature. The continuity of the earthly and risen humanity of Christ means that the same human nature exists in heaven, but in an imperishable state, such

---

23   Ibid.

24   *Theol, in Reconcil.*, p. 82.

25   CAC, vol. 1, p. 290.

26   *Space, Time and Resurrection* (cited afterwards as STR) (Grand Rapids: Eerdmans, 1976), pp. 135-136. The Incarnation as the "hermeneutical horizon" for authentic humanity is developed by Ray S. Anderson in *On Being Human*, p. 199.

as the angels'. This is how one should interpret the saying in Matthew 22:30 about the abolition of marriage in the resurrected state.[27]

Torrance retains the eschatological sense of the resurrection, even with his doctrine of vicarious and risen humanity. The resurrection and ascension of the humanity of Christ as the "consummation" of the work of atoning reconciliation has done away with the "darkness" of this world, for it is into this "darkness" which Christ descended and over which he was victorious. "Even the human nature he took from our dark and fallen existence is completely and finally restored in the light of God (II Cor. 4:6)."[28] However, the darkness is obviously not fully eradicated in this life. This eschatological tension is pictured in the Gospels by the fleeting glimpses which the disciples get of the resurrected Christ. A theology of the resurrection is not a *theologia gloriae* without a *theologia crucis*. Nevertheless, as far as we let the uncreated light of the Spirit fall upon us, "we may discern the reality of God's ways and works in a deeper and more triumphant mode."[29] This eschatological living is seen most clearly in the sacraments, when the risen humanity of Christ is recognized to correspond to the physical nature of the elements.

We seek now to summarize Torrance's thought on the vicarious humanity of Christ and salvation into nine thesis statements.

1. Christology includes the "double movement" of the way of God to humanity and the way of humanity to God, *contra* Docetism and Ebionitism. The "Creator Son," "the Word of God," is identical with Jesus of Nazareth (Athanasius). Thus, the radical significance of Christology is "the coming of God himself into the universe he created."[30]

2. God coming *as* a human being, not just *in* a human being removes all possibility of a "deistic disjunction" between God and creation. The possibility of the interaction of the living God with space and time is opened up.

---

27 Ibid., pp. 135-136, n. 12.
28 Ibid., p. 139.
29 Ibid., pp. 141-142.
30 DCO, p. 134.

3. The vicarious humanity of Christ is the heartbeat of salvation history. From the circumcision of Abraham to the Incarnation, crucifixion, resurrection, and ascension, the interaction of the humanity of Christ with creaturely form provides a basis for the knowledge of God and the reconciliation of humanity within the structures of space and time.

4. However, the reality of the humanity of Christ, as the reality of the "Creator Son," "the Word made flesh," is not limited to the structures of space and time. This is what is expressed in the Reformed doctrine of the so-called *extra Calvinisticum*, the significance of the vicarious humanity of the risen and exalted Christ.

5. The reality of the vicarious humanity of Christ stresses the inability of fallen humanity to know and respond to God. The Lutheran emphasis on *finitum capax infiniti* paved the way for the nineteenth century doctrine of the religious capacity of the human spirit .

6. This integration of the divine and creaturely provides the basis for the mediatorial ministry of Christ.

7. The divine Logos in human flesh, as the vicarious humanity of Christ, communicates the very life of God in humanity (Campbell). Salvation is based on the communication of this life (Irenaeus, Athanasius). In this way, Christology is dynamically related to soteriology. In effect, Christ becomes the "very matter and substance of salvation."

8. The work of the vicarious humanity of Christ is based on the twin moments in salvation of substitution/representation and incorporation. Christ not only takes our place, and becomes our representative, thereby creating a new humanity (substitution/representation), but also incorporates us into this new humanity (incorporation). Our actions become his actions. Our life becomes his life, the life of God.

9. The "correlation and correspondence" produced by the vicarious humanity of Christ provides an "inner determination" of life. There is a "reciprocity" of being which creates "wholeness" and "integrity" and presents a "contradiction" to the forces of darkness.

In this next section, we will examine how Torrance relates
the saving humanity of Christ to several different areas of theological reality: knowledge of God, revelation, the inspiration and
authority of the Scriptures, God and creation, justification, faith,
the church, the sacraments, and eschatology.

KNOWLEDGE OF GOD, REVELATION, AND INSPIRATION

Knowledge of God in Jesus Christ means that Truth has
taken on human being. As God is true in himself, so has the humanity of Christ become the truth which is made manifest from the
side of humanity.[31] This is an integral part of Torrance's desire to
bridge the object-subject chasm of modern theology.[32]

The Incarnation allows theology to be based on "empirical
correlates."[33] This is absolutely essential if our theology is going
to be related, not only to God and humanity, but also to the world.
In addition, a genuine humanity within the structures of space and
time allows itself to be exposed to a rigorous historical-critical
method.[34]

It is through the humanity of Christ that God actually works
upon our thinking and speaking.[35] This gives our thinking and
speaking an "inner obedience to his Word through our participation in the holy communion of Father, Son, and Holy Spirit." In
this confrontation with God in the humanity of Christ, we are face
to face, not only with knowledge of God, but also with knowledge of true humanity. The perfect humanity of Jesus reveals our
being to be diseased and self-willed. It is an exhortation for us not
to read our own humanity back into God.[36] Torrance maintains
the famous "infinite qualitative difference" between God and
humanity in Kierkegaard, even in the midst of his emphasis on the

---

31 *Theol. in Recons.*, pp. 133-134.
32 *TS*, pp. 1ff.
33 *Reality and Evangelical Theology* (cited afterwards as *RET*) (Philadelphia:
    Westminster Press, 1982), p. 35.
34 *TS*, p. 295. However, the limitations of the historical method are maintained
    strongly by Torrance: See *TS*, "The Relevance of Historical Science," pp. 312-
    336; *RET*, "Theological Questions to Biblical Scholars," pp. 52-83.
35 *Theol. in Recons.*, pp. 133-134.
36 *TS*, pp. 309-310.

humanity of Christ and salvation as participation in the life of God.

Torrance has long championed a "scientific" theology which allows the object studied to determine the means by which we know it. According to Torrance, this is the great heritage of patristic theology in antiquity, and of natural science as seen in Einsteinian physics in modern times. This "realist" view of knowledge decries the entrance of any alien principle into the field of study, since the object determines the means by which we know it. The Incarnation provides the means by which the tyranny of an alien systematic principle entering into theology is to be avoided. The scientific interest in coherence is not bound to a system in theological science, but to the actuality of Christ as the divine-human being.

The subjective aspect of God's knowing and how it relates to human knowledge is integral to knowledge of God, according to Torrance. The impasse in modern theology is so deep because of the refusal to acknowledge the actuality of the subjectivity of God. Karl Barth avoided the "epistemological Apollinarianism" of Bonhoeffer in *Act and Being*[37] by asserting the importance of the humanity of Christ for theological epistemology.[38] It is only God who is able to know himself as God. Any attempt to know God solely based on human effort results in only a reflection of human, not divine, being. The humanity of Christ reveals not only the saving act of God, but within that act, also genuine knowledge of God. This is the manifestation of the freedom of God to disclose his divine being. The humanity of Christ reveals not only the saving act of God, but within that act, also genuine knowledge of God. This is the manifestation of the freedom of God to disclose his divine being in humanity so that humanity is enabled to share in his divine life.[39] One of the "radical consequences of justification" is the calling into question of all natural knowledge.[40] Since Christ died for the whole person, it is imperative that the human way of knowing be called into question and crucified, especially in regard to knowledge of God. Torrance considers the purpose of

---

37 Dietrich Bonhoeffer, *Act and Being*, trans. Bernard Noble (London: Collins, 1962), p. 92.
38 *TS*, p. 292.
39 *GR*, p. 139.
40 *Theol. in Recons.*, p. 162.

dogmatics to be the unification of "the objective content of revelation with the subjective actualization of it in the humanity of Christ."[41] This is the basis for the ability of dogmatics to transcend our thoughts and language, but yet still use very human forms of language and thought. In this "Christological pattern" in thought and language, there should be both a genuine "correspondence" to the Word of God and a "coherence" of the forms of our doctrine to the structures of Christology.[42]

The problem of religious language takes on a new character, Torrance claims, when the implications of the Incarnation are considered. The gap between the contingent statements (human language) and God as Wholly Other is bridged by the Incarnation, the bridge between "not only the Word of God and the word of man, but also between the uncreated Truth of God and the created truth of this world."[43] Since God has joined himself with "creaturely and physical forms of thought," there is real knowledge of God, although, in the words of Hilary, the language only "suggests" and does not "exhaust" God as he is in himself *(intelligentiam magis significet, quam expleat).*[44] Theological concepts become "the medium of transcendental reference" to God.[45]

The communication of divine truth through human speech does not make the speech any less human. In fact, the humanity of Christ is the epistemological basis for a true correspondence between God and humanity. Since the humanity of Christ is not an appearance of humanity, but genuine humanity, this provides a genuine correspondence from the human side, between God and humanity.[46] It is true that the nature of theological statements is such that they bring a great burden to bear upon themselves. This is where the overlap between the divine and the human in Jesus Christ becomes epistemologically important.[47] Not only is the humanity of Christ essential for a true creaturely correspondence, but

---

41 Ibid., pp. 147-148.
42 David Tracy speaks of Torrance's "strict coherence" model for theological knowledge, whereas Reinhold Niebuhr is characterized as having a "rough coherence" model. *The Analogical Imagination,* p. 62.
43 *RET,* p. 125.
44 *De Trinitate* 1.19; cited by Torrance, STI, p. 21.
45 Ibid.
46 *TS,* p. 149. Cf. Jesus as the Sacrament, p. 150.
47 Ibid., p. 293.

also, the divine reality of Christ becomes "the creative Ground and the controlling Center for all our thoughts and statements about God."[48]

The epistemological problems of both Roman and Protestant theology stem from a lack of emphasis on the epistemological implications of the humanity of Christ.[49] Roman Catholicism suffers from "the subordination of revelation to the natural forms of man's rationality and piety." The lordship of Christ expressed as the humanity of Christ provides a critique of both its thought forms and its piety. Protestantism suffers from the view of revelation as the subjectivity of the religious consciousness (Schleiermacher), Christian experience, or of faith. The humanity of Christ expresses "the subjective embodiment" of the act of God. What Protestantism needs is

> a critical reorientation of faith in a repentant self-denial of its own subjectivity and a renewed subjection of itself to its object, Jesus Christ, as true God and true Man.[50]

In Book Three of the *Institutes*, Calvin has a chapter entitled, "The Sum of the Christian Life: The Denial of Ourselves."[51] Torrance draws out the epistemological implications of the Reformed doctrine of the Christian life as self-denial, based on the vicarious humanity of Christ. Our epistemological problem is that we cannot divorce ourselves from the question which we ask of God, and therefore we bring along all too much excess baggage, cultural and philosophical, into the question. "To learn what is new we have to learn how to forget; to take a step forward in discovery we have to renounce ourselves."[52] This is possible only in Jesus Christ, who enables us to renounce ourselves "by making us share His life and what He has done with our human nature in

---

48   *RET*, p. 151.
49   *Theol. in Recons.*, p. 134.
50   Ibid. Jacques de Senarclens, among others, sees a basic resemblance between the epistemologies of Thomism and Neo-Protestantism. *Heirs of the Reformation*, trans. and ed. G. W. Bromiley (London: SCM Press, 1963), p. 29.
51   John Calvin, *Institutes of the Christian Religion*, 2 vols. trans. F. L. Battles, ed. J. T. McNeill (Philadelphia: Westminster Press, 1960), 3.7.
52   GR, p. 54.

Himself."[53] It is obvious that any concept of a religious *a priori* in humanity is anathema to Torrance.[54] Therefore, Torrance concludes, dogmatic statements of the church should be based on the humanity of Christ, and not on the church's acts of consciousness, which would only result in the self-deification of the church.[55]

Knowledge of God comes through the means of revelation. The preparation for the Incarnation came through revelation in salvation history to Israel. In Israel, God created "a community of reciprocity," a basis for speaker-hearer relationships between God and humanity. This is what was meant for Israel to be seized by the Word of God. As Israel's language and societal structures were bent into conformity to the will of God, it was able to be the unique bearer of God's Word to humanity. This is most of all reflected in the Servant of the Lord motif—the model of obedient response.[56] Thereby, "a matrix of appropriate forms of human thought and speech for the reception of the Incarnational revelation" was formed.[57] The revealing activity of the Word in Jesus Christ is revelation, not a phenomenological analysis of the life situations of Israel or the apostolic church.[58] The transient correlation and response which exists in Israel is transcended and relativized by the Incarnation. In the Word made flesh, a "profound integration" takes place in which the Word of God and the word of humanity can no longer be separated from each other.[59] The humanity cannot be discarded, but is "indissolubly bound up with its material content."[60]

To see the humanity of Christ is to see the revelation of who God really is. This is the importance for Torrance of the equation of the economic Trinity with the immanent Trinity.[61] There is no true revelation of God if this is not so. While the Incarnation does

---

53 Ibid.
54 See as an example Carl F. H. Henry, *God, Revelation, and Authority*, Vol 1 (Waco: Word Books, 1976), pp. 280-394.
55 *TS*, pp. 351-352.
56 *GR*, pp. 146-149. Cf. *The Mediation of Christ*, chs. 1 and 2.
57 *GR*, p. 149.
58 Ibid., pp. 149-150.
59 Ibid., p. 149.
60 Ibid., p. 150.
61 Torrance, "Toward an Ecumenical...," pp. 338ff.

not bind God to the structures of space and time, it does affirm the reality of rationality of created space and time for God in his relations with us "and binds us to space and time in our relations with him."[62] The Incarnation is not an abrogation nor intrusion, but God's chosen means of revealing himself in the midst of the space and time of which he is master.

The apostolic authority of the New Testament has its basis for Torrance in its correlation with the saving humanity of Christ. The apostolate is the place where revelation, based on the Incarnation, is "earthed."[63] One wonders whether Torrance is stating it too strongly when he says that the apostolate was "the human expression of his [God's] Word."[64] Should not such strong language be reserved for the Incarnation alone? However, he does stress that Scripture, the writings based on the apostles' teaching, like the apostolate, stands with sinners under the judgment and redemption of the cross. Torrance is quick to point out that this "creaturely correspondence of the Holy Scriptures to God's Word" is "a human expression based on the Humanity of Jesus Christ."[65] Thus, since it is related to the historical humanity of Christ, Scripture must have the character of "learned obedience to the Father." "Just as we speak of his [Jesus'] life in terms of obedience, so we must speak of the Bible as obedience to the Divine self-revelation."[66] Therefore, the doctrine of verbal inspiration should not mean the inerrancy or infallibility of the Bible in a literary or historical sense. "It means that the errant and fallible human word is, as such, used by God and has to be received and heard in spite of its human weakness and imperfection."[67] This fallible human expression then must point beyond itself "to what it is not in itself, but to what God marvelously makes it to be in the adoption of his grace."[68] If revelation [and, therefore, inspiration of Scripture] takes place in the midst of fallen humanity, we must allow the "fallenness" of the humanity of the Scriptures to have its proper place if it is to be

---

62   *STI*, p. 24.
63   *Theol. in Recons.*, p. 136.
64   Ibid., p. 138.
65   Ibid.
66   Ibid., p. 139.
67   Ibid.
68   Ibid.

regarded as truly human.[69] It is on the basis of such a consideration of atonement as taking place within the realm of fallen humanity that has caused Torrance to call for a serious interrelationship between revelation, Scripture, and "a doctrine of atoning mediation between the Word of God and the word of man."[70] Our doctrine of the human written Word must be seen in correlation, but not to be identified with, the human living Word.

Torrance finds crucial hermeneutical implications in such a view of Scripture. The real text of which we are to be concerned with, according to Torrance, is not the letter of Scripture but the humanity of Christ "as the actual objectification of the Word of God for us within our human mode of existence in space and time. It is to this which the Scriptures refer."[71] The "this-worldly reality," the human aspect of hermeneutics is inherent in the genre of Scripture itself. This is best seen in the parables of Jesus. As they relate their humanness to the humanity of Christ, they point to Christ as the real text of Scripture. "He is God's exclusive language to us and He alone must be our language to God."[72] It is a mark of the New Testament authors, according to Torrance, that

> Far from obtruding themselves and their own spirituality upon us, the New Testament writers serve the gospel by directing us back to the representative and vicarious humanity of Christ as the creative ground and normative pattern for actualization of every response to God on our part. It is in fact the humanity of Jesus Christ himself which is the real text underlying the New Testament Scriptures; it is his humanity to

---

69 *RET*, pp. 162-163, n. 3. It may be asked whether the human nature of Christ also demands his "fallibility." This raises many implications but suffice it to say that the humanity of Christ is indwelled with the divine Logos, which we cannot claim for the Scriptures, although Torrance can speak of the "imprint" of the Word of God on the human word of Scripture. *Theol. in Recons.*, p. 139. See also the discussion of the doctrine of the humanity of Christ in relation to original sin and salvation in Harry Johnson, *The Humanity of the Savior* (London: Epworth Press, 1962). Torrance is considered on pp. 170-173.
70 *RET*, pp. 162-163, n. 3.
71 *TS*, p. 193; RET, p. 93.
72 *GR*, pp. 150-151.

which they refer and in terms of which they are to be interpreted.[73]

GOD AND CREATION

We have previously stated in our thesis statements that, for Torrance, the reality of salvation involves the importance of the vicarious humanity of Christ as the point of integration between the fallen world and the Creator God. It would perhaps be better to speak of this as the "context" of integration, for it is not a mere incident or "point" in time which Torrance is speaking of, but the participation of divine life with human life.

The full participation of the Creator in our creaturely and human life is the foundation of soteriology according to the Fourth Gospel. "Without the Incarnation of the Creator Word the fallen world would crumble away finally and irretrievably into nothingness."[74] But it is also true that the humanity of Christ is a commitment by God to humanity that reconciliation will take place in the context of God's own being. This is Torrance's view of "the Incarnation as falling within the life of God himself."[75] The true humanity, as well as the true deity, of Christ falls within the life of God. Not only is this a definition of atonement, it is also a qualification of transcendence. The "kenotic" or "historical" aspect of transcendence allows the revelation of God itself to define the meaning of the transcendence of God, i.e. a transcendence expressed in the power to take on human creatureliness and weakness.[76]

Creation is obviously a much broader reality than humanity. What makes humanity unique? According to Torrance, it is the reality of the Incarnation. The fact that God has entered into "contingent existence" and has effected a reconciliation within the "ontological foundations" of humanity means that humanity has a

---

73 *RET*, p. 93.
74 *GR*, p. 144. Cf. a similar reason for the necessity of the Incarnation in Augustine in F. H. Kettler, "Versöhnung," *Die Religion in Geschichte und Gegenward*, Vol. 6 (Tubingen: J. C. Mohr [Paul Siebeck], 1962), p. 1374.
75 Torrance, "Toward an Ecumenical...," p. 339. Cf. Athanasius' stress on the "creative relation" between Christ and creation in the humanity of Christ, discussed in *Theol. in Recons.*, p. 217.
76 Cf. Ray S. Anderson, *Historical Transcendence and the Reality of God.*

special place in the universe.[77] But within that special place is a special responsibility, "man's priestly function" in "the pattern of a redemptive mission to nature," in the sense of both scientific explanation and physical healing. However, it is only in the context of the healing of humanity itself that humanity can function as a priest for creation.

JUSTIFICATION, FAITH, AND SANCTIFICATION

Justification, for Torrance, can never be separated from Christ.[78] The center of justification is the saving humanity of Christ, "his positive obedience and filial life in the flesh." Justification comes from participating in the obedience of Jesus, in his worship, his prayers, his love. Only on this deep ontological basis can we stand before God. The vicarious humanity of Christ enables us to receive not only forgiveness of sins but a new righteousness, a righteousness which comes from beyond us, which we have through union with Christ. Therefore, justification is not the beginning of a new self-righteousness, "but the perpetual end of it."[79]

Torrance speaks of the double-sided nature of justification as both "objective" and "subjective."[80] "Objective" justification includes both the active and passive obedience of Christ in the context of his whole life of atonement.[81] His obedience is not only the passive obedience of the death on the cross, but also the active obedience of a life of love, faithfulness, praise, and prayer. Both aspects make up his obedient humanity. Within this obedience in human flesh, "the sanctification of our human nature" takes place.

But it is also true that justification has its "subjective" side. This, too, has already taken place in Christ, our substitute and representative, "who appropriated the divine Act of saving

---

77 *DCO*, p. 138.
78 *Theol. in Recons.*, pp. 150-151.
79 Ibid., pp. 151-152, 161. Cf. the discussion of "objective" and "subjective" justification in Hans Küng, *Justification: The Doctrine of Karl Barth and a Catholic Reflection*, pp. 22-226.
80 Ibid.
81 Ibid., pp. 153-156. Cf. John McLeod Campbell's view of the Incarnation as the presupposition of the atonement. *The Nature of the Atonement* (London: Macmillan and Co, 1867), xx.

Righteousness for us."[82] He is "the great Believer." In a sense, Torrance tends at this point to blend justification and sanctification. In one respect, this is in accord with Karl Barth's enlightening discussion on the unity between justification and sanctification as "the one totality of the reconciling action of God, of the whole and undivided Jesus Christ, and of His one grace."[83] But Torrance seems not to follow Barth's teaching on the "two genuinely different moments" of justification and sanctification.[84] But does that mean that Torrance does not have a place for a genuine human response?

Torrance defines sanctification as "the continual unfolding and maintaining of our justification."[85] He sees it as a "continual renewing" and "reenacting" in the believer of justification. Torrance's concern is that sanctification should not be regarded as "a response of man that must be added to justification." The experience of sanctification takes place in the Word and sacrament, through which the believer is "nourished with the new humanity of Christ."[86] Already we can see the importance of the relationship between the humanity of Christ and the sacramental and liturgical life of the church for an understanding of the reality of salvation in Torrance's theology. This will be developed much more in the next section.

What place, then, does Torrance have for a genuine human response to God? This question must be considered, first of all, in light of nothing less than the nature of the revelation of God, that is, the Incarnation. This is the significance of the "double movement" of salvation: Christ as the way of God to humanity and as the way of humanity to God. The way of humanity to God in Jesus Christ is expressed in Jesus as "the hearing man" in "a final

---

82 *Theol. in Recons.*, pp. 153-156.
83 Barth, *CD* IV/2, p. 502.
84 Ibid., p. 503. Cf. Barth's warning concerning merging sanctification into justification: "If we do not give any independent significance to the problem of sanctification, do we not necessarily obscure in a very suspicious way the existential reach of the atonement, the simple fact that justification always has to do with man and his action, and that faith in it, even though it is a work of the Holy Spirit, is still a decision of man?" CD IV/2, p. 504.
85 *CAC*, Vol. 1, p. 66.
86 Ibid.

and definitive way."[87] The message of the Gospel documents is not simply a divine revelation with a human response required. In Jesus of Nazareth there is both a divine revelation and a human response, if one takes seriously the Incarnation. Both the divine revelation and the human response are predicated on "the all-significant middle term, the divinely provided response in the vicarious humanity of Jesus Christ."[88] In relation to human beings, his humanity is both representative and substitutionary in all our relations with God "such as trusting and obeying, understanding and knowing, loving and worshipping." This relationship is available to those whom, in the teaching of the Fourth Evangelist, having received and believed in him, are given power and freedom to become children of God, "who were born, not of blood nor of the will of the flesh nor of the will of man, but of God" (Jn. 1:12-13).

Thomas Smail, while expressing appreciation for Torrance's emphasis upon the objective nature of the vicarious humanity of Christ, objects to his leaving out the importance of the individual personal response of faith. This must take place so that Christ's response "can take effect in me."[89] Peter's confession, in other words, the rock on which the church is built (Mt. 16:18), needed to be made. This "yes" of mine is not just an "echo" of Christ's "yes," as Torrance says, but is rather "the result and consequence" of his. Jesus' response is not enough, "but what he has done for me, I need to go on and do for myself." "The worship, the teaching; the life and witness of the Church" are parts of that response. Torrance's failure to acknowledge the place of my individual response is a reflection of his "wider failure" to distinguish clearly enough between the work of Christ and the work of the Spirit.

Smail's criticisms of Torrance are plain enough. But does Torrance really disallow the importance of one's personal response of faith? A careful reading, it seems, would answer, no. Torrance is concerned with the radical implications of the vicarious humanity of Christ. Therefore, Christ takes our place in *"all* the

---

87 *GR,* pp. 145-156. The entire essay in this book, "The Word of God and the Response of Man," pp. 133-164, is very important for our study.

88 Ibid.

89 Thomas Smail, *The Giving Gift: The Holy Spirit in Person* (London: Hodder and Stoughton, 1988), pp. 109-112.

basic acts of man's response to God."[90] Yet both liberals and
evangelicals have quite a problem with the concept of Christ's
"total substitution" for us.[91] It comes from a feeling that "the inner
citadel of human freedom is being threatened." But such a way of
thinking only reveals the poverty of our Christology. We do not
take the Incarnation that seriously. So, we contrive to "juxtapose
God and man, divine grace and human freedom, in a *logical* way
in which 'all of God' logically excludes 'anything of man'." The
vicarious humanity of Christ is not meant to *destroy* humanity, but
to *restore* it. Unfortunately, as Torrance suggests,the influence of
Latin theology is great. Such a theology rejects the Greek patristic
principle of "the unassumed is the unhealed" and the truth that our
minds are alienated from God. Such an opening for "autonomous
reason" and "unbaptized rationalism" bypasses the total substitutionary work of Christ.

Smail's critique seems to reflect these epistemological and
Christological problems. He is concerned with the "effect" of
Christ's work in a person. Certainly the work of Christ has an effect on the individual. But is it in the sense of a Newtonian mechanistic universe of simply causes and effects, as Torrance has so
often warned us against? Our relation to Christ is much more dynamic and ontological. We are not just the "effects" of Christ as
"cause." He did not simply *enable* us to respond. No, our situation of sin and death is much too desperate. He acts on our behalf,
when we are unable; not to *destroy* our responses, but to *establish*
them, in order to provide a *basis* and *foundation* for them!

Smail's critique seems to reflect a lack of concern for the
ontological reality of salvation. My "yes" to God becomes only
"the result and consequences" of Christ's "yes" to the Father,
rather than participating by faith in the Spirit, in Christ's own
"yes". Smail misreads Torrance when he says that the latter does
not have a place for my individual human response. Torrance
would agree with Smail when he says "what he (Christ) has done
for me, I need to go on and do for myself." The problem is that
Smail needs to add to the last sentence, "...in Christ"! We have no
power nor wisdom of our own to respond faithfully to God. But
we can and should respond as we participate in his one perfect re-

---

90 T. F. Torrance, "Karl Barth and the Latin Heresy", *Scottish Journal of
      Theology* 39 (No. 4), 1986, p. 479.
91 Ibid., p. 480.

sponse. This is the hope of the reality of salvation: a genuine human response *has* been made, which we are called to participate in by faith, through the Spirit. *Contra* Smail's belief that Torrance has failed to clearly distinguish between the work of Christ and the work of the Spirit, Smail seems to develop too much of a cleavage between the Second and Third Persons of the Trinity, forgetting that only the Son has taken on human flesh. The Spirit has no incarnation of his own. But the absolutely crucial ministry of the Spirit is to enable us to participate by faith in the perfect obedience of the Son to the Father.

Therefore, there is a place for a definite human response in Torrance's theology. However, it is grounded on the priority of the representative and substitutionary response of Jesus, which "invalidates all other ways of response." It is "the sole norm and law" of an acceptable human response to God. The result of this is a human response which is not arbitrary self-determination of independent self-expression on the part of humanity, but a response which is "derived from, grounded in, and shaped by the very humanity of the Word."

It is the "ring of faithfulness," the faithfulness of Jesus Christ which "undergirds" our faith.[92] Torrance defines faith as the faithfulness of humanity grounded on the faithfulness of God.[93] The basis of this is in the consistency between word and event.[94] It is the place of the Incarnation to illustrate this unity of word and event in the being and action of God.[95] Therefore, the Word of God is to be understood as, 1) a physical act in space and time, 2) creating an indissoluble connection between spiritual and creaturely realities, and 3) within the levels of created rationality. The unity of God's person, word, and act in the Incarnation "gathers within its embrace... the differences in human person, word, and act." The "assent" and "consent" to the lordship of the Word comes in the encounter between the unity of the Word and

---

92 *GR,* p. 114.
93 *GR,* pp. 153-154. Cf. Torrance's discussion, "One Aspect of the Biblical Conception of Faith," *The Expository Times* 68 (1956-57), 111-114, 221-222 and CAC, Vol. 2, pp. 74-82. James Barr's well-known linguistic criticism of Torrance is in *The Semantics of Biblical Language* (Oxford: Oxford University Press, 1961), pp. 161-205.
94 *GR,* pp. 153-154.
95 Ibid., pp. 141-142.

the Being of God.[96] Since the Word of God came in a human medium, it requires an appropriate human response of "articulate acknowledgment and thanksgiving." In summary, the humanity of Christ is "the embodiment of our salvation... the very substance of our salvation and anchor of our hope."[97] "He believed for us, was faithful for us, and remains faithful even when we fail Him, again and again...."[98]

THE CHURCH

The church is related integrally to the humanity of Christ in Torrance's thought in both its ministry, and in its life of worship. As the body of Christ, the church is the continuing expression and agent of the inner structure of being within creation and redemption, within space and time, yet contingent to space and time. This is the continuing importance of the twin doctrines of *anhypostasia* and *enhypostasia*.[99] *Anhypostasia* means that the church does not have an existence apart from Christ. *Enhypostasia*, however, speaks of a genuine *hypostasis* given in Christ through incorporation. "That is why to speak of the Church as the Body of Christ is no mere figure of speech but describes an ontological reality, enhypostatic in Christ and wholly dependent on Him."

Torrance believes that an *anhypostatic/enhypostatic* understanding of the church provides an answer to the cleavage between the "eschatological" and "ontological" views of the church.[100] If we view the church as only an eschatological event, anhypostatically, we rob the church of its grounding in the person of Christ. If we view the church only from an ontological viewpoint, that is, enhypostatically, only in terms of the Incarnation and incorporation, we rob the uniqueness of the Incarnation and tend to see the church as the continuation of the Incarnation.

The church is the "effective operation" of the humanity of Christ in the world.[101] It is the "subjective actualization of revelation and reconciliation," sharing in the election and assumption of

---

96   Ibid., pp. 155-156.
97   *CAC*, Vol. 2, pp. 81-82.
98   Ibid.
99   *CAC*, Vol. 1, p. 248. Cf. Barth, CD III/2, p. 70; I/2, pp. 163ff.
100 Ibid., p. 249.
101 *Theol. in Recons.*, p. 135.

humanity in Christ and assimilated to Christ's humanity in life and thought. As such, its physical relationship to the physical humanity of Christ speaks of its concrete unity in space and time. There should be no dichotomy between spiritual and physical unity, as there was no dichotomy between the "human" and "spiritual" Jesus.[102] The task of dogmatic theology is to help the church test its conformity to Christ, in order that it may grow up into "the full stature of the humanity of Christ."[103]

The vicarious humanity of Christ expresses the reality of salvation in Torrance's theology as presenting a radical critique and foundation for the ministry of the church. Christian service arises out of the ministry of Jesus Christ on behalf of the world. Therefore, its basis is not the spontaneous, autonomous love of the individual Christian with its own "intrinsic intelligibility."[104] No, the true spontaneity and freedom of the church comes from its roots in the Incarnation. It is free from the anxiety and the ulterior motivation of the individual because Christ has become the basis of its love for the world. The church rests on the purity of motive within "the commanding reality of Jesus Christ." Pastoral ministry is neither a Catholic nor a Protestant sacerdotalism but "a displacement of our humanity by the humanity of Christ" in worship.[105] Here Torrance brings his emphasis on the substitionary nature of the atonement to bear on the ministry of the church. Since our humanity is "displaced" by the humanity of Christ, we do not have to appear before God in our own names, but solely in the name of Christ, our Priest.

As we have seen, the "correlation and correspondence" produced by the vicarious humanity of Christ provides an "inner determination" of life, a "reciprocity," which creates wholeness and integrity within the structures of created being. The ministry of the church takes place in this world in which "the hidden presence of the incarnate, crucified and risen Christ" is the basis for overcoming evil and promoting the inner structures of wholeness and integrity.[106] Since spiritual and physical existence have been reconciled in the humanity of Christ, we can neither hold apart "the

---

102 *CAC*, Vol. 1, p. 138.
103 *Theol. in Recons.*, p. 146.
104 *GR*, p. 162.
105 *Theol. in Recons.*, pp. 161-166.
106 *GR*, pp. 162-163.

ministry of love from the act of service, nor the act of service from the ministry of love." This is all a part of the profound ethical implications of Torrance's unitary thought which have yet to really be developed.[107]

Worship takes on a vital meaning if it is seen in the context of the vicarious humanity of Christ.[108] The two aspects in salvation of substitution/representation and incorporation play an essential part in Torrance's understanding of worship. If Christ has not taken on our humanity, our death, then worship does not take place in Christ.[109] Substitution is absolutely essential to incorporation. On the other hand, the implications of union with Christ are also essential for our understanding of worship if we are going to avoid the typical over-intellectualism caused by an overemphasis on justification by faith.[110] The implications of this for both a theologically grounded worship and a theology which takes shape in the context of godliness and worship are profound.

Worship is integrally related to the soteriological reality of the reconstruction of the world from its fragmentation and darkness into a unity of wholeness and integrity. The vicarious humanity of Christ becomes the place where human nature is healed, sanctified, and offered up to the Father on our behalf. This is the doxological exegesis of the "Our Father" in the Lord's Prayer. He became one with us in order that we might pray with him.[111] When the vicarious humanity of Christ is left out, worship be-

---

107 See the discussion of dualism vs. a unitary world view in T. F. Torrance, "Emerging from the Cultural Split," in *The Ground and Grammar of Theology* (Charlottesville: University Press of Virginia, 1980), pp. 15-43. Cf. Todd Speidell, "The Incarnation as Theological Imperative for Human Reconciliation: A Christocentric Social Ethic" (unpublished Ph.D. dissertation, Fuller Theological Seminary, 1986).

108 Cf. the contributions by James B. Torrance, "The Place of Jesus Christ in Worship," in Ray S. Anderson, ed. *Theological Foundations for Ministry,* pp. 348-369; "The Vicarious Humanity of Christ," in T. F. Torrance, ed., *The Incarnation* (Edinburgh: Handsel Press, 1981), pp. 127-147; cf. J. J. von Allmen, *Worship, its Theology and Practice* (New York: Oxford University Press, 1961) and J. A. Jüngmann, *The Place of Jesus Christ in Liturgical Prayer,* 2nd rev. ed., trans. A. Peeler (Staten Island: Alba House, 1925), pp. 176ff.

109 *Theol. in Reconcil.,* p. 150.

110 Ibid., p. 208.

111 Ibid., p. 106.

comes only "man's self-expression."[112] As salvation is the communication of the very life of God through the vicarious humanity of Christ, worship and prayer participate in that atoning life. So the prayer we offer in the name of Christ is "the worshipping form of the life and sonship which we have received in Christ."[113] "It is in fact the eternal life of the Incarnate Son in us that ascends to the Father in our worship and prayer through, with and in him, in the unity of the Holy Spirit."[114] Forms of worship are certainly to be flexible, according to different cultures, as long as the "invariant element" is maintained: "The normative pattern of the Incarnate love of God in Jesus Christ."[115]

The revelation of the inability of fallen humanity through the revelation of the vicarious humanity of Christ is also related to the foundations of the life of prayer. "The invocatory character of Christian prayer" is based on our recognition of our inability to pray (Rom. 8:26).[116] Shaped and adapted in the humanity of Christ, it is prayer which is turned away from itself, asking the ascended High Priest to help us in our weaknesses. Worship and prayer as participating in the worship of the Son to the Father, participating in a life, are a continuation of the saving work of Christ, who is "the very matter and substance of salvation."[117]

THE SACRAMENTS

The ultimate meaning of the sacraments is found for Torrance in the vicarious obedience of Christ to the Father.[118] Christ as the Act of God is the primary *mysterium* or *sacramentum*. This is "the whole historical Jesus Christ from his birth to his resurrection and ascension," who has incorporated himself into our humanity. The integration of creation and redemption is born witness to by the "prophetic signs" in the sacraments of a healing between spiritual and physical existence.[119] The sacraments become the counterparts in our lives to the acts of grace and power in the life

---

112 Ibid., p. 206.
113 Ibid., p. 212.
114 Ibid.
115 Ibid., p. 213.
116 Ibid., p. 212.
117 *Theol. in Reconcil.*, p. 289.
118 Ibid., pp. 82-83.
119 *GR*, p. 161.

of Jesus.[120] Therefore, this becomes a call for the integration of spiritual and physical existence in our lives in anticipation of the new creation. Since Christ is the essence of our sacramental response, the sacraments will not allow our response to the proclamation to be in a purely intellectual or spiritual way. The unity of being means a unified life of response. In this way, the proclamation of the word and the sacramental response live in a unitary relationship in Torrance's theology, but only in the context of the vicarious humanity of Christ as the one who has already responded.[121] The essence of the sacraments is centered on what God has already done in the humanity of Christ. Thus, the meaning of the sacraments is the essence of grace. We do not baptize ourselves, nor do we come to the Eucharist on the ground of what we have done.

> The Sacraments provide the natural basis within our daily physical existence for free and spontaneous response to the word in which we do not have to keep looking over our shoulders to see whether our response is good enough.[122]

Baptism as the act of God is the living manifestation of the risen Christ effectively operative in the church.[123] Therefore, it is not a ritual act which has meaning in itself, nor is it an ethical act that has meaning in the response of the recipient. It is related essentially to the entire event of the Incarnation, not just to the death and resurrection.[124] At this point, the relation of baptism to substitution/representation and incorporation becomes important. Baptism is usually spoken of as our incorporation into Christ, but this is only true in light of the prior movement of the Incarnation of the Word into humanity, that is, Christ as the substitute for and representative of humanity. It is only because of his union with us that we can share in his human life and ministry on our behalf. Baptism is not only "the Sacrament of the death and resurrection of Christ, " but also "the Sacrament of the Incarnation."

---

120 Ibid.
121 Ibid., pp. 159-160.
122 Ibid.
123 *Theol in Reconcil.*, pp. 82-83.
124 *CAC*, Vol. 2, pp. 117-118.

As the sacrament of the Incarnation, baptism is the sacrament of the obedience of Christ offered in our place. "Baptism is the Sacrament of the fact that in Jesus Christ God has bound Himself to us and bound us to Himself, before ever we have bound ourselves to Him."[125] In baptism we participate in a righteousness which is not our own, in which "we renounce our reliance upon ourselves."[126] Therefore, if baptism is something done to us, solely by grace, Torrance concludes that we should have no problem with the doctrine of infant baptism.[127]

Torrance is fond of quoting Calvin's teaching on the place of the humanity of Christ in our understanding of the Lord's Supper.[128] According to Calvin, Christ is the "substance" of our salvation, so that the meaning of the sacrament is the substance of Christ himself. Once again, we return to Torrance's theme of Christ as the sum of salvation in the context of the humanity of Christ. Through our union with Christ's human nature, we can truly share in his obedience and obtain life from his "vivifying flesh." The Lord's Supper is the mode in which Christ communicates his life to us, but only based on our prior union with Christ.[129]

The "vivifying flesh" which Calvin and Torrance speak of is not the flesh of divinized humanity but the "kenotic" flesh of humiliated humanity.[130] This signifies the depth to which Christ takes on the flesh of humanity, in order to make it alive, to turn it into the "vivifying flesh" of Christ. This is the mystery which the Eucharist points to, not to itself. Therefore, to speak of the presence of Christ in the Eucharist is to speak of a presence in "the

---

125 Ibid., p. 123.
126 Ibid., p. 124.
127 Ibid., p. 125.
128 Ibid., pp. 143-144. Cf. "The Place of the Humanity of Christ in the Sacramental Life of the Church," *Church Service Society Annual* 26 (1956), pp. 4ff. Torrance also mentions the remarkable comment of William Cunningham concerning Calvin's view that "real influence" was "exerted by Christ's human nature upon the souls of believers" in the sacrament. "This is, perhaps, the greatest blot in the history of Calvin's labours as a public instructor." *The Reformation and the Theology of the Reformation*, 2nd ed. (Edinburgh: T & T. Clark, 1861), p. 240; cited by Torrance, "The Place...," p. 7.
129 Calvin, *Institutes*, 4.17.7-12.
130 *Theol. in Reconcil.*, pp. 108-109.

form of humiliation."[131] That is the significance of the breaking of
his body and the shedding of his blood. Torrance contends that in
the Reformed tradition, it has been the sense of the vicarious,
priestly ministry of Christ which does not allow the "real presence" in the Eucharist to be maintained by itself, but only in connection with the humanity of Christ.[132] He considers the characteristic Catholic and Protestant views on the Eucharist to have the
same basic problem: "a damaged understanding of the relation
between God and the world, affecting the doctrines of creation and
incarnation."[133] Thus, the eucharist becomes either a "holy mystery" enshrined and controlled by the church, or an appointed
ordinance for the moral and spiritual prodding of believers. The
inherent oneness between who the Offerer is and what is offered is
destroyed. Therefore, his offering is not unique, and what is not
unique is not vicarious for all. In eucharistic practice, we lose the
basis of going boldly before the throne of grace because we do not
do so *through* Christ, but only "for Christ's sake."[134]

For all his emphasis on the sacraments as acts of God,
Torrance maintains his doctrine of the "double movement" of
Christology in relation to the Christological reality of the Lord's
Supper: it is both a movement from God to humanity and a
movement from humanity to God, based on the vicarious humanity of Christ. [135] The "deistic disjunction" between God and creation is healed because the Eucharist reveals the Son of God acting
not just *in* humanity, but *as* a human being. Although in the
Eucharist it is the "Godward" aspect which is prominent, a non-
dualist view of the Eucharist will take into account the action of
Christ as our Priest in the eucharistic sacrifice, based upon both
substitution and incorporation.[136] It is our participation in his offering before the Father which nourishes and makes alive. This is
"the mind of Christ" in John McLeod Campbell's language, the
only worship which the Father accepts.[137] Our partaking of this
worship is an eschatological pledge of the resurrection and re-

---

131   Ibid., pp. 120ff.
132   Ibid., p. 128.
133   Ibid., p. 131.
134   Ibid., pp. 133-134.
135   Ibid., pp. 117-118.
136   Ibid., pp. 135-136.
137   Ibid., p. 139.

demption of the body, since the physical elements are vitally related to the physical, risen humanity of Jesus Christ.[138]

ESCHATOLOGY

In Torrance's theology, eschatology is essential to faith because of the reality of union with Christ.[139] This Christ with whom we are united is risen, but not without his humanity. Torrance's contention is that many people cannot see the importance of eschatology because various forms, expressed in such movements as demythologization and chiliasm, do not take the humanity of Christ seriously. The result is that their eschatologies deal with a Christ who is dehumanized and unrelated to humanity. But our very future is based on the humanity of Christ seen in a vicarious sense, Torrance contends.

The resurrection loses its full significance unless the Risen One is identified with the full historical humanity of Christ. "The resurrection is the fulfillment of the incarnate mission of the Son of God who has taken up our worldly existence and history into himself and remains regnant over all space and time."[140] The only difference between the earthly and risen Christ is that he has now taken on "the depth of our corruption" and "fixed it to death" through the cross and the resurrection.[141] In the resurrection and the ascension "the goal of the incarnation" is accomplished: "the exaltation of man into the life of God and on to the throne of God."[142] This does not mean that humanity is swallowed up into divine Being, because of the risen humanity of Christ. "Human nature, remaining creaturely and human, is yet exalted in Christ to share in God's life and glory."[143] "The humanizing in Jesus of dehumanized man" is vindicated by the resurrection.[144] The dark and fallen human nature which Christ took is restored and renewed in the light of God (II Cor. 4:6).[145]

---

138 *STR*, pp. 141-142.
139 *CAC*, Vol. 1, pp. 98-100.
140 *STR*, p. 171.
141 Ibid., pp. 74-75.
142 Ibid., pp. 135-136.
143 Ibid.
144 Ibid., p. 79.
145 Ibid., pp. 135-136.

But this eschatological renewal is lived now in the midst of tension. The resurrected Christ is real and present, but much like the fleeting glimpses of the resurrected Christ which the early disciples had.[146] The sacraments have an eschatological function as the physical elements anticipate the full union of our physicality with the risen humanity of Christ.

However, a vital part of the ministry of the risen Christ is his ministry as High Priest, as intercessor in our behalf.[147] This necessitates both the substitutionary and representative aspects of the atonement. He not only acts on our behalf, but also in our place in order that the prayers issued out of our human nature would be worship and praise before God.

THE RECONCILING LIFE OF GOD; POSSIBILITY OR ACTUALITY?

If our rather hurried survey of T F. Torrance's thought on the vicarious humanity of Christ and salvation has any merit, it will be at least to impress upon us the incredible extent to which Torrance has gone to draw out the implications of the vicarious humanity of Christ for virtually every area of what has traditionally been called "dogmatic" theology. Certainly Torrance's many expositions and interpretations merit detailed criticisms at several different levels. This we cannot do at this time. But it does remain for us to look critically at the explicit implications his teaching has for the question of the reality of salvation.

Certainly the aforementioned *scope* of Torrance's theology of the vicarious humanity of Christ is the place to start. Salvation for Torrance is not a point in either universal or salvation history, nor is it an existential moment in the life of the individual. Salvation in Jesus Christ grasps both the totality of life and its particularity. One of Torrance's great contributions is to present a theology of salvation in the midst of the riches of theological existence. It is the vicarious humanity of Christ which created such a "correlation" and "correspondence." The very physicality of God made flesh, and that flesh substituting for us and representing us, enabling us to be incorporated into Christ, affects the heart of the

---

146 Ibid., pp. 141-142.
147 Ibid., pp. 116-117.

knowledge of God. To know God is to know the humanity of God in the face of Jesus of Nazareth. In the words of Karl Barth,

> We do not need to engage in a free-ranging investigation to seek out and construct who and what God truly is, and who and what man truly is, but only to read the truth about both where it resides, namely, in the fullness of their togetherness, their covenant which proclaims itself in Jesus Christ.[148]

So also creation itself is restored and renewed because of the "correlation" and "correspondence" worked out by the Incarnation of the divine Word into human flesh. Salvation takes on a flesh and blood reality because of this ontological relationship between the physicality of creation and the physicality of the atoning human flesh of Jesus. Since it is genuine human flesh in which this divine Word partakes, justification, faith, and sanctification, based on the obedience of Christ, is "enfleshed." It is the communication of a life, not simply a legal acquittal, or a moral example. The vicarious humanity of Christ brings a "fleshly" reality to the church, which gives both ontological significance to the church as the body of Christ, and provides a critique of the church's attempts to establish its own humanity, its own agenda, apart from the humanity of its Lord, whether it be in issues of authority, polity, ministry, or liturgy. Finally, the eschatological dimension of the gospel takes on a new reality when eschatology is grounded on and consists of the presence of the coming humanity of the risen Christ. The "otherworldliness" of eschatology is supplemented by the "thisworldliness" of the continuity between the earthly humanity of Christ and the risen humanity of Christ our High Priest.

In the context of the breadth and depth of such a contribution as Torrance's, we observe four major contributions to a contemporary statement on the reality of salvation, summed up in the following statement: The reality of salvation as understood in the context of the vicarious humanity of Christ is *unitary, ontological, contingent,* and *human.*[149]

---

148 Karl Barth, *The Humanity of God,* p. 47. Cf. Eberhard Jüngel, "On the Humanity of God," *God as the Mystery of the World,* pp. 299-398.

149 The first three categories are similar to those of Ray S. Anderson, in his short study of Torrance's epistemology, "Toward a New Basis for Natural Theology

The reality of salvation is *unitary* in that the vicarious humanity of Christ teaches us not to divorce form from being in our cosmology, nor the empirical from the theoretical in our epistemology.[150] Ray S. Anderson cautions us not to misunderstand Torrance at this point:

> It would be a mistake, however, to assume that Torrance does not allow for a differentiation in his unitary view of reality, between God and the created world. A differentiation, in Torrance's view, is itself a rational or logical order, whereas, dualism leads to an irrational, or mythical relation.[151]

Torrance is not an epistemological nor cosmological monist, as seen from his statement that "there is only one basic way of knowing," but "different modes of rationality" according to the intrinsic intelligibility of the object.[152] A non-dualist, unitary framework of theological knowledge allows for the unity between form and being expressed in the Incarnation, which in turn is the basis for a creative interaction between God and his creation.

Secondly, the reality of salvation is *ontological*. There is an "intrinsic intelligibility" in salvation which derives from salvation as the communication of God himself in Christ.[153] Therefore, the concrete reality of salvation is certainly an implication of such a theology which, since it integrates the Act and Being of God,

---

in the Tradition of Karl Barth: A Critical Analysis of the Theology of Thomas F. Torrance," (unpublished paper presented to the American Academy of Religion, Group on Evangelical Theology, San Francisco, CA, Dec. 19-22, 1981), pp. 8-13. A revised version of this paper is "Barth and a New Direction for Natural Theology," in *Theology Beyond Christendom: Essays on the Centenary of the Birth of Karl Barth, May 10, 1886*, ed. John Thompson, pp. 241-266.

150 The best extended discussion by Torrance of the problem of dualism is in the chapter "Emerging from the Cultural Split" in *The Ground and Grammar of Theology*, pp. 15-43. Cf. "Theology in the Scientific World," GR, pp. 89-111.

151 Anderson, "Toward...," p. 22, n. 25.

152 Torrance, *The Ground and Grammar of Theology*, p. 9.

153 Anderson, "Toward...," p. 9. Cf. "Theological Rationality," in GR, pp. 3-25 and "Creation and Science" in Torrance, *The Ground and Grammar of Theology*, pp. 44-47.

means that salvation is rooted in what is most real, the divine Being. Torrance puts it very eloquently in this way:

> Since the Act and Word of God we meet in Jesus Christ are eternally inherent in the Being of God, and since none other than the very Being of God himself is mediated to us through the Incarnation of his love in Act and Word in Jesus Christ, God's Being is revealed to be his Being in Act and Word—Being that is intrinsically dynamic and eloquent, the Being of the ever living, acting and loving God.[154]

The being of God is the life of God communicated in the vicarious humanity of Christ. Soteriology can be based on no less an important foundation.

Thirdly, the reality of salvation is *contingent*. The relationship between God and the world in Jesus Christ is based on the contingent purpose of God.

> By contingence is meant, then, that as created out of nothing the universe has no self-subsistence and no ultimate stability of its own, but that it is nevertheless endowed with an authentic reality and integrity of its own which must be respected.[155]

In a soteriological sense, this is a way of speaking of the reality of salvation as "salvation *ex nihilo*," that is, there is no innate way in which humanity can recognize the reality of salvation apart from the gracious act of God, an act which is contingent upon his initiative and sustenance. This brings a new perspective to the question of the reality of salvation. The reality of salvation does not have a "self-subsistence," but it does have "an authentic reality of its own, which must be respected." That is to say, we must not determine beforehand the boundaries, limits, and criteria for salvific reality. The vicarious humanity of Christ, understood in a contingent sense, means that there is a structure of reality which we can understand and live within, which can be known and explored. It is at this point that the ecclesial and sacramental aspects of the reality of salvation become important. However, they must always be understood as contingent upon the gracious act of God.

---

154 Ibid., p. 67.
155 Barth, *CD* III/2, "Jesus, Man for Other Men," pp. 203-221.

Most of all, the reality of salvation is *human*. A Christology has lost its heart when it is so obsessed with defending the "deity," "sinlessness," "holiness," or "spirituality" of Jesus, that it ceases to see the deep implications of his vicarious humanity. It is within space and time that creation and redemption are united in the reconciling humanity of Jesus Christ.

The very humanity of the reality of salvation is a great strength in Torrance's presentation. To speak of salvation as less than human is to fall into idealism and far from the reality of the Incarnation. It is for this reason that Torrance follows Karl Barth in his teaching on the humanity of Christ as the basis for our humanity.[156] Humanity is not simply an ontological "given," but a contingent reality, grounded in the Being (cf. the *imago Dei*) and Act of God. Berkouwer criticizes Barth, claiming that the presupposition of the Incarnation is that Jesus "becomes like us" (Phil. 2:7-8; Heb. 2:14-17).[157] But surely this is because Berkouwer does not take into account either the humanity of Christ as based on the eternal being of God,[158] nor the implications of the twin doctrines of substitution and incorporation. One's interpretation of the *imago Dei* would have implications also.[159] But suffice it to say that the vicarious humanity of Christ avoids the unreality of a "divinized" human Jesus who is the savior because he possesses more piety than other human beings. A "degree Christology" such as this really tears asunder the relationship between Christ's humanity and ours.[160] Such a "super-spiritual" person is far removed from the "sinners and publicans" with whom Jesus ate and lived (not to mention the bulk of humanity!). There is a certain humility to the atonement which the vicarious humanity of Christ brings. Weak, frail human nature becomes the arena of salvation. And in that humanity there is the meeting of creation and redemption, the establishment of wholeness, integrity and hope.

---

156 *DCO*, pp. vii-viii.
157 G. C. Berkouwer, *Man: the Image of God*, trans. Dirk W. Jellema (Grand Rapids: Eerdmans, 1962), pp. 72f., 93-97. See the discussion in Anderson, *On Being Human*, p. 224.
158 Barth, "The Humanity of God," in *The Humanity of God*, pp. 37-65.
159 Anderson, *On Being Human*, pp. 69-87, 215-216.
160 An example of this is John A. T. Robinson, *The Human Face of God* (Philadelphia: Westminster Press, 1973). See the discussion by Colin E. Gunton, "Degree Christology," in *Yesterday and Today*, pp. 15-17.

CHAPTER SEVEN

VICARIOUS HUMANITY AS EPISTEMOLOGICAL
AND HERMENEUTICAL REALITY:
JOHN McLEOD CAMPBELL

T.F. Torrance has provided us with a sweeping survey of the *scope* of the implications of the vicarious humanity of Christ for theological reality. In the remaining chapters of Part Two we will look in detail at some particular, crucial theological concerns. Through John McLeod Campbell's classic study, *The Nature of the Atonement,* we will examine the implications of the humanity of Christ for *theological epistemology* and *hermeneutics.* The heart of soteriology will then be explored through the doctrine of the vicarious *repentance* of Christ in the theology of Campbell, R. C. Moberly, and James B. Torrance. Then, we will climax Part Two with a discussion of the eschatological reality of the *exalted* humanity of Christ as seen in the Epistle to the Hebrews.

JOHN McLEOD CAMPBELL: THEOLOGIAN OF "HOLY SORROW" IN HUMANITY

One of the most intriguing figures in the history of Scottish theology is John McLeod Campbell (1800-1872), who spent most of his life as a pastor in Glasgow, but is chiefly known for his deposition from the Church of Scotland ministry in 1831 for believing in and preaching universal atonement and assurance as be-

longing to the essence of faith.[1] After Campbell began his ministry
in Glasgow, his thoughts on the atonement matured with the publication of his book *The Nature of the Atonement* (1856).[2] It is
this work which has won Campbell a place in the history of
theology. From his early days of questioning the *extent* of the
atonement, Campbell now turned to what he considered a more
basic issue, its *nature*.[3] His unique treatment of this crucial
doctrine earned Campbell instant praise, and its importance since
then has not been slighted by historians of doctrine. The *London
Times* of June 9, 1868, spoke of it as "one of the most remarkable
books ever written," while admittedly regretting the "painful
involution" of Campbell's writing.[4] The nineteenth century
German historian, Otto Pfleiderer, in his definitive work, *The
Development of Theology in Germany Since Kant, and Its
Progress in Great Britain Since 1825*, called the ideas of

---

[1]   Primary sources for Campbell include *Memorials of John McLeod Campbell*, ed.
Donald Campbell, 2 vols. (London: Macmillan, 1877), consisting of letters
collected by his brother; and the autobiographical *Reminiscences and
Reflections, Referring to His Early Ministry in the Parish of Row, 1825-31*, ed.
Donald Campbell (London: Macmillan, 1873). The best studies of Campbell
include Eugene Garrett Bewkes, *Legacy of a Christian Mind* (Philadelphia:
Judson Press, 1937); James B. Torrance, "The Contribution of McLeod
Campbell to Scottish Theology," *Scottish Journal of Theology* 31 (August,
1973), pp. 295-311; John Macquarrie, "John McLeod Campbell, 1800-1872,"
Expository Times 83 (June 1972), pp. 263-268; George Milledge Tuttle, "The
Place of John McLeod Campbell in British Thought Concerning the
Atonement," (unpublished Ph.D. dissertation, Victoria University of Toronto,
1961); and *So Rich a Soil: John McLeod Campbell on Christian Atonement*
(Edinburgh: The Handsel Press, 1986) and B. A. Gerrish, *Tradition and the
Modern World: Reformed Theology in the Nineteenth Century* (Chicago:
University of Chicago Press, 1978), pp 71-98.

[2]   Cited afterwards as *Atonement* (London: Macmillan and Co., 1867). We will
refer to the third edition, which contains additional appendices and an
analytical table of contents. See Gerrish, p. 276 for further bibliographical
information.

[3]   Ibid., p. 3.

[4]   Cited by Gerrish, p. 80.

Campbell, along with those of his friend, Thomas Erskine, "the best contribution to dogmatics which British theology has produced in the present century."[5] He concluded that the exclusion of Campbell from the Scottish church had arrested the development of its theology for half a century. R. S. Franks, the noted historian of the doctrine of the atonement, regarded Campbell's book as "the most systematic and masterly book on the work of Christ produced by a British theologian in the nineteenth century."[6] P. T. Forsyth advised his readers, "I hope you have read McLeod Campbell on the Atonement. Every minister ought to know that book, and know it well."[7] H. R. Mackintosh said that *The Nature of the Atonement* " belongs to that very small class of treatises on theology which are also felt to be great books of devotion."[8] More modern theologians and scholars have cited the importance of Campbell. J. H. S. Burleigh considers his book to be "Scotland's greatest contribution to theology."[9] James S. Stewart speaks of Campbell's "great work on the atonement."[10] Campbell achieves the acclaim as "one of the greatest (if not the greatest) of our Scottish theologians" from James B. Torrance.[11] From John Macquarrie comes the following comments, "He [Campbell] was a man ahead of his times and his ideas are relevant to current theological discussion. After one hundred years his work has still much to teach us and opens up

---

[5] Otto Pfleiderer, *The Development of Theology in Germany Since Kant, and Its Progress in Germany Since 1925,* trans. J. Frederick Smith (New York: Macmillan, 1923), p. 382.

[6] R. S. Franks, *A History of the Doctrine of the Work of Christ* (London: Hodder and Stoughton, 1918), p. 665.

[7] P. T. Forsyth, *The Work of Christ* (New York: Hodder and Stoughton, 1910), p. 148.

[8] H. R. Mackintosh, *Some Aspects of Christian Belief* (New York: George Doran, n. d.), p. 81.

[9] J. H. S. Burleigh, *A Church History of Scotland* (London: Oxford University Press, 1960), p. 332.

[10] James S. Stewart, *A Man in Christ* (London: Hodder and Stoughton, 1964, 1935), p. 193.

[11] J. Torrance, "Contribution," p. 295.

avenues that are still worth exploring."[12] An entire chapter in B. A. Gerrish's work, *Tradition and the Modern World: Reformed Theology in the Nineteenth Century*, is devoted to Campbell.[13] But the most moving testimony to the significance of Campbell is found in one who differed with him often in his own studies on the atonement, James Denney:

> Of all the books that have ever been written on the atonement, as God's way of reconciling man to Himself, MacLeod (sic) Campbell's is probably that which is most completely inspired by the spirit of the truth with which it deals. There is a reconciling power of Christ in it to which no tormented conscience can be insensible. The originality of it is spiritual as well as intellectual, and no one who has ever felt its power will cease to put it in a class by itself. In speculative power he cannot be compared to Schleiermacher, nor in historical learning to Ritschl, and sometimes he writes as badly as either, but he walks in the light all the time, and everything he touches lives.[14]

Certainly most of these witnesses would not endorse everything which Campbell says. But their universal acclaim for him points to a significant theologian worthy of serious study.

In this chapter, it will be argued that John McLeod Campbell's book, *The Nature of the Atonement*, offers a unique hermeneutic by which the humanity of Christ is involved in an integral way in the reality of the atonement. The essence of this hermeneutic is found in his conviction that the Incarnation is the presupposition of the atonement. As such, it has epistemological significance in Campbell's emphasis on the life of Christ as "the light of life." This is not simply a moral or spiritual significance, but also epistemological. The meaning of this life is seen in Christ's revelation of the Father through his obedient sonship. Within these themes, Campbell weaves two concurrent threads.

---

[12] Macquarrie, p. 263.

[13] Gerrish, ch. 3.

[14] James Denney, *The Christian Doctrine of Reconciliation* (New York: George Doran, 1918), pp. 119-120.

One is that the meaning of atonement is found in this "life" which brings "light." Second, is that the fulfillment of this atonement is seen in the *participation* of humanity in this obedient sonship. Our thesis is that one's *formal* approach, i.e. hermeneutical method, determines the possibility of a dynamic relationship between the vicarious humanity of Christ and atonement as much as the *material* aspect, i.e. the dogmatic understanding. This chapter is content to consider this epistemological and hermeneutical concern.

PRELIMINARY CONSIDERATIONS

There are several preliminary considerations which led Campbell down the road to seeing the importance methodologically of the Incarnation as the presupposition of the atonement. One of these is the sheer reality of the Incarnation of the Son of God in Jesus Christ which Campbell calls "the primary and highest fact" of the history of the relationship between God and humanity.[15] There is no other light than the cradle at Bethlehem. Theism may have its place, but it is soon superceded by "the divine fact." *Cur Deus Homo?* ceases to be a speculative question when we are confronted with "the divine mind in Him."[16] Campbell cautions against a surrender to "principles," even such a statement as "God is love," instead of the divine reality revealed in Jesus Christ, "the facts of the gospel."[17] These "facts" concern the eternal relationship between the Father and the Son, which becomes the axiom of the uniqueness of the gospel. The proclamation of the revelation of "the mind of God" is not sufficient. "The mind of God" is revealed only in this relationship of love, trust, and obedience.[18] Apart from this, there is categorically no participation in the divine life, for the divine life means divine sonship. Revelation is not made on the basis of the identity of will between the Father and the Son exclusively, but on their relationship. As Campbell puts it, a father is only a father when one knows his

---

15 *Atonement,* xvii.
16 Ibid., xviii.
17 Ibid., xxi.
18 Ibid., xliv. It must be admitted, however, that the relationship between "theism" and "religion" in Campbell is a topic which deserves further study.

son. His indebtedness to Matthew 11:25-27 is obvious at this point.

The transcendent esoterica of these lofty ideas are evident to Campbell. But he answers this with a unique emphasis on the combination of the humanity of Christ and the Reformed doctrine of the internal witness of the Holy Spirit. There is a certain accessibility to "the divine mind" since it takes shape in "the life of Christ," which is "the light of life to us."[19] However, the finitude of human understanding limits this. This is the place of the epistemological work of the Holy Spirit.[20]

Campbell draws heavily upon Luther's emphasis on the humility which comes in meditating upon the Babe in the manger. There is an "epistemological chastening" taking place when one looks upon God as helpless human flesh. It is as if God were imploring us not to look into heaven in order to fill our minds with theistic speculations as countless as the stars.[21] *"In Him was life and the life was the light of man,"* and *"He that hath seen me hath seen the Father"* have epistemological, as well as soteriological significance for Campbell. Indeed, the weaving of the epistemological and the soteriological creates an emphasis on the revelation of knowledge, not just for knowledge's sake, but for the practical doing of the will of God.

Campbell draws several deductions from the primacy of the Incarnation. One concerns "individualism." A contemporary reviewer of Campbell's book had objected to his emphasis on the corporate nature of humanity. Recent study on the importance of the individual contradicted that. Campbell replied that he had a theological right to ascertain the meaning of "individual" from "his relation to Christ," rather than from "a form of metaphysical or psychological thought on the subject of personality accepted by the reviewer."[22] This assumes a basic stance concerning the theological knowledge of the nature of humanity. In a similar sense, the

---

19   Ibid., xviii. See Calvin, *Institutes* 1. 7. 4.
20   *Atonement,* xix.   Cf. a similar thought in T. F. Torrance, "The Epistemological Relevance of the Holy Spirit," in *God and Rationality*, pp. 165-195.
21   *Atonement,* p. 43. Cf. Bewkes, p. 41.
22   *Atonement* p. 401.

conscience may signify to us the need for atonement, and thus be a halfway point between Christ and humanity, but only in the context of Christ as the revelation of true humanity.[23] The humanity of Christ has epistemological as well as soteriological import.

Thus, we have a continuity with our previous discussion of the wide ranging *scope of* the vicarious humanity of Christ as presented by Torrance. The scope extends to epistemological and hermeneutical implications of the atonement and salvation. The reality of salvation is not found in religious, political, or world experience, but in God himself, the vicarious humanity of Christ as the external expression of the eternal humanity of God. Therefore, *knowledge of* God (epistemology) and *interpretation* of that knowledge (hermeneutics) are found in the humanity of Christ, a humanity which takes upon, heals, and restores our fallen humanity.

THE INCARNATION AS THE PRESUPPOSITION OF THE ATONEMENT

The incarnational theological method implicit throughout his work is made explicit by Campbell at the very beginning in his introduction to *The Nature of the Atonement:* The atonement is to be seen as the "development" of the Incarnation.[24] Campbell lists three distinct implications which follow from this premise: 1) The relationship between the two is "indissoluble." 2) It is a "natural, not an arbitrary relationship." 3) This speaks of one overriding divine purpose in love.

The first point is a warning against an "incarnational" religion which does not take atonement seriously. The Scriptures clearly teach a soteriological motive for the Incarnation: "God commendeth his love toward us, in that, while we were yet sinners, Christ dies for us,"[25] and "Herein is love, not that we loved God, but that he love us, and sent his Son to be the propitiation

---

23 *Atonement,* pp. 13, 170. Cf. Macquarrie, p. 265. The similarities to the thought of Karl Barth are striking. See *CD* III/2, pp. 203-221.

24 *Atonement,* xx.

25 Romans 5:8.

for our sin."[26] There is a "remedial" character to the gospel which is left out when the Incarnation is seen apart from atonement.[27]

Secondly, Campbell speaks in an almost "organic" way of the relationship between the atonement and our participation in Christ: It is "not arbitrary, but natural." Even eternal life directly involves Christ as the "divine life in humanity." Otherwise, atonement becomes an appendage to an independent doctrine of a divine human being. In Campbell's thought, the life of Christ as a whole had atoning effect. This is the basis on which to understand Campbell's controversial teaching of Christ as providing a "vicarious repentance" for our sins. This is an integral part of the true humanity of Christ, which only could have been made possible by the Incarnation. Not only is a vicarious repentance made possible by Christ, but the Incarnation creates a necessity for the proper response within humanity to the sin of humanity, in light of the divine mind.[28] A similar implication is seen in the question of the reason for Christ's sufferings. A typical forensic view of atonement will see a necessity for "suffering as suffering" or "pain as pain," as Christ bears the punishment for our sins. But if the atonement is the development of the Incarnation, the sufferings of Christ can be nothing less than the sorrow in the Father's heart toward the sin of humanity. And in that sorrow, there is atonement.[29] The sufferings of Christ arose naturally out of who he was, the divine mind in humanity. It is important to notice that although he does not use the term, the Nicene doctrine of the *homoousion* between the Father and the Son is very alive in the thought of Campbell.[30] For whatever emphasis he puts on the humanity of Christ, it is not engulfed into an Ebionite abyss.

Thirdly, Campbell sees a "unity and simplicity" in the relationship between the Incarnation, atonement, and participation in

---

26 I Jn. 4:10.
27 *Atonement,* xxi.
28 Ibid., p. 138.
29 Ibid., pp. 114-115.
30 For the significance of the *homoousion* for theology today, see A. I. C. Heron, "Homoousion with the Father" in *The Incarnation,* ed. T. F. Torrance (Edinburgh: The Handsel Press, 1981), pp. 54-76.

the divine nature, which points to "one purpose of divine love."[31] A continuity exists in the entire gospel story which cannot be dichotomized into "law/grace" or "law/gospel." As the atonement moves out from the reality of the Incarnation, the same reality of Immanuel, "God with us," is present at Calvary. Again, one senses an "organic" understanding of salvation in Campbell, based on the manifestation of the divine life in humanity through Jesus Christ.

THE LIGHT OF CHRIST

Campbell is fond of speaking about salvation as "divine light fulfilling humanity."[32] "Light" becomes an important picture for Campbell which helps to portray the epistemological significance of the life of Christ. "Light" is neither a purely mystical experience nor a purely rational understanding for Campbell. "Light" is only found, in a theological sense, in the life of Christ. This is the core of Campbell's argument with John Owen and Jonathan Edwards, the famous paragons of Calvinist orthodoxy.[33] If justice is seen as the primary necessity laid upon humanity, then "the atonement *ceases to reveal that God is love.*"[34] Justice is seen to be the essential attribute of God. Mercy and love become "arbitrary," of merely secondary status.

The light of the life of Christ reveals the honoring of the eternal Father.[35] To know God is to honor God. This is not simply external lip-service, but an honoring which proceeds from the depths of one's being. Such is the picture of Jesus as recorded in the Gospels: "I do nothing of myself, as I hear, I judge" (Jn. 5:30), "The Father dwelleth in me, He doeth the works" (Jn. 14:10), "The Son doeth nothing of Himself, but whatsoever the Father doeth, the same doeth the Son likewise" (Jn. 5:19), "Why

---

31 *Atonement,* xix.
32 A contemporary discussion of the significance of "light" in physics and theology is found in T. F. Torrance, *Christian Theology and Scientific Culture* (Belfast: Christian Journals Ltd., 1980), pp. 73-104.
33 *Atonement,* p. 53.
34 Ibid., p. 64.
35 Ibid., p. 166.

callest thou me good? There is none good but one, that is, God"
(Mt. 19:17 par.). The depth of this honoring of the Father is seen
when "through the eternal Spirit He offered Himself without spot
before God" (Heb. 9:14).

The light in the life of Christ which honors the Father is our
participation in the Son's relationship with the Father.[36] This is
the "gift" of the Father to us in the Son and the answer to the
prayer of Jesus in John 17:4, 11:

> I glorified thee on the earth, having accomplished the
> work which thou gavest me to do. And now I am no
> more in the world, but they are in the world, and I am
> coming to thee. Holy Father, keep them in thy name,
> which thou hast given me, that they may be one, even
> as we are one.

Two points are to be noted. First, the glorification of the Father
takes place "on the earth," i.e., in the Incarnation. In the midst of
this glorification there is genuine knowledge of God. So to speak
of the "transcendence" of God, one must always define this qual-
ity in light of the "transcendence" which has walked the sands of
Galilee.[37] However, the second point is also important: There is
no "historical transcendence," to use R. Gregor Smith's and Ray
S. Anderson's term, apart from the participation of humanity in
the oneness which exists between the Father and the Son. As
Campbell stresses, this theology is far from certain forms of fed-
eral Calvinism which emphasize imputed righteousness as the legal ground of justification. The gift of this oneness between the
Father and the Son is made manifest through the "light" of the
Incarnation, the Word made flesh.

Campbell makes a strong case against any sense of modalism in regards to the life of the Son. His was a real life, not just
the playing of a part.[38] The epistemological importance of this can
be readily seen. Theological knowledge for the Christian does not
come as an idea, nor even primarily as an experience, but through
the Life of One Person. Salvation means to participate in that life

---

[36] Ibid., p. 178.
[37] Cf. Ray S. Anderson, *Historical Transcendence and the Reality of God.*
[38] *Atonement,* pp. 230-231.

through faith. Along the same lines, recent theologians have emphasized the importance of the identification of the "economic" Trinity with the "immanent" Trinity.[39]

The vicarious humanity of Christ as epistemological "light" is not sheer *humanitas* apart from having concrete external incidents affecting that humanity, as well as a conscious will responding in love to the Father. Without such features, we would not have true humanity. With such features, our understanding of the atonement broadens and deepens as we realize we participate in that particular life. As T. F. Torrance is fond of putting it, quoting the Fathers, "the Logos became man and did not just enter into man."[40] How truly human is the Word made flesh? That is the question which has been asked *Christologically*, but how often in the history of the church has it been asked *epistemologically* and *hermeneutically*? This is the significance of the vicarious humanity of Christ and its relation to the atonement, as we find it in the work of John McLeod Campbell.

In the New Testament, in both the Synoptics and the Fourth Gospel, the foremost characteristic of this particular human life of Jesus is his obedience to the Father. Campbell brings the obedience of Christ into focus as "light," i.e. in an epistemological sense. In light of this obedient life, the death of Christ becomes not darkness for Campbell, but light.[41] His obedience was an "obedience unto death" (Phil. 2:8), but that death was never separated form his life of obedience. There is a revelation of God in the midst of the sufferings of Christ, not merely in connection with them.[42] The obedience of Christ means that there is a sorrow in God's heart, a sorrow over humanity's sin. But it is a problem which he himself takes up: not by coming *into* humanity but by *becoming* human.

---

[39] Barth, *CD* I/1, p. 479; T. F. Torrance, "Toward an Ecumenical Consensus on the Trinity," *Theologische Zeitschrift* 31 (1975), pp. 335-350.

[40] T. F. Torrance, *Theol. in Reconcil.,* (Grand Rapids: Eerdmans, 1975), p. 157.

[41] *Atonement,* p. 320.

[42] Ibid., p. 141.

THE LIFE OF CHRIST

It remains for us to look more closely at the epistemological significance of the atoning "life" of Christ as it relates to the life of humanity. First of all, life is not an eternal given in the universe for Campbell. God is "the fountain of life." As "the fountain of life," God himself is able to bring humanity from death into life.[43] This is the soteriological significance of *creatio ex nihilo,* a much maligned, but vitally important doctrine.[44] It is at this point that salvation passes from simply a forensic concern to an *ontological* reality for Campbell, much like the Greek Fathers:

> The question of salvation is seen to be simply the question of *participation* in that favour [of the Creator-Father] as it is the outgoing of a living love, the love of the Father's heart, and not as the mere favourable sentence of a judge and a ruler, setting the mind at ease in reference to the demands of the law of His moral government.[45]

For Campbell, eternal life is not to be separated from the life of the Son. Since the Son has become flesh and dwelt among us, eternal life should not be seen as only a future promise, but also as a present gift.[46] This is a life of active self-sacrificing love which both represents God before humanity and humanity before God, as well as dealing with both the past and the future of humanity.[47] This is the "simplicity" and "unity" of eternal life in the life of the Son. Campbell expresses a strong aversion to any dualisms between Incarnation/cross, death/resurrection, law/gospel, and most of all, the wrath of God versus the love of God.[48] There is one life of the Son which mirrors the singleminded love of the Father.

---

43 Ibid., p. 219.

44 See the contemporary case for *creatio ex nihilo* made by T. F. Torrance in *The Ground and Grammar of Theology,* p. 53 and *Divine and Contingent Order.*

45 *Atonement,* p. 220.

46 Ibid., pp. 14-15.

47 Ibid., pp. 127-128.

48 "Unitary" knowledge versus "dualistic" thinking has been discussed recently by T. F. Torrance in *The Ground and Grammar of Theology,* pp. 15-44.

According to Campbell, occupying ourselves with a future blessedness, as was common in Reformed piety,[49] may actually cause our minds to stray from Christ, whose life brings eternal life into the present.[50] The communion between the Father and the Son is the life in which we participate in the present.[51] The essence of this life is the obedience of sonship, which culminates in the death on the cross. This "must be not only apprehended by our faith, but also spiritually shared in by us."[52] Since there is an essential unity between the life and death of Christ (again, *contra* dualistic forms of thought), to receive Christ as our life is also to participate in his death. What can it mean to participate in his death, apart from participating in the mind which willingly accepted that death? This is "the mind in which he lived," the mind which condemned sin in the flesh (Rom. 8:3). The essential unity in the life of Christ extends to both "inward" and "outward" obedience.[53] It is "inward" as Christ submits himself to the Father ("opening ears as the learner, morning by morning") and "outward" as he lives among humanity and is confronted by its sin ("not hiding his face from shame and spitting"). These are, of course, Campbell's terms for what has been known in classic Reformed theology as "the active and passive obedience of Christ."[54] Campbell sees the effect of the "outward" obedience

---

[49] See Richard Baxter, *The Saints' Everlasting Rest* (Westwood:Revell, 1962) and Calvin, *Institutes, 3.9.*

[50] Contemporary biblical theology has often stressed the present reality of the kingdom of God. See C. H. Dodd, *The Parables of the Kingdom* (New York: Scribners, 1935); George E. Ladd, *The Presence of the Future* (Grand Rapids: Eerdmans, 1974); H. Ridderbos, *The Coming of the Kingdom* (Philadelphia: Presbyterian and Reformed Pub. Co., 1962); R. Schnackenburg, *God's Rule and Kingdom,* trans. John Murray (New York: Herder and Herder, 1963), and most recently, Dale C. Allison, Jr., *The End of the Ages Has Come: An Early Interpretation of the Passion and Resurrection of Jesus* (Philadelphia: Fortress Press, 1985).

[51] *Atonement,* p. 173.

[52] Ibid., p. 308.

[53] Ibid., pp 242,244.

[54] See L. Berkhof, *Systematic Theology* (Grand Rapids: Eerdmans, 1941), pp. 379-381; F. Schleiermacher, *The Christian Faith,* eds. and trans. H. R. Mackintosh and J. S. Stewart (Edinburgh: T. & T. Clark, 1928), pp. 451-466.

upon the "inward" as a progression throughout the life of Jesus, so that he can say: "The elements of the atonement gradually developed themselves with the gradual development of His humanity, and corresponding development of the eternal life in His humanity."[55] This is another example of how Campbell deals seriously with the phenomenon of the life of the individual man Jesus as essential to understanding the theological humanity of Jesus as it relates to the atonement. For that reason, Campbell takes pains in devoting an entire chapter to "The Atonement, As Illustrated by the Details of the Sacred Narrative" (chapter ten).[56]

Participation in the life of obedience unto death brings a fresh perspective to the teaching of Jesus.[57] What does it mean to hate one's kindred, as well as one's own life, in order to be a disciple of Jesus (Mt. 10:37-38; Lk. 14:26-27)? Campbell refuses to separate the teaching of Jesus from the person of Jesus. Therefore, he notes that Jesus fulfilled his own teaching by "hating" his own life: "Jesus lived that life which he was commanding."[58] "Obedience unto death" is the mark of the disciple as well as of the master. On a practical level, this is what it means to participate in the life of the Son.

If it is said that Jesus lived the life which he commanded by "hating" one's own life for the sake of obedience to the Father, then for Campbell this takes on the form of the "naturalness" of death as a part of the life of the only one who truly has lived a full and sinless human life.[59] As a truly human being, life was given to Jesus as a gift.[60] Death was the withdrawal of that gift. So Jesus truly felt the withdrawing of the gift of life in a way that sinful humanity cannot. The sufferings of Jesus are always to be related to his life.

---

[55] *Atonement*, p. 244.

[56] Ibid., p. 242.

[57] The necessity for uniting the teaching of Jesus with his person has been argued by both Karl Barth, *CD* II/2, p. 690, and T. F. Torrance, *Reality and Evangelical Theology*, p. 93.

[58] *Atonement*, p. 250.

[59] Ibid., pp. 301-302.

[60] See the similar emphasis on the theological value of life in Dietrich Bonhoeffer, *Ethics*, pp. 143-187.

In the life of obedient sonship, Jesus reveals the mind of the Father. His life is not just a prelude to the real drama, the crucifixion and resurrection. Nor is it simply the life of a religious teacher, which one is called to imitate. In the life of the Son, the mind of the Father is revealed in the midst of the oneness of mind between the Father and the Son.[61] Campbell's theological method understands the life of Christ as a hermeneutical key. This is a particular life, not as simply generic humanity, but as partaking in the fullness of human experience. In this sense he is preparing for a comprehensive relationship between the vicarious nature of the humanity of Christ and salvation. In this he seems to be following no less a theologian than the author of the Fourth Gospel, who declares concerning the Word: "In him was life, and the life was the light of men" (Jn. 1:4).

THE SONSHIP OF CHRIST

It has been stated that in Campbell's thought, the life of Christ which is given in humanity as a present gift, in order for humanity to participate in it, is a *particular* life and not simply generic humanity. The "particularization" of the vicarious humanity of Christ in the theology of John McLeod Campbell is especially seen in the emphasis he places on the sonship of Christ. Sonship is the context of the life of Christ which is the light of the Father's heart. The place of the sonship of Christ is considered by George M. Tuttle to be "the crowning and most inclusive feature of Campbell's understanding of Christ's work," which has often been overlooked in studies of Campbell.[62] It may be looked at from the perspective of an emphasis upon the general religious experience of Jesus. Otto Pfleiderer likens Campbell and Thomas Erskine in this regard to the transition from "forensic externality" to "ethical inwardness" centered on religious experience, found in Kant and Schleiermacher.[63] Campbell was certainly interested in the details of the life of Jesus, as was most of the nineteenth cen-

---

[61] *Atonement,* p. 261

[62] Tuttle, "The Place of...", p. 203.

[63] Pfleiderer, p. 382.

tury, but not to the exclusion of the Christ of faith.[64] It is much
more accurate to see, with James Torrance, Campbell's teaching
on the sonship of Jesus in light of his parallel doctrine of the vicarious humanity of Christ.[65] Sonship is not simply a reflection of
ethical inwardness nor religious experience, but a full-orbed
manifestation of the fatherhood of God, its reconciling power, and
the reality of the participation of humanity in that sonship. The
arena for this is "the whole history of the human Jesus," in which
the Father-Son relationship mirrors the two movements of the
Incarnation, according to Torrance: the "God-manward" movement, the revelation of the Father and the kingdom of God, and
the"man-Godward" movement, the faithful and obedient life of
sonship offered to the Father by the human Jesus.[66]

In Campbell's teaching, sonship means a revelation of God.
To speak of sonship means to speak of the knowledge of God.
Campbell makes much of the Johannine verse, "He that hath seen
me hath seen the Father" (Jn. 14:9).[67] This is not meant to be
simply the mind of God in human flesh. No, there is a real
revelation of the Father himself. This is what Jesus means when
he says, "I am the way, and the truth and the life, no man cometh
to the Father but by me" (Jn. 14:6). In no uncertain terms,
Campbell weds his hermeneutic to the Word made flesh. His
concern for the alternative is expressed when he states that apart
from John 14:6, no "light" is shed on the divine fatherhood, the
divine sonship, "and the participation in the Divine Life of
Sonship to which it is the grace of God in Christ to raise us."
Since it is a son revealing his father, it is no question of a simple
unity of wills, however. For when one knows the son, one knows
the father: "A father as such is known only in his relation to his
son." It is as if my claim to be a son leaves you with no alternative

---

64 Tuttle, "The Place of...", p. 172.
65 J. Torrance, "Contribution," pp. 305-306.
66 Ibid., p. 306.
67 *Atonement,* xliv.

than to admit that because this son exists, there must also be a father.[68]

Much discussion among theologians concerns "objective" versus "subjective" theories of the atonement. Campbell is usually placed within the "subjective" category because of his emphasis on "vicarious repentance" and his opposition to the forensic theory. However, Eugene G. Bewkes sees a genuine "objective" side to Campbell in his emphasis on Jesus' communion with the Father.[69] This is a "true objectivity" which stands over against us because it is unique. "Objectivity" is not simply a forensic act done once and for all on Calvary, but an eternal relationship of mutual love revealed to humanity in the humanity of Jesus. It is this "objective" side of the Incarnation which also has an epistemological function.

The priority of the "filial" over the "judicial" in Campbell has caused James Torrance to see a connection between Campbell and Calvin's doctrine of "evangelical repentance."[70] "Forgiveness, therefore repentance" lays the basis for repentance in Calvin, not "repentance, therefore forgiveness," which he understands as a "legal repentance." This may be extended to the atonement as a whole. The message of the gospel is not "atonement, then forgiveness," but "forgiveness, then atonement." This was certainly the burden of Campbell in his struggle against the prevailing forensic theories of his day.

Campbell's characteristic emphasis on the sonship of Jesus as the revelation of God as Father is expressed in many ways. It is typical of Campbell to see a revelation of the love of God even in the midst of pathos. So it is not surprising to find him exegeting the declaration of faith by Jesus on Calvary as the archetypal expression of true sonship: "Father, into thy hands I commend my spirit" (Lk. 23:46). The Son proclaims the worthiness of worshipping the Father, even in the midst of the tragedy of the cross.

---

[68] See the work by Thomas Smail, *The Forgotten Father* (London: Hodder and Stoughton, 1980). Cf. George E. Ladd, *A Theology of the New Testament*, (Grand Rapids: Eerdmans, 1974), p. 87.

[69] Bewkes, pp. 268-270.

[70] J. Torrance, "Contribution," p. 311; Calvin, *Institutes,* 3.3.1.

Through the example of Jesus, there is a revelation of the
gift of the Son: the right to call God "Father." The Incarnation not
only reveals the heart of the Father, but also the desire of the
Father for humanity to walk in that sonship:

> Our confidence is to be the fellowship of His confi-
> dence; our worship, the fellowship of His worship:—
> for the sonship is that sonship, in spirit and truth,
> which the Father seeketh.[71]

Campbell definitely has a doctrine of the *imitatio Christi*, but on
the basis of a participation in, not simply following of, the life of
Christ. As usual, he contrasts this filial understanding of salvation
with the "Calvinists" who ground salvation on a legal standing
given to us by Christ. If this is so, then the Christian life has no
place for being led by the spirit of Christ, "for our experience is no
repetition of, no fellowship in His experience, nor the breathing of
our new life the free breathing of the life of sonship."[72] If this is
"strictly adhered to," the most tragic outcome is that "all direct
dealing on our part with the Father's heart as the Father's heart, in
other words, all experimental knowledge of God, would become
impossible."[73] For Campbell, the revelation of "the heart of the
Father" is integrally related to the act of atonement within the humanity of Christ. The Incarnation is the epistemological key into
the heart of God.

Sonship has important implications for our understanding of
the obedience of Christ. A logical place to begin to understand the
obedience of Christ is in terms of the two great commandments as
expressed by Jesus himself (Mt. 12: 28-34; Lk. 10:25-28). "The
spirit of sonship" provides the relationship between the two commandments and Jesus.[74] (See also our discussion of the command
of self-denial and its fulfillment by Jesus, p. 168.) The spirit of
obedient sonship in Jesus loved the Father with all his heart,
mind, soul and strength. The second commandment according to
Jesus, to love your brother as yourself, is "like it." How is it "like

---

71 *Atonement,* p. 107.
72 Ibid., p. 107.
73 Ibid., p. 108.
74 Ibid., p. 125.

it"? In one way, according to Campbell, in that it is also fulfilled in "the spirit of sonship." As the perfect Son, Jesus also becomes the perfect elder brother of humanity who, unlike the elder brother in the parable of the Prodigal Son (Lk. 15), sympathizes with the yearnings of his Father for his wayward brethren. As the perfect brother, the Son participates in the humanity of the brethren in order to sympathize with them (Heb. 4:15). In an interesting insight, Campbell speaks of the power of sonship to fulfill the law, as summarized in the two great commandments.[75] The closeness of this eternal relationship between the Father and the Son now made manifest in humanity has a power within itself which becomes an integral part of the meaning of "atonement."

The power and strength of obedient sonship within humanity is seen by Campbell in its greatest depth through the cross. Sonship is fulfilled to the uttermost when the blood of Christ is offered. But it must be remembered that the death of Christ is the offering of the Son before the Father. The eternal filial relationship between the Father and the Son is the spiritual dynamic which defines for us the meaning of the atonement, according to Campbell. The access to the Holy of Holies achieved for us by the blood of Christ, as taught by the writer of the Epistle to the Hebrews (Heb. 10:19), is based on the eternal filial relationship between the Son and the Father ("He who has seen me has seen the Father").[76] The Christologies of both John and Hebrews coincide in the vicarious sonship of Christ. The "cleansing" from sin which the First Epistle of John speaks of (I Jn. 1:9), is not based on a legal justification, but on the "fellowship" between the Father and the Son in which we now participate (I Jn. 1:2-3, 6-7).[77] Notice that even in this context of "fellowship" soteriology, the blood of Jesus is an integral act of atonement, not as a means, but as an expression of forgiveness through a life (I Jn. 1:7). This is the same blood as contemplated in Hebrews:

> If the blood of bulls and of goats, and the ashes of a heifer sprinkling the unclean, sanctifieth to the purifying of the flesh; how much more shall the blood of

---

75 Ibid., p. 70.
76 Ibid., p. 193.
77 Ibid., p. 195.

> Christ, who through the eternal Spirit offered himself
> without spot to God, purge your conscience from dead
> works to serve the living God (Heb. 9:13-14)?[78]

Campbell presents the death of Christ as a great "victory of sonship," for it showed the extent to which sonship could trust the Father. In the depths of this grim event there is a revelation of God as the Father who is worthy of trust.[79]

Campbell's counsel not to go outside the life of Christ in which we partake, and settle for an "unknown future blessedness" involves also the need for the yielding of our wills to the law of the Spirit of the life which is Christ. This life to which we yield ourselves has a definite content and a definite form: the life of sonship.[80] Bewkes calls this partaking of sonship in Campbell, "active living reconciliation," in which intercession for others becomes a natural expression of life in Christ.[81] This is the dwelling of divine love in the human heart.

The theme of participation in Christ once again becomes prominent in Campbell, this time in relation to sonship. Participation in sonship is an integral part of a definition of salvation. Is not salvation anything more than orphans finding their lost Father? Campbell asks.[82] His "universalistic" tendencies come through at this point, and in a refreshingly biblical way. The misery of this "orphan state" is "the ultimate contradiction to the original law of our being." Campbell cites Paul's Areopagus address as an example of the apologetic thrust of this point ("For we are also His offspring," Acts 17:28). If we are God's offspring, it is fitting that he should send the Son to save us. This emphasis is interesting once we remember that the teaching of "universal atonement" (but not "universal salvation") was one of the criteria for dismissing

---

[78] Ibid., p. 196.
[79] Ibid., pp. 261-262.
[80] Ibid., p. 169.
[81] Bewkes, p. 274.
[82] *Atonement,* p. 169.

Campbell from the ministry of the Church of Scotland in 1831.[83] Campbell is compelled by his incarnational theological method to see a continuity between creation and redemption, even in the heart of his soteriology. The Father who created gives his Son to redeem.[84]

Salvation through the Son reveals both the need of humanity and the heart of the Father.

> It is the cry of the child that reveals the mother's heart. It is the cry of Sonship in humanity bearing the burden of humanity, confessing its sin, asking for it the good of which the capacity still remained to it, which being responded to by the Father has revealed the Father's heart.[85]

This is humanity as God desires it to be: dependent on God as Father, based on the filial, not legal, relationship. According to Tuttle, this is "one of the pivotal points in Campbell's thought."[86] It was to cause a great strain between Campbell and the view of salvation which saw Christ as a human being working out a legal righteousness (although Campbell definitely had a place for the obedience of Christ, as we shall see later in detail).

The declaration by the Father concerning Jesus at the Transfiguration ("This is my beloved Son, with whom I am well pleased," Mt. 17:5; cf. the baptism of Jesus, Mt. 3:17; Mk. 1:11) is not to be understood as simply the commissioning for the messianic task, but also as the call for humanity to participate in the sonship of Jesus. This is the call to "listen to Him" (Mt. 17:6), the "quickening of humanity."

---

83 J. Torrance, "Contribution," p. 295. However, at least some semi-Pelagian views can be seen in Campbell's thoughts on the "capacity" of restoration to sonship. p. 22; cf. *Atonement*, p. 236; cf. Emil Brunner, "Nature and Grace," in Emil Brunner and Karl Barth, *Natural Theology*, p. 31.

84 A similar claim can be made for Karl Barth in his teaching on the relationship between creation and covenant ("creation as the external form of the covenant" and "covenant as the internal basis of creation"), *contra* the attempts of his opponents to drive a wedge between nature and grace in his thought, *CD* III/1, pp. 94-330.

85 *Atonement*, p. 236.

86 Tuttle, "The Place of...", p. 192.

Participation in sonship has its definite epistemological implications for Campbell. As we have seen, "the light of life" in Christ has strong relevance for our knowledge of God. This includes "participation" in "the light of life," since this life is the communion between the Father and the Son given to humanity as a gift.[87] Included within this life is the gift of the righteousness of Christ in the context of sonship.[88] The Reformed doctrines of imputed righteousness and satisfaction find a place in Campbell if they are understood within the context of the priority of the filial relationship between the Father and the Son. This is atonement as the reality of who God is and who humanity is in the midst of its relationship to Christ.[89] The ethical power of the filial relationship as explicated by Campbell is acknowledged by R. S. Franks. In answer to the criticism that Campbell's doctrine is less morally demanding than the traditional doctrine, Franks remarks that the demand of a judge, as in a forensic theory of the atonement, is limited once justice has been done. But the father presents a continual demand on his son because of their filial relationship. The heavenly Father, therefore, demands nothing less than "a complete and perfect holiness of life."[90] But it must be added that this demand comes in the context of the Father's grace. Being the Father means that he loves his children eternally and what demands he gives are given in the context of love. This is certainly true if we have a doctrine of the One who existed in an eternal relationship of love with the Father, and who is now made manifest in the flesh of humanity.[91]

THE OBEDIENCE OF CHRIST

We have gone from the "light of life" in the Incarnation to its "particularization" in the sonship of Jesus. Closely related to

---

87 *Atonement,* p. 173.

88 Ibid., p. 225.

89 Tuttle, "The Place of...", p. 195. This is true in spite of Campbell's strong criticism of the doctrine of "imputed righteousness." *Atonement,* pp. 155-158.

90 Franks, *History* , Vol. 2, p. 399.

91 Cf. Karl Barth's statement, "Even when man does not keep the command, the command keeps him. *CD* III/4, p. 239.

Campbell's understanding of the vicarious sonship of Christ is his teaching on the obedience of Christ. To know the Son is to know him as the Obedient Son. To understand atonement in the Son is to understand the participation of humanity in the obedience of the faithful Son. The *formal basis* for his teaching is found in his emphasis on the perfect response of Christ as the ground of redemption. This obedience, extending to the point of suffering and death, achieves atonement and yields victory over sin and death. The *material content* of his teaching is found in the honoring of the Father and the fulfilling of the law by the Son, in which humanity now participates.

The obedience of Christ is based on the "perfect response" of the Son to the Father's judgment on sin. In Campbell's famous words, this was "a perfect Amen in humanity to the judgment of God on the sin of man."[92] Notice the emphasis: "a perfect Amen *in humanity*." The vicarious humanity of Christ is always at the forefront of Campbell's thought.

Campbell certainly has a place for the wrath of God, but it is a wrath centered on *sin*, not the *sinner*. The Incarnation was "a peculiar development of *the holy sorrow* in which He bore the burden of our sins" (emphasis mine). Christ understands and receives the burden of human sin and is able to provide the perfect atonement: a perfect response; a perfect "yes" to the judgment of the Father, which only God can do. It is important at this point to see Campbell's roots in the Reformed doctrine of total depravity and inability. The *inability* of humanity to provide the "perfect repentance," "perfect sorrow," "perfect contrition" provides the context for the Incarnation as atonement.[93] This is the ground of God's redemption in history.[94]

Campbell is often criticized for not placing enough emphasis on the sufferings and death of Christ.[95] However, it is evident from *The Nature of the Atonement* that the death of Christ has a special place in his theory of the atonement. Campbell sees the

---

92 *Atonement*, p. 136.
93 Ibid., pp. 137-138.
94 Ibid., p. 238.
95 Macquarrie, p. 268.

death of Christ as an extension of the work of atonement in the Incarnation. The sufferings of Jesus express the "living will and heart" of Jesus, not simply a fate or necessity.[96] His baptism which he is to undergo (Lk. 12:50), his troubled soul (Jn. 12:27), and the terror of Gethsemane (Mk. 14:33-36; Lk. 21:44) express a genuine human will in obedience to the Father. This obedience is expressed in "the strength of sonship," for the cup of bitterness is accepted, not from the Judge or from Necessity, but from the hand of the Father. The filial relationship provides the basis for the endurance of such suffering: "The cup which *my Father* hath given me to drink, shall I not drink it?" (Jn. 18:11)[97] The sufferings of the Son express the *extent* to which sonship in humanity could trust the Father and the development of his life of love.[98] The death of Christ becomes the "perfect manifestation" of the faith which existed in obedient sonship.[99] In other words, Campbell maintains the creative continuum between the life and the death of Christ, while still maintaining a unique significance for his death.

In summary, the obedience of Christ is based on its achievement of atonement and the victory which Christ's righteousness brings. Campbell relates the story of Phinehas, the son of Eleazar, in Numbers 25:10-13, who achieves "atonement" because of his "zeal" for Yahweh.[100] The "moral element" in "the mind of Phinehas' achieved atonement, just as Christ's death, was atoning "because of the condemnation of sin in his spirit."[101] In the same vein, Hebrews 10:4-10 speaks of the impossibility of the blood of bulls and goats to take away sin, and the complete sufficiency of the atoning obedience of Christ. He is the one who says, "Lo, I have come to do thy will, O God." This verse is "the great key-word on the subject of atonement" for Campbell.[102] The center of atonement is not the fact of a death, but the obedient will of

---

[96] *Atonement,* pp. 251-252.

[97] Ibid., p. 253.

[98] Ibid., p. 261.

[99] Ibid., pp. 299-300.

[100] Ibid., p. 120.

[101] Ibid., p. 121.

[102] Ibid., p. 124.

which the submission to death is the outcome. "By the which will we are sanctified, through the offering of the body of Jesus Christ once for all" (Heb. 10:10). The doing of the will of God by Christ is "the essence and substance of the atonement." As in Luther's thought, which Campbell is fond of quoting, the righteousness of Christ meets the sinfulness of humanity and achieves the victory.[103] This is the formal basis of the obedience of Christ as atonement.

The material content of the obedience of Christ as atonement includes its *goal* in honoring the Father, its *context* in fulfilling the law of God, and its *actualization* in the participation of humanity in this obedience. The honoring of the Father by Jesus is a result of the oneness of mind between the Father and the Son.[104] As a result, the Son freely and joyfully declares the name of the Father: "I have declared thy name and will declare it" (Jn. 17:26). This does not refer to merely the plan of redemption, but to the actual reality of atonement. The very act of obedience in declaring the name of the Father is atonement. According to Campbell, that "which caused the shedding of His blood to have a virtue which was not in that of bulls and goats" is "the will of God done, the mind of God manifested, the name of the Father declared by the Son."[105] The prayers of Jesus are the highest expression of his trust in the Father.[106] In the boldness of prayer we see the "knowledge of the Father's will and confidence in His love" as moving Jesus to prayer. "Such intercession was the fitting form for His bearing of our burdens to take."

But the honoring of the Father by Jesus took place in the context of sinful humanity. Jesus was not unaffected by the surroundings in which he lived, according to Campbell. Honoring the Father, a manifestation of brotherly love, and a perfect walk of godliness, resulted in dishonor, hatred, and unbelief among his

---

103   Ibid., p. 143.
104   Ibid., p. 239.
105   Ibid., p. 125.
106   Ibid., p. 235.

brethren.[107] But this was not a sorrow which came without a profound sense of joy in doing the will of the Father (Heb. 12:2).

There was joy in honoring the Father, in spite of the rejection, because of the power of a righteous life before God. This obedience had the power to "arrest the course of judgment" as he acknowledged the divine wrath against sin through his perfect confession of our sins.[108] The confession of Christ was "a perfect Amen in humanity to the judgment of God on the sin of man." Atonement means the honoring of the Father. At this point, Campbell's debt to Anselm is obvious.[109] But Campbell sees satisfaction of God's honor in the provision of a perfect repentance. Since the atonement presupposes the epistemological necessity of the Incarnation, the Word made flesh, the humanity of Christ assumes a strategic place in the *ordo salutis*. True knowledge of God only comes through participation in his reconciliation. As Campbell thinks through the "inner logic" of Incarnation and atonement, he is able to see an epistemological implication of the atonement which does not occur in Anselm: the honoring of the Father has atoning value in the perfect confession of our sins by the Son, who represents our humanity to the Father.

The fulfillment of the law by Christ communicates the extent to which Campbell is willing to draw out the soteriological implications of the humanity of Christ in every way, including the perfect repentance. Campbell rightly centers upon Jesus' exposition of the two great commandments in order to understand his relationship to the law (Mt. 22:34-40; Mk. 12:28-34; Lk. 10:25-28).[110] The spirit of sonship is seen in the fulfillment of the command to love God. The second is "like it." Jesus as the perfect elder brother, unlike the elder brother in the parable of the Prodigal Son, sympathizes with the yearnings of the Father's heart for his children. Campbell cites Jonathan Edwards' acknowledgement of the depth of Christ's identification with humanity, but criticizes

---

107   Ibid., p. 130.

108   Ibid., pp. 135-136.

109   Anselm, "Why God Became Man," ed. and trans. Eugene A. Fairweather, in *A Scholastic Miscellany: Anselm to Ockham* (New York: Macmillan, 1970), I. 11.

110   *Atonement*, pp. 125-126.

him for failing to see its implications for the love of all humanity, not just for a select few. The law is not the "dark side" of God, but it is a mirror of his grace. As Jesus fulfills the law, according to Campbell, he is dealing directly with the heart of the Father.[111]

But the purpose of fulfilling the law is not for the sake of drawing humanity once again under its bondage. Quoting Galatians, Campbell sees the purpose of the Incarnation in redeeming those who were under the law "that we might receive the adoption as sons" (Gal. 4:5).[112] This is the unique power of Christ's sonship.[113]

THE DIVINE MIND AND THE MIND OF CHRIST

Campbell strives to see atonement from the perspective of the heart of the Father. What significance could atonement have apart from the heart, the attitude, the feelings, the mind of the Father concerning an estranged world and a rebellious creation? All of Campbell's probings into the light of life revealed in the Incarnation as obedient sonship creating atonement are reflected back and forth upon the divine mind and the mind of Christ.[114] It is as though in the Incarnation, God has ended his own weary traveling through the desert of an unreconciled world and has now reached an oasis. The dry skin and parched throat of God look into the oasis of the Word made flesh and see reconciliation. For in Jesus Christ, the mind and the feelings of the Father's love for humanity pour out as "living water" upon the desolate land of sinful humanity.[115] But how important is it to see the face in the pool as the same face which has taken upon dry skin and a parched throat! *Naked* divine "mind" is not gospel. *Clothed* divine "mind," clothed in the flesh of fallen humanity, is gospel.[116] And as the gospel, it is the only means by which we know the heart of the Father which eternally beats for humanity: "I am the way, the truth

---

[111] Ibid., p. 70.
[112] Ibid., p. 69.
[113] Ibid., p. 70.
[114] Ibid., xvii.
[115] Campbell, *Memorials,* Vol. 1, p. 62. Cf. Bewkes, p. 52.
[116] *Atonement,* xliv.

and the life; no man cometh unto the Father but by me." Again, the *soteriological* is inseparably bound to the *epistemological*. The divine mind *is* the divine Word.

To know the divine mind is to know the revelation of the Father in the Incarnation, to the depths of suffering and death. The sufferings of Christ do not express punishment but revelation of what our sin is to the Father's heart.[117] And if it is revelation, then our knowledge of God (epistemology) is wrapped around our method of interpretation (hermeneutics). For what greater criteria, whether it be philosophic, sociological, or historical, could the creature have for discerning the reality of the Transcendent apart from the Transcendent taking upon the dry skin and the parched throat of estranged humanity? What is atonement, according to Campbell?

> The feeling of the divine mind as to sin being present
> in humanity and uttering themselves to God as a living
> voice from humanity, were the true atonement for the
> sin of humanity.[118]

The above statement deserves careful consideration. For not only is there a revelation of the Father in the Incarnation, but there is also the gracious atoning response of obedient, faithful humanity. The confession by Christ of our sins means that the divine mind has penetrated into the deepest recesses of our humanity.[119] This was not in order to change the heart of the Father, but to mirror the heart of the Father within humanity.[120] The divine mind becomes the mind of Christ, and therefore, the mind of humanity. Even to the point of suffering and death, the divine mind is expressed in the light of life in the obedient sonship of Jesus Christ. This is the "new mind" which is contained in the blood of Christ.[121] But the atonement has significance only for us when we appropriate "the mind of Christ" (cf. I Cor. 2:16). The call of the gospel is to participate in Christ's honoring of the Father. Satis-

---

[117] Ibid., p. 133.
[118] Ibid., p. 143.
[119] Ibid., p. 148.
[120] Ibid., p. 238.
[121] Ibid., p. 184.

faction, the honoring of the Father in Anselmic doctrine, must not end at the cross. It is not simply one moment in time. It is not punctiliar, but linear. The continuous honoring of the Father is true "satisfaction" to God for those who possess and are possessed by "the mind of Christ."[122]

THE LIGHT OF THE LIFE OF THE OBEDIENT SON: THE "SACRED DANCE" BETWEEN THEOLOGICAL EPISTEMOLOGY AND HERMENEUTICS

Christian dogmatics speaks of the knowledge of God. To fail at this is to be less than faithful to the reality of the revelation of God in Jesus Christ. A theology which speaks of the *possibility* of revelation apart from the *actuality* of that which has already occurred, is occurring, and will occur, has passed from theology into only the realm of the study of the phenomena of religion.

Christian dogmatics deals with the problem of hermeneutics: How do we interpret the data of theology? One of the true contributions of the Enlightenment was to stress how much our subjectivity influences our interpretation of the world. Often the subject of hermeneutics is restricted to the Bible. But does it not include also the entirety of the questions which are posed by theology?

When theological epistemology and hermeneutics are discussed, it is rare when the questions of Christology and soteriology are raised in the midst of them. Are not Christology and soteriology to be dealt with *after* one considers the proper epistemological and hermeneutical method? But why? Our contention is that John McLeod Campbell provides an example of a theologian who takes seriously the epistemological and hermeneutical implications of the Incarnation in his teaching on the relationship between the vicarious humanity of Christ and the atonement. And these are implications which affect both theological epistemology and hermeneutics as well as Christology and soteriology.

Campbell takes pains to stress the "light" which comes from the life of Christ. This life involves the eternal relationship between the Father and the Son, the historical life of Jesus of Nazareth, and the resurrected life of the ascended Lord. Campbell

---

[122] Ibid., p. 166.

is wiser than some in seeing the danger of creating an ontological
chasm between the "three moments" of the life of Christ. But the
question of what this "light" reveals may take many forms. This
"light" may reveal only Jesus as the moral teacher in whom true
humanity was embodied. However, in the context of the aforementioned "three moments" in the life of Christ, this cannot be
so.[123] The "light" of God in Jesus Christ is the "light" of God as
he is in himself.[124]

Eschatology is brought into deep interrelationship with the
atonement in the theology of John McLeod Campbell. Eternal life
has a "realized" ring throughout his writing which has great implications for the knowledge of God and how we know him. If eternal life is a present possession, to be realized to some extent in the
present, that means that the One who is Life is in our midst. This
is the danger and blessing of Christian existence. Therefore, to
understand atonement and salvation as participating in the life of
the humanity of God is to come to terms with the call and command of God. The immediacy of salvation means a serious encounter with a God who is not far away, but in our midst.
"Behold, now is the acceptable time; behold, now is the day of
salvation" (II Cor. 6:2).[125] Campbell stresses this immediacy
through seeing the atonement as integrally related to the knowledge of God in the humanity of Christ. To know God is to know
eternal life in the life of the Obedient Son.

Campbell is not content, as we have seen, to settle for a
"content-less" soteriology. If his soteriology involves the communication of a life, it is of utmost importance to go beyond the

---

123 We will relate the epistemology of the life of Christ to a theology of the
present and eschatological Christ in chapter nine.

124 It is remarkable how Campbell's interrelationship between Christology and
soteriology brings a fresh approach to Christology, as well as to
soteriology. Campbell does not speak of the "two natures" of Christ in
themselves, i.e., apart from their soteriological life. Cp. Athanasian
Patristic theology to its later development. Wolfhart Pannenberg,
"Christologie, II. Dogmengeschlictlich," *Die Religion in Geschichte und
Gegenwart,* 3rd ed., I (Tubingen: J. C. B. Mohr, 1956-1962), p. 1772.

125 The immediacy of salvation and discipleship is, of course, a hallmark in the
writings of Søren Kierkegaard. See the discussion in Martin J. Heinecken,
The Moment Before God (Philadelphia: Muhlenberg Press, 1956).

formal to the material aspects of that life. The material aspect of
this life is sonship. It is through the sonship of Jesus that
knowledge of God comes. The Son is the hermeneutical key for
this knowledge, for only through a Son do we know that one is a
Father. And in the Father we see the origins of a movement of
divine love which mirrors an eternal love which exists between the
Father and the Son. This love is now "poured out" in Jesus Christ
through the Holy Spirit (Rom. 5:5). At this crucial point, the
atonement presents a "sacred dance" (*perichoresis*, to borrow a
term from Trinitarian theology) between theological epistemology
and hermeneutics. Knowledge of God is communicated through
the one hermeneutical key, the atoning flesh of Jesus Christ.[126]
And in that interdependence, the freedom of God breaks through
the confines of our epistemological straitjackets in order to confront and to heal.[127] Theological epistemology and hermeneutics
have a dogmatic basis in the vicarious humanity of Christ and the
atonement. *How* we know is based on *who* we know.[128]

A further definition of sonship is emphasized by Campbell in
the obedience of Christ. In the obedience of Christ, Campbell
seeks to draw out the characteristics of the sonship of Christ. He
does this with both remarkable success and yet some questionable
emphases.

The obedience of Christ brings out the "moral and spiritual
elements" of the atonement. This is a genuine contribution by
Campbell, for he was not satisfied by a "moral influence" theory
of the atonement apart from the soteriological implications of the
filial relationship between the Father and the Son communicated
by the Son's humanity. However, does "moral and spiritual" sum
up the depth of the atonement in Jesus Christ? Is this a dualistic

---

[126] Cf. T. F. Torrance: "It is in fact the humanity of Jesus Christ himself which is
the real text underlying the New Testament Scripture." *Reality and
Evangelical Theology*, p. 93.

[127] As we have seen, T. F. Torrance is the best contemporary representative of
Campbell's approach.

[128] Cf. the relation of faith to knowledge in Dietrich Bonhoeffer, *Christ the
Center*, trans. Edwin H. Robertson (San Francisco; Harper and Row, 1978),
p. 76, and as it relates to scientific knowledge in T. F. Torrance, "The
Framework of Belief," *Belief in Science and In Christian Life*, T. F. Torrance,
ed. (Edinburgh: The Handsel Press, 1980), pp. 1-28.

emphasis in Campbell which does not include the physical, social, and emotional aspects of humanity?

Secondly, there may be an overemphasis on the *active* obedience of Christ as opposed to his *passive* obedience. There is a certain "triumphalism" in Campbell's passion story in which he sees only the faithful obedience of the Son to the Father in even what seem the darkest hour: the cry of dereliction —"My God, my God, why hast thou forsaken me?" (Mt. 27:46; Mk. 15:34) But does this not neglect the *passive* obedience of Christ, in which God, through the Son, genuinely suffers, to the point of abandonment, as J. Moltmann and D. Bonhoeffer have recently emphasized?[129] There may be a dialectic here which needs to be maintained. Should we choose between "abandonment" by the Father and the "faith" of the Son? Campbell may neglect the passive obedience of Christ, but not to the extent of undermining the suffering of God. The heart of Campbell's doctrine of the atonement is the "holy sorrow" of the Father toward the sin of humanity. This "holy sorrow" is expressed *in the humanity of Christ.*

We have seen in T. F. Torrance's theology the *comprehensive* nature of the vicarious humanity of Christ in relation to the problem of the reality of salvation: it affects all theological existence. In Campbell, we have seen that this does not exclude the relationship between epistemology and hermeneutics. "In him was life and the life was the light of man" has great epistemological and hermeneutical implications, as well as soteriological implications. In the vicarious humanity of Christ, the reality of salvation is seen in the God who is Lord of all reality and, as such, provides the means (hermeneutics) by which we know him (epistemology) through his taking upon the totality of human life. Thus, our understanding of far-reaching implications of the reality of salvation in God himself has been deepened.

From the standpoint of the *scope* and *breadth* of the reality of salvation (all of theological reality, including epistemology and hermeneutics), we turn now to the *depth* of the soteriological implications of the reality of salvation, as we look at the vicarious *repentance* of Christ, in our next chapter.

---

129   Jürgen Moltmann, *The Crucified God,* pp. 227-235; Dietrich Bonhoeffer, *Letters and Papers From Prison,* p. 361.

CHAPTER EIGHT

VICARIOUS HUMANITY AS SOTERIOLOGICAL REALITY: THE VICARIOUS REPENTANCE OF CHRIST

As we mentioned in the preceding chapter, the name of John McLeod Campbell is well-known among historians of Scottish church history. A pastor who spent most of his life in Glasgow, Campbell is remembered best for his deposition from the church of Scotland in 1831 because of the preaching of universal atonement and assurance as belonging to the essence of faith.[1] Among historians of doctrine, Campbell's notoriety stems from his later work, *The Nature of the Atonement*.[2] The book aroused controversy from the moment of it publication. Among the highly original themes set forth by Campbell, one continues to stand out as the most perplexing and controversial: Campbell's teaching on Christ as providing a "perfect response," a "perfect repentance," a "perfect sorrow," and a "perfect contrition" toward the judgment of the Father on the sins of humanity.[3] It is usually stated that the Anglican theologian R. C. Moberly (1845-1903) follows Campbell in his teaching on Christ as the "perfect penitent" in his book, *Atonement and Personality*.[4] Among modern writers, the Christian apologist C. S. Lewis has used Moberly's nomenclature

---

[1] Cf. Eugene Garrett Bewkes, *Legacy of a Christian Mind.*

[2] John McLeod Campbell, *The Nature of the Atonement* (cited afterwards as *Atonement*).

[3] Ibid., p. 137.

[4] R. C., Moberly, *Atonement and Personality* (London: Murray, 1917).

and theme for a chapter on the atonement in his book, *Mere Christianity.*[5]

However, this line of thought has predictably run up against widespread criticism. Immediate questions are raised: How can one person confess the sins of many? Does not repentance necessitate a personal consciousness of sin? If Jesus is divine, how can he repent? If repentance is a "change of heart," how can Christ be said to repent? How can the "One" repent for the "Many"?

James B. Torrance, in his essay, "The Contribution of John McLeod Campbell to Scottish Theology," suggests that Campbell's theology of the atonement should be understood from two premises: 1) The Father-Son relationship between Christ and God, which is the basis of the adoption of humanity as sons and daughters, and 2) The vicarious humanity of Christ, through which we come to know the Father in the context of the perfect response of the Son.[6] The purpose of this chapter is to compare and contrast Campbell's and Moberly's teaching on this subject in light of these premises. Our proposal is that the way in which Campbell integrates these two premises helps him to avoid many of the objections usually raised to "vicarious repentance" in a way which Moberly was not able to do.

CAMPBELL: "THE PERFECT CONFESSION"

Under his chapter entitled "Retrospective Aspect of the Atonement," John McLeod Campbell examines the aspect of the atonement which deals with the problem of the past guilt of humanity.[7] Campbell finds in Jonathan Edwards a helpful description of the two alternatives God had in order to deal with human sin: either a vicarious punishment for our sins or a vicarious repentance.[8] Either of these would vindicate the holiness and majesty of God. Unfortunately, Campbell relates, Edwards chose

---

[5] C. S. Lewis, "The Perfect Penitent," in *Mere Christianity* (New York: Macmillan, 1952), pp. 56-61.

[6] James B. Torrance, "The Contribution of John McLeod Campbell to Scottish Theology," *Scottish Journal of Theology* 26 (1973), pp. 295-311.

[7] *Atonement,* p. 129.

[8] Ibid., p. 137. Jonathan Edwards, "Satisfaction for Sin" in *The Works of President Edwards* (New York: J. Leavitt and J. F. Trow, 1843), II, 1-3.

the former alternative, instead of vicarious repentance, "which is surely the higher and more excellent, being a moral and spiritual satisfaction."[9] A. B. Bruce has traced an idea of vicarious repentance back to Rupert of Deutz (c. 1075-1129), a German schoolman.[10]

In Campbell's thought, the vicarious repentance of Christ takes the form of accepting the condemnation of sin which occurs in "Christ's dealing with the Father on behalf of humanity."[11] It was "a perfect confession of our sins... a perfect Amen in humanity to the judgment of God on the sin of man."[12] It is within this "holy sorrow" caused by the combination of God's love for humanity and his abhorrence of their sins that atonement takes place. Christ takes the feelings of the divine wrath against sin into "the bosom of divine humanity," and receiving it, responds with "a perfect response and in that perfect response... absorbs it." It is a "perfect repentance," a "perfect sorrow," a "perfect contrition," with all the elements of repentance "excepting the personal consciousness of sin."[13]

The need of humanity is seen in the "cry of sonship" expressed in the humanity of Jesus:

> It is the cry of the child that reveals the mother's heart.
> It is the cry of Sonship in humanity bearing the burden
> of humanity, confessing its sin, asking for it the good
> of which the capacity still remained to it, which re-
> sponded to by the Father has revealed the Father's
> heart.[14]

In line with Torrance's aforementioned premises, George M. Tuttle considers the sonship of Christ to be "the crowning and most inclusive feature of Campbell's understanding of Christ's work," and a factor which has often been overlooked by schol-

---

9 *Atonement*, p. 137.
10 A. B. Bruce, *The Humiliation of Christ* (Edinburgh: T. & T. Clark, 1895), pp. 319-320, 442.
11 *Atonement*, pp. 135-136.
12 Ibid., p. 136.
13 Ibid., p. 137.
14 Ibid., p. 256.

ars.[15] The cry of the child reveals the need of the child for the mother, as well as revealing the mother's heart. It speaks of the total need of humanity, the total inability of humanity to repent. For it is only in the Son's knowledge of the Father that our sins can truly be confessed.[16] In the words of Edgar P. Dickie, who comments upon Campbell's teaching, "He [Christ] did for us that which in our best moments we would fain do for ourselves if only we could."[17]

However, as Torrance makes clear, a great misunderstanding of Campbell can occur if his teaching on *vicarious repentance* is not seen in light of his emphasis upon the *vicarious humanity* of Christ. Campbell considers vicarious repentance to be the answer to the problem of the "legal fiction" that he found in other theories of the atonement. Since Christ has taken on the same "nature" as humanity, and has become the "brother" of humanity, the atoning work of his confession of our sins is a reality akin to the reality of the Incarnation.[18] It is not a "fiction" if one takes seriously that, in the Incarnation, God participates in human flesh.

The truth of vicarious confession is not known apart from understanding the identification of Christ with humanity.[19] The Incarnation not only reveals the gravity of the sins of humanity but also "its great capacity of good."[20] Campbell characteristically describes this as

> the revelation of an inestimable preciousness that was hidden in humanity, hidden from the inheritors of humanity themselves, but not hid from God, and now brought forth into manifestation by the Son of God. For the revealer of the Father is also the revealer of man.[21]

---

[15] George M. Tuttle, "The Place of ...", p. 203.

[16] *Atonement,* p. 149.

[17] Edgar P. Dickie, "Introduction to J. M. Campbell" in John McLeod Campbell, *The Nature of the Atonement* (London: J. Clarke, 1959), xviii.

[18] *Atonement,* p. 146.

[19] Ibid., p. 159.

[20] Ibid.

[21] Ibid., p. 160.

Atonement, according to Campbell, is not simply a salvific work, but also revelation, a revelation of both God and humanity. The vicarious *repentance* of Christ is, in a wider sense, the vicarious *confession* of Christ, the "confession" which "confesses" both the heart of God and the response of humanity, for the confession of true humanity through the humanity of the Son is not merely a confession of sin, but also of the "inestimable preciousness" of humanity to the Father.

So much does Campbell wed the vicarious repentance of Christ to his humanity, that he can even speak of the *necessity* for such a form of atonement based upon the fact of the Incarnation.

> But the incarnation of the Son of God not only *made possible* such a moral and spiritual expiation for sin as that of which the thought thus visited the mind of Edwards, but indeed caused that it *must* be.[22]

This is the ministry of the Word taking upon our "nature" and becoming our "brother."[23] In Campbell's scheme, it is an integral part of Christ's "dealing with God on the behalf of men."[24]

MOBERLY: "THE PERFECT PENITENT"

R. C. Moberly was to develop Campbell's ideas on vicarious repentance, but with his own distinct emphasis. In his thought we once again see the importance of the vicarious humanity of Christ for any idea of vicarious repentance. Whether or not he was more successful than Campbell in his formularization is another matter.

Moberly's similarities with Campbell's thought are obvious. This is so much so that Eugene Bewkes, in his study on Campbell, remarks in an appendix on Campbell and Moberly how often historians of doctrines assume that their teaching is identical in every respect.[25] It is true that Moberly also emphasizes that sin is condemned when the perfect penitent confesses the sin of human-

---

22 Ibid., p. 138.
23 Ibid., p. 139.
24 Ibid., p. 135.
25 Bewkes, p. 295.

ity.[26] The past life of sin is genuinely contradicted by a repentance which is "perfect." This is atonement, for Moberly.[27] Campbell's emphasis upon the obedient will of Christ is also prominent in Moberly. The obedience of Christ is not separate from atonement. Although obedience might emphasize life and atonement emphasize death, their interrelationship must be upheld.

> Obedience is atoning; and the atonement itself can be exhibited as one great consummation of obedience.... Only in death is the climax of obedience reached; while the life is a sacrifice from end to end.[28]

The purging of human nature was consummated by the will which was obedient unto death. This was a part of "the impossible demand of a perfect repentance."[29]

Moberly, with Campbell, stresses the reality of "sorrow" as the motivation for repentance.[30] Sorrow in effect marks the destiny of a person. Whatever a person is sorrowful over is a sign of what is important to them. But, while penitence expresses itself in sorrow, the cause of sorrow is love. This was the case with the woman who was a sinner in the Gospels (Lk. 7:36-50; Mt. 26:6-13; Mk. 14:3-9, Jn. 12:1). "Her sins, which are many, are forgiven, for she loved much" (Lk. 7:47). Her sorrow was caused by the love she felt for Jesus, a love created by his love and acceptance of her.

But, Moberly asks, is true penitence something even possible for a sinful human being? If the truly penitent person becomes personally identified with righteousness rather than sin, can it be said that any fallible human being could attain this perfection?[31] A change must take place, a change from a desire for sin and a loathing of righteousness to a loathing of sin and a desire for righteousness. True penitence is "a real killing out and eliminating

---

26 Moberly, p. 22.
27 Ibid., p. 110.
28 Ibid., p. 99.
29 Ibid., p. 117.
30 Ibid., p. 28.
31 Ibid., pp. 38-39.

of the past from the present 'me.'"[32] This is restorative, redeeming, and atoning, but it is not a practical possibility when the capacity for sin still lives within us.[33] Therefore, perfect penitence is possible only for one who has never sinned.[34] "Penitence, in the perfectness of its full meaning, is not even conceivably possible, except it be to the personally sinless."[35] The effect of sin on one's life is always present.[36]

Still, it is true that Christian repentance, based on Christ as the perfect penitent, has a powerful effect:

> Do we not recognize it at once as more than humanly
> profound and tranquilizing? as beautiful almost beyond
> all experience of beauty? as powerful, even to the
> shattering of the most terrible of powers?[37]

This is penitence which is not simply a shallow half-regret, but a loathing of sins in the same way in which they are loathed by God.[38]

On these points, and others, Moberly heartily concurs with Campbell. But it is at the very point which we have stressed, along with Torrance, that of the vicarious humanity of Christ, that Moberly departs from the view of vicarious repentance held by Campbell. Indeed, Moberly expresses a reticence about using the term "vicarious."[39] This leads to misunderstandings, he contends, such as that individuals do not have to repent because Christ has already done so for them. "Representative," one of Campbell's favorite descriptions of Christ's work, is not acceptable either. Both of these terms deny the completeness of the identification of Christ with humanity. For Moberly, Christ is "the inclusive total

---

[32] Ibid., p. 41.
[33] Ibid., p. 42.
[34] Ibid., p. 43.
[35] Ibid., p. 117.
[36] Ibid., p. 42.
[37] Ibid., p. 44.
[38] Ibid., p. 46.
[39] Ibid., p. 283.

of true Humanity."[40] Individuals are only potentially a part of that humanity. The aim of the penitence of Christ is not to excuse our penitence but to provide the "true possibility of repentance." Therefore, one cannot speak of a loss of our personal identity when we speak of identification with Christ. He is our true freedom, wisdom, and personality, "the consummation of the meaning of ourselves."[41] Atonement is nothing less than Christ himself. "Our atonement is real in proportion to the reality of Christ in us."[42]

According to Moberly, Campbell fails to relate humanity properly to Christ because he does not view Christ as "the inclusive total of true humanity."[43] This is expressed finally in the church through the Spirit in sacramental communion.[44] Moberly finds further evidence of this lack in Campbell's emphasis upon the phrase, "Christ's confession of our sins." He quotes R. W. Dale:

> Had he simply made a confession of sin in our name.... He would still have remained at a distance from the actual relation to God in which we were involved by sin.[45]

According to Moberly, Christ's confession of the sin of humanity is based upon nothing less than Christ "being" humanity:

> He confessed the sin of humanity by being the very manifestation of humanity, in its ideal, reality of penitential holiness, before the Father.[46]

According to Moberly, in Campbell's theology, Christ's suffering is made the suffering of an individual holy man rather

---

40 Ibid., p. 284.
41 Ibid., p. 285.
42 Ibid., p. 286.
43 Ibid., p. 402.
44 Ibid., p. 404.
45 R. W. Dale, cited by Moberly, p. 405.
46 Moberly, p. 405.

than an immensity of suffering which can come only from his "inclusive humanity."[47]

OBJECTIONS TO 'VICARIOUS REPENTANCE'

Irrespective of their differences, both Campbell and Moberly have encountered strong opposition to their views on the vicarious repentance of Christ. These objections can be summarized into two basic questions: 1) How can a sinless Holy Being confess sin? and 2) How can one person represent/substitute or be "included" in another, let alone in many? The first problem has even led to the doctrine being held up to ridicule. A. B. Bruce, in his work, *The Humiliation of Christ*, says that the idea of a personal confession of sin being made apart from the consciousness of sin "is certainly absurd enough. It is the play of Hamlet without the part of Hamlet."[48] T. J. Crawford considers the very nature of penitential sorrow as argument enough against a "vicarious repentance" on the part of Christ:

> For the very thing which characteristically distinguishes *penitential* sorrow from every other kind of sorrow is just that deep personal consciousness of sin which, in the case of our Saviour's affliction, was entirely wanting.[49]

Repentance cannot be the act of both humanity and Christ. According to "any reasonable or Scriptural notion we can form of it," repentance is the individual act of one who repents for wrongs which he has done.[50] Repentance is not simply a sorrow for sin, according to Crawford, but "a change of heart and mind with respect to sin.... 'Godly sorrow worketh repentance' (II Cor. 2:10), not 'godly sorrow is repentance.'"[51] Indeed, even Moberly

---

[47] Ibid., p. 406.

[48] Bruce, p. 320.

[49] T. J. Crawford, *The Doctrine of Scripture Respecting the Atonement* (Edinburgh: W. Blackwood, 1871), p. 323.

[50] Ibid., p. 324.

[51] Ibid., p. 326.

stresses the place of a chance of heart in repentance.[52] But, as
H. R. Mackintosh asks, "Can we transfer *this* to Jesus?"[53]

A common opinion is that Campbell's doctrine of vicarious
repentance only increases the old problem of vicarious punishment: How can one person represent/substitute himself for
many?[54] John Macquarrie finds an even greater problem in
Moberly's concept of "inclusive humanity", which he calls
"Hegelian."[55] This seems to him to be a "greater fiction" than any
found in Campbell. How one person can be included in another is
a mystery to Macquarrie.

TOWARD A CONSTRUCTIVE UNDERSTANDING
OF 'VICARIOUS REPENTANCE'

The objections to a doctrine of vicarious repentance cannot
be ignored. However, there is much in Campbell's and Moberly's
presentations, and even in their differences, which can help us to
answer the two main objections: How can a sinless Holy Being
confess sin? and How can one person represent/substitute or be
"included" in another, let alone in many? Drawing upon J. B.
Torrance's suggestion that the Father-Son relationship and the vicarious humanity of Christ are both needed in order to understand
Campbell's theology of the atonement, we will discuss their
implications for vital doctrine of vicarious repentance, with a particular look at the relevance of the differences between Campbell
and Moberly on this issue.

The Inability of Humanity and the Nature of Repentance

It is immediately apparent from critiques of vicarious repentance how little they ground their own doctrine of repentance on

---

52 Moberly, pp. 53-54.
53 H. R. Mackintosh, *Some Aspects of Christian Belief* (New York: George B.
    Doran, 1924), p. 91.   Cf. James Denney *The Christian Doctrine of
    Reconciliation* (New York: Doran, 1918), p. 259.
54 J. K. Mozley. Cf. G. B. Stevens, *The Christian Doctrine of Salvation,* (New
    York: Scribners, 1905). Both cited in Bewkes, p. 181.
55 John Macquarrie, "John McLeod Campbell, 1800-1872," *Expository Times*
    83 (1972), pp. 263-268.

the equally important (and equally Reformed) doctrine of the total salvific inability of humanity.[56] Unless the "man-Godward" movement of Christology (J. Torrance) is a constituent part of the atonement, then it leaves one to ask how Christ could be called our "wisdom," our "righteousness," and our "sanctification" by the apostle (I Cor. 1:30). Paul certainly does not mean that redeemed humanity will not possess its own wisdom, righteousness, or sanctification. But he does mean that the basis for our wisdom, our righteousness, and our sanctification is in Jesus Christ.[57] So it is also true with repentance. For, irrespective of the fact that, as many have commented, vicarious repentance is not taught explicitly in the New Testament, it can be argued that, in keeping with the doctrine of the Trinity, vicarious repentance is a legitimate theological deduction based upon the importance of the doctrine of the vicarious humanity of Christ. Vicarious repentance finds its origin in the same reality of Christ's humanity as expressed in his worship, trust, communion, prayer, and obedience to the Father.[58] Moberly rightly saw the problem of "objective" versus "subjective" atonement as based on an understanding of "subjective" atonement as only the human, creaturely response,

---

[56] "Total inability" is usually seen in Reformed theology as one aspect of "total depravity" Charles Hodge, *Systematic Theology, II* (Grand Rapids: Eerdmans, 1977), pp. 261f.; Augustus Strong, *Systematic Theology* (Philadelphia: Judson Press, 1907), pp. 637-644; Donald Bloesch, *Essentials of Evangelical Theology,* I (San Francisco: Harper and Row, 1978), p. 90. L. Berkhof draws a distinction with "total inability" as referring to "its effects on man's spiritual powers" *(Systematic Theology* (Grand Rapids: Eerdmans, 1939), pp. 246-248). The emphasis is upon sin involving every aspect of the person (Calvin, *Institutes,* II.9), and thus humanity has "wholly lost all ability of will to any spiritual good accompanying salvation" *(Westminster Confession,* 9:3). Barth concludes that if reconciliation and justification involve the whole person, "then there can be no reservations with regard to his corruption" *(CD* IV/1, pp. 499-500). Hodge, interestingly enough, relates inability directly to repentance: "What the Bible and all the Confessions of the churches of the Reformation assert is, that man, since the fall, cannot change his own heart; he cannot regenerate his soul; *he cannot repent with godly sorrow* [emphasis mine], or exercise that faith which is unto salvation" (p. 264).

[57] Paul also mentions Christ as our "redemption." We have no salvific parallel to this, but this in no way invalidates the previous pictures of wisdom, righteousness, and sanctification.

[58] J. Torrance, "Contribution", p. 306.

rather than as based on Christ in his perfect humanity as the "perfect penitent."[59]

George Whitefield summarizes for Campbell this link between the total inability of humanity and the nature of repentance. Sin affects our humanity so deeply that, "our repentance needeth to be repented of, and our tears to be washed by the blood of Christ."[60] This is a blunt critique of a false sense of "spirituality" which seeks to boast in its own achievement of "repentance."

The sufficiency of Christ for atonement reveals the insufficiency of humanity's efforts. This must also include those of the Christian, in whom the effects of sin are still present.[61] In C. S. Lewis' version of Moberly's "The Perfect Penitent," love and reason become possible because God's love and reason "holds our hands" as the basis for our love and reason.[62] Says Lewis: "Only a bad person needs to repent: only a good person can repent perfectly."[63] The echo of Moberly in Lewis is obvious. Lewis' distinct contribution to our subject is centered in his teaching on our need to participate in the living, dying and rising of Christ.[64] This is the one act which it is impossible for humanity to do.

Moberly finds in "the Humanity of Deity" the power to help humanity in its predicament.[65] (Shades of Karl Barth's "humanity of God"!) The power behind "the Perfect Penitent," the difference between ordinary humanity and Christ, is his deity. It is the deity of the Holy One which confronts sin with his holiness. This is "penitential holiness" according to Moberly.[66] Only in the context of such perfect holiness can the depth and horribleness of sin be truly known, and thus, can repentance truly take place.

---

[59] Moberly, pp. 136-153.
[60] Cited by Campbell in *Atonement*, p. 144.
[61] Moberly, p. 42.
[62] Lewis, p. 60.
[63] Ibid., p. 59.
[64] Ibid., p. 60.
[65] Moberly, p. 90.
[66] Ibid., p. 66.

Likewise, Campbell stresses the subjective benefits which Christ's confession of our sins provides for us. Is it not the *power* to confess our sins, in our "Amen to Christ's confession of them"?[67] It is statements like this in Campbell which more than put to rest the criticism that vicarious repentance is a substitute for our personal confession of sins. On the contrary, it provides the true basis for our own personal confession. No longer is repentance centered in the vicissitudes of the flesh, but in the obedient life of the Son.

The Reality of Participation in Christ

In the above passage, C. S. Lewis suggests the importance of our participation in Christ's humanity for understanding vicarious repentance. James Torrance makes a strong case for the importance of "participation" in Campbell's thought.[68] Participation should not be taken to mean a grandiose metaphysical scheme with pantheistic overtones. Rather, it is simply the gospel as seen from its results. In an interesting passage, Campbell speaks of the reality of the atonement not in the "transaction in humanity... viewed in itself," but rather in the relationship of Christ in humanity which is presupposed by the "transaction."[69] Therefore, one starts *a posteriori*, viewing the results of salvation as a key to understanding salvation. The meaning of the atonement is a "prospective", as well as a "retrospective", in Campbell's words.[70] Certainly this leads us closer to the meaning of the reality of the atonement.

Participation in Christ for Campbell is based on the divine participation in human nature. God sent his Son "in the likeness of sinful flesh" (Rom. 8:3). Motivated by love, the Son of God as-

---

[67] *Atonement*, p. 178.

[68] J. Torrance, "Contribution", p. 310.

[69] *Atonement*, p. 377.

[70] Ibid., pp. 129-191. Campbell contends that while penal substitution relieves one from having to die, which is a "legal fiction," representative repentence is based on the *prospective* purpose that one will come to repentence, based on Christ's repentance; *Atonement*, p. 392; Tuttle, *So Rich A Soil*, p. 129.

sumed human flesh in order to take on the burden of our sin.[71]
Christ's identification with humanity provides the basis and the
imperative for the vicarious confession of our sins. [72]

James Denney emphasizes the significance of Christ's
identification with humanity in Campbell's though. Campbell's
concern, according to Denney, is to avoid understanding what
Christ has done for us apart from what he produces in us.[73]
Therefore, language of imputation is superceded by language of
identification. As Denney puts it, "His identification of Himself
with us must have as its aim and issue an identification on our part
of ourselves with Him."[74]

Identification is the preliminary stage for participation in
Campbell. Whereas the first movement is "manward," the movement of God into humanity in Jesus Christ, the "Godward"
movement is the participation of humanity in the humanity of
Christ. Of primary importance to this is the reality of the sonship
of Christ. To participate in the humanity of Christ is to participate
in the filial relationship of love and trust between the Father and
the Son. In one of his favorite phrases, Campbell describes the
filial relationship as "the very light of life to us."[75] This is particularly seen in the First Epistle of John where salvation is viewed as
participating in the fellowship between the Father and the Son
(I Jn. 1:3).[76]

Moberly extends this relational approach to the atonement
into an ontological reality. Atonement is not real unless it affects
who I am.[77] This is surely the strength in Moberly's presentation.
Atonement is a reality which works within the structures of what
is and what it may become, rather than something which is only
external to that humanity. In the fullest sense, "Christ is our

---

71   Ibid., p. 127.
72   Ibid., p. 159.
73   James Denney, *The Christian Doctrine of Reconciliation*, p. 118.
74   Ibid.
75   *Atonement*, p. 173.
76   Ibid., p. 195.
77   Moberly, pp. 137-138.

atonement,"[78] and the reality of the atonement is true in proportion to our identification with Christ. But in Moberly we also find a problem. Moberly speaks of becoming increasingly identified with Christ as the process of "surrendering the sovereignty of our proper personality by identification with Him."[79] This raises an important question, however: is our individuality or distinctness from Christ's humanity necessarily a reflection of sin and alienation, as Moberly seems to imply? Does not this turn the vicarious humanity of Christ, and thus, his vicarious repentance, into an abstract "Christ principle" which denies the distinction between God and humanity and the specific effect of salvation upon the individual person? Is this the only way to view "participation"?

The Sonship of Christ and the Sonship of Humanity

In Campbell's view of participation we have a corrective to Moberly's problem. His view of participation in Christ is seen in terms of the sonship of Christ and our participation in that sonship. The "Our Father" of the Lord's Prayer indicates for us the significance of sonship for participation.[80] It is through the sonship of Christ that Campbell avoids the semi-pantheistic conclusions of Moberly and helps to answer the problems of how a sinless Holy Being can repent and how the One can represent the Many.

The vicarious humanity in which we participate in Christ is not an abstract, ideal humanity, but the humanity of the Son. If we know the Son, then we know the Father also (Jn. 8:19). It is the intimate relationship between the Father and the Son which is communicated to humanity through the Spirit of the Son (Rom. 8:29). Thus, human beings become brethren of Jesus (Heb. 2:10f.) with a destiny to be conformed to his image (Rom. 8:29). It is in this sense that sonship as salvation is defined simply and beautifully by Campbell when he calls us "orphans who have found their lost father."[81] This is in stark contrast to Moberly's

---

[78]   Ibid., p. 286.
[79]   Ibid., p. 285.
[80]   *Atonement*, p. 249.
[81]   Ibid., p. 345. Cf. xxv.

refusal to see the Father-Son relationship as a mirror of the eternal being of God.[82] In Campbell's thought, sonship means a revelation of God. To speak of sonship means to speak of the knowledge of God. As we have seen previously, Campbell makes much of the Johannine saying, "He that hath seen me hath seen the Father" (Jn. 14:9).[83] Humanity participates in the Father-Son relationship which is the mirror of the eternal being of God.[84] The significance of this is profound. If he is the Son of the Father, then it is by the Father's initiative, power, and most importantly, by his shared life with the Son, that the Son is able to provide the repentance which becomes the basis for the repentance of others. Moreover, as we have seen, this is absolutely needed because of the inability of humanity to provide a perfect repentance. This is the "manward" side of vicarious repentance.

The "Godward" side of the vicarious repentance of Christ in Campbell is the *character* of the sonship of Christ; his *obedience*. It is in light of his *perfect* obedience that he provides a perfect confession on behalf of the many. This is a perfect obedience made possible by the oneness of being between the Father and the Son ("He that hath seen me hath seen the Father"). Certainly, if one cannot affirm the *homoousion* of the Son with the Father, as is common in contemporary circles, this argument will not hold. Nevertheless, when one grants this, the problems with vicarious repentance are substantially lessened.

But does such an understanding meet a typical objection to vicarious repentance, such as Macquarrie's, that questions whether one person can represent or substitute himself for many? But are Macquarrie's objections only with Campbell, or also with the biblical teaching on the basis of the new humanity in the shared sonship of Christ? The issue here is theological anthropology. We cannot start with an *a priori* notion of human being and end up with a distinctly Christian insight into the realities of repentance,

---

[82]   Moberly, pp. 191-192.

[83]   *Atonement,* xliv.

[84]   Martin Hengel concludes in his New Testament study, *The Son of God,* trans. John Bowden (Philadelphia: Fortress Press, 1976), pp. 92f., that "Son of God" was a "metaphor" used in early Christian theology for "expressing both the origin of Jesus in God's being. . .and his true humanity."

participation, and sonship. This is the difference between "theological" anthropology and "non-theological" anthropology, as stated so well by Karl Barth.[85] A non-theological anthropology is not simply an anthropology which leaves out the determinate of God. A "mystical" or "philosophical" anthropology can be concerned with God, yet be thoroughly Cartesian in its approach to the epistemology of human beings.[86] As Ray S. Anderson states, "the fundamental problem with all non-theological anthropologies is that they proceed from *anthropos* rather than *theos*."[87] Macquarrie's objection seems to be based on such an *a priori* anthropology.

The theological implications of vicarious repentance are many. Space allows us to make only one observation. It is simply this: Vicarious repentance enables one to see the depth of the vicarious humanity of Christ as an indication that salvation is completely the work of God, *sola gratia*, yet it leaves a place for a genuine human response, based upon the response freely given in the obedient sonship of Christ. The vicarious repentance of Christ signifies the soteriological *depth* of the place of the reality of salvation in God himself, but not God apart from his union with our humanity.

The way in which the New Testament writers were at least implicitly aware of such an implication is seen in the use of the Christological title "Son of God." O. Michel calls this "the essential confessional term of early Christianity."[88] It is interesting to note the strategic use of this title in the confessing acts of the early

---

[85] Barth, *CD* III/2, pp. 19ff.

[86] Ray S. Anderson, *On Being Human*, p. 8.

[87] Ibid., p. 14. In addition, Macquarrie's objection would be equally true of any soteriology (apart from a strict "moral influence" theory) which seeks to relate the individual Jesus of Nazareth to all of humanity in a salvific sense. One wonders whether Macquarrie would wish to press his objection this far.

[88] O. Michel, "Son of God," *New International Dictionary of New Testament Theology,* (cited afterwards as *NIDNTT*) ed. C. Brown, Vol. 3 (Grand Rapids: Zondervan, 1978), p. 639. Cf. Oscar Cullmann, *The Christology of the New Testament,* trans. Shirley C. Guthrie and Charles A. M. Hall (Philadelphia: Westminster Press, 1959), p. 290, and Ray S. Anderson "Son of God," *International Standard Bible Encyclopedia,* revised edition, vol. 4, ed. G. W. Bromiley (Grand Rapids: Eerdmans, 1988), pp 571-574.

church. In the Gospels, it is centrally located in Peter's confession in Matthew (16:16),[89] as well as being the climax to Mark (15:39; cf. 1:1; 14:61).[90] Both demons and pagans, and even the Tempter, confess him to be the Son of God (Mk. 5:7; 15:39; Lk. 4:41; Mt. 8:29; 4:3,6, par. Lk. 4:3,9). It is an integral part of an early trinitarian catechism in the church (Mt. 28:19). Johannine literature goes on to speak of a participation, or "abiding," in the being of the Son (Jn. 15:4; I Jn. 4:15; 5:5). Faith in the Son equals faith in God (I Jn. 5:10).[91] To confess the Son is to confess the Father. (I Jn. 2:23). In fact, true confession can be done only in "the name of the Son" (I Jn. 3:27; 5:13). In this confession of the Son we simultaneously confess our sonship, which then becomes the motivation for genuine repentance on our part.[92] Thus, confession of the Son, as a genuine human act, becomes the primary human act, the act in which we participate in the life of the eternal Son, including his vicarious repentance. Consequently, the way is paved for our personal acts of repentance.

---

[89] S. E. Johnson, "Son of God," *The Interpreter's Dictionary of the Bible,* ed. G. A. Buttrick, Vol. 4 (Nashville: Abingdon Press, 1962), p. 410.

[90] Ibid., p. 409. It is also tempting to see the baptism of Jesus as recorded in Matthew as an indication of how vicarious repentance and the sonship of Jesus are intertwined. John's baptism is a baptism "for repentance" (εἰς μετάνοιαν) (3:11). He is genuinely surprised when Jesus comes to be baptized by him (v. 14) (a response similar to the modern opposition to "vicarious repentance"?). Jesus states that its purpose is "to fulfill all righteousness" (v. 15, only in Mt.). (πληρῶσαι πᾶσαν δικαιούνην.) Is it coincidental that the baptism is crowned with the pronouncement by the Father, "This is my beloved son..." (v. 17)?

[91] Eduard Schweizer, "υἱός," *Theological Dictionary of the New Testament* (cited afterwards as *TDNT*) eds. G. Kittel and G. Friedrich, trans. G. W. Bromiley, Vol. 8 (Grand Rapids: Eerdmans, 1972), p. 378.

[92] See the successive order of forgiveness before repentance in Calvin's theology (*Institutes* III.3.1, 2) Cf. J. Torrance, "Contribution", p. 311.

CHAPTER NINE

VICARIOUS HUMANITY AS ESCHATOLOGICAL REALITY: THE EXALTED HUMANITY OF CHRIST IN THE EPISTLE TO THE HEBREWS

As we have seen, the vicarious humanity of Christ is the gracious act of the eternal humanity of God in reaching onto the *breadth* and *depth* of the human plight. The breadth we have seen in our discussion of the implications of Torrance's doctrine of the vicarious humanity of Christ from epistemology to the sacraments. The depth we have seen in Campbell and Moberly's emphasis upon the vicarious repentance of Christ, where in the deep recesses of human need, Christ comes to be our representative, even in the act of repentance. But what now? Where is Christ after incarnation and resurrection? Where is the reality of salvation after the Incarnation? The answer is provided in the Epistle to the Hebrews: he is exalted, ascended to the Father. This is the answer of Christ's eschatological destiny, which for Hebrews, as we shall see, does not leave his *humanity* behind. Therefore, we too, in our humanity, continue to be sustained by the exalted eschatological, yet present, Christ.

Eschatology has an obvious significance in the Epistle to the Hebrews. This significance is profoundly Christological. Jesus is the "great high priest," superior to the Levitical priesthood. (4:14). Why superior? Because he "has passed through the heavens," that is, he lives now, continually, in his eschatological destiny.[1] This

---

[1] R. McL. Wilson. *Hebrews* (Grand Rapids: Eerdmans and Basingstoke: Marshall, Morgan, and Scott, 1987), p. 91.

high priest has been *"crowned* with glory and honor" (an eschatological act) (2:9). Therefore, the Christian believer can "with confidence draw near to the *throne* of grace" (where the One who has been crowned sits) in time of need (4:16). Where is this throne? At the right hand of God. Even the angels have not been given the invitation to "sit at my right hand, till I make thy enemies a stool for thy feet" (1:13, citing Ps. 110:1). As the great high priest at the right hand of God, Jesus ministers in a new heavenly sanctuary, made by God, not by man (8:2), of which the earthly tabernacle is but shadow and figure (8:5). Still, since he is a high priest, even in heaven, he is *human,* always living to make intercession for humanity (7:25).

The eschatological, exalted Christ has a ministry and continues to have a ministry because eschatology in Hebrews, as Barrett reminds us, is, as is characteristic of the New Testament, in some ways *realized* and in other ways *to come. Already* Christ is sitting on the throne of grace, exalted, yet Christians have not yet attained their goal, as the author of Hebrews exhorts his readers (12:1). Still, for them, the unseen truth which God will one day enact is no longer entirely unseen: it has been manifested in Jesus.[2] The reality of salvation is found in God himself, in the person of Jesus, not in religious, political, or world experiences. The early Christian believer could have hope because the one who took upon his humanity is on the throne of grace, still ministering for the sake of humanity.

The emphasis which the Epistle to the Hebrews puts upon the humanity of Christ has long been recognized and has been an item of great interest for New Testament scholars: "No New Testament book emphasizes the humanity of Jesus more emphatically than does Hebrews."[3] "Nowhere in the New Testament is

---

2   Charles K. Barrett, "The Eschatology of the Epistle to the Hebrews" in
    W. D. Davies and David Daube, eds., *The Background of the New Testament
    and Its Eschatology: C. H. Dodd Festschrift* (Cambridge: Cambridge University
    Press, 1954), pp. 364, 382.

3   George E. Ladd, *A Theology of the New Testament* (Grand Rapids: Eerdmans,
    1974), p. 574.

the humanity of Christ set forth so movingly."[4] Nevertheless, the implications of the humanity of Christ for the theology of the epistle has been seen by some to create quite a dilemma. The reason for this is obvious. In Hebrews, not only is the depth of the passion and the human experience of Jesus stressed, but at the same time, the divine sonship and pre-existence of Christ is also emphasized.[5] This "dilemma" has been characterized in several ways. James D. G. Dunn describes the dichotomy in these terms: the view of Christ as a heavenly being on the one hand, whose earthly life is incidental, and on the other hand, the view of Christ as a "son by appointment."[6] The importance of the "pre-existence" of Christ is one reason for this situation. According to Dunn, the pre-existence of Christ is taught more clearly in Hebrews than in any other New Testament book, with the exception of the Fourth Gospel. This is evidenced by 1:2: "In these last days God has spoken to us by a Son, whom he appointed heir of all things, through whom also he created the world." The teaching on Christ as belonging to the order of Melchizedek also speaks of pre-existence: Melchizedek is "without father or mother or genealogy, and has neither beginning nor end of life, but resembling the Son of God he continues a priest forever" (7:3, cf. 10:5). But, at the same time, "adoptionistic" language is used by Jesus: by his passion and exaltation he became superior to the angels (1:4) and by his exaltation he was begotten as God's Son and by virtue of his passion was appointed God's high priest (1:5; 5:5-10).

Dunn believes that the ultimate reason behind this "odd juxtaposition of seemingly contradictory themes" is Hebrews' "unique synthesis of Platonic and Hebraic world views, or more precisely Platonic cosmology and Judaeo-Christian eschatology." "The awkward tensions of his presentation of Christ are the result of his merging there two world views."[7]

---

[4] H. R. Mackintosh, *The Doctrine of the Person of Jesus Christ* (Edinburgh: T. &. T. Clark, 1912), p. 79. Cf. Vincent Taylor, *The Person of Christ in New Testament Teaching* (New York: St. Martin's Press, 1958), p. 91.

[5] Martin Hengel, *The Son of God*, p. 88.

[6] James D. G. Dunn, *Christology in the Making* (Philadelphia: Westminster Press, 1980), p. 52.

[7] Ibid., p. 53.

The "poignant dilemma" of Hebrews presented by John Knox is similar.[8] Both adoptionism and pre-existence are found side by side in Hebrews, as is made immediately evident by 1:1-4. T. E. Pollard states the case similarly, but stresses the emphasis on the use of the human name "Jesus" (2:9; 3:1; 6:20; 7:22; 12:2, 24) in contrast with his "Christology from above."[9] The theological implications of this dilemma have been aptly stated by Knox:

> How could Christ have saved us if he was not a human being like ourselves? How could a human being like ourselves have saved us?[10]

Certainly the author of Hebrews was concerned with this problem. It seems evident that one of the greatest obstacles to his argument for the superiority of the Son is the Son's humanity.[11] But instead of avoiding the issue, the author sees it as a strength, in light of the implications of the humanity of Christ for salvation. As Calvin states, Hebrews does not merely assert the truth of the humanity of Christ, but shows him in the context of the salvific fruit which it bears.[12]

The purpose of this chapter will be to examine the significance of the "vicarious" humanity of Christ, that is, how the humanity of Christ relates to common humanity in a vicarious sense, and the perspective which the author of Hebrews has on the reality of salvation. Our thesis is that the full identification of the pre-existent Son with humanity is not a "dilemma" but a significant contribution to New Testament theological constructions of the reality of salvation. This involves the importance of his "developmental" view of Christ's humanity, a humanity which "learned obedience"

---

8 John Knox, *The Humanity and Divinity of Christ* (Cambridge: Cambridge University Press, 1967), pp. 35-36.

9 T. E. Pollard, *Fulness of Humanity: Christ's Humanness and Ours* (Sheffield: Almond Press, 1982), pp. 76-77.

10 Knox, p. 52.

11 Donald A. Hagner, *Hebrews* (San Francisco: Harper and Row, 1983), p. 24.

12 John Calvin, *The Epistle of Paul the Apostle to the Hebrews and the First and Second Epistle of St. Peter.* (cited afterwards as *Hebrews*) trans. William B. Johnston, eds. David W. Torrance and Thomas F. Torrance (Edinburgh: Oliver and Boyd, 1963), p. 30.

by suffering (5:8) and which was made "perfect by suffering" (2:10). This "developmental" aspect of Christian existence is a call for the readers to "go on to maturity" (6:1) in their Christian experience. The salvific humanity of Christ involves an integral place for the faith of Jesus as the basis for humanity's faith (chs. 11 and 12).[13] The concrete expression of this faith is the obedience of Christ, mainly expressed by his role as the high priest who is also the pre-existent Son of God. The author stresses the continual, eschatological reality of salvation by emphasizing the exalted state of the humanity of Christ and the present ministry of intercession on the basis of that exalted, shared humanity. Therefore, the Incarnation is not simply an event reserved for the earthly life of Jesus, but a reality which is the basis for present Christian existence.

IDENTIFICATION WITH HUMANITY

The real and total identification of Christ with humanity is emphasized early on in the epistle:

> Therefore he had to be made like his brethren in every respect, so that he might become a merciful and faithful high priest in the service of God, to make expiation for the sins of the people.[14]

The identification of Christ with humanity is real and total to the extent that humanity becomes brethren with Christ in the strictest sense of the word (v. 11), and especially in sharing suffering and mortality.

2:14 also expresses well the identity between the human nature of Christ and common humanity:

> Since therefore the children share (κεκοινώηκεν) in flesh and blood, he himself likewise partook (μετέσ-χεν) of the same nature...

Bruce refuses to admit a distinction between the two verbs because the emphasis is on the commonality of human nature between

---

[13]   G. Delling, "ἄρχω," TDNT, Vol. 1. p. 488.

[14]   C. Spicq, *L'Epître aux Hébreux,* (Paris: J. Gabalda, 1952-53), vol. 2, p. 46.

Christ and humanity, not their difference.[15] However, Westcott argues for a distinction in meaning.[16] Κεκοινώηκεν "marks the common nature ever shared among men as long as the race lasts." Μετέσχεν, in contrast, expresses the unique fact of the Incarnation as a voluntary acceptance of humanity, The aorist tense speaks of its punctiliar nature, presumably in the past. A similar contrast between tenses is found in I Corinthians 15:4; I John 1:1; Colossians 1:16; John 20:23, 29, as well as in the examples of the difference between κοινωνέω and μετέχω in I Corinthians 10:17-21 and II Corinthians 6:14. If one relies primarily on the context in this case, Bruce's explanation seems to be the best. The main point is the reality of the shared nature. The niceties of Westcott's exegesis do not seem to be present in this author's argument.

2:16 is a controversial verse involving the verb ἐπιλαμβάνεται. It is translated in the RSV as "to be concerned with": "For surely it is not with angels that he is concerned but with the descendants of Abraham." Verse seventeen continues to explain that he had to be made like his brethren "in every respect." According to Davidson, ἐπιλαμβάνεται means to "take hold of" for the purpose of helping (cf. Isa. 41:9-10; Jer. 31:32). It does not mean to assume the nature of, as some patristic writers supposed.[17] Montefiore adds that the γὰρ at the beginning connects it with the preceding verse on deliverance from fear of death rather than the following verse on assuming a common nature.[18] However, this is to ignore the broader context of the verse, starting with verse fourteen: "Since therefore, the children share in flesh and blood, he himself likewise partook of the same nature."

---

15 F. F. Bruce, *The Epistle to the Hebrews* (Grand Rapids: Eerdmans, 1964), pp. 48-50.

16 Brooke Foss Westcott, *The Epistle to the Hebrews* (Grand Rapids: Eerdmans, 1974), p. 52.

17 A. B. Davidson, *The Epistle to the Hebrews* (Edinburgh: T. & T. Clark, n.d.), p. 71.

18 H. W. Montefiore, *The Epistle to the Hebrews* (London: Black, 1964), p. 64.

Bruce relates that it is the same verb as that used in 8:9, where God recalls how he "took hold" of Israel in Egypt.[19]

However, this is not to say that champions of the patristic exegesis "to assume the nature of" are without compelling arguments. The context of the verse is instructive for some. P. E. Hughes asks pointedly: "Could anyone have imagined that Christ came to earth for the purpose of assisting angels?"[20] In addition, when Christ is spoken of in the immediate passage as the one who helps us in our hour of need (v. 18), it is with a different verb (βοηθῆσαι). Luther's exegesis seems to accomplish a combination of the two options through his quaint saying: Christ "captured everybody by getting to know them."[21] In doing so, Luther follows Chrysostom's Latin *apprehendere* ("to seize") rather than *suscipere* ("to take up").[22] Christ "pursued after human nature and overtook it when it was fleeing from him." Spicq also emphasizes the meaning of "to seize" in, ἐπιλαμβάνεται,[23] as does G. Delling, with interesting implications: "to draw someone to oneself to help, and thus to take him up in to the fellowship of one's destiny."[24] Luther, Spicq, and Delling all show that it is possible to unite the meanings "to take hold of" or "help" with "to assume the nature of." Thus, in our judgment, such a translation as Hagner's "to become like in order to give help" is entirely appropriate.[25]

10:20 presents another controversial issue in the investigation of Christ's identification with humanity in Hebrews. The RSV translates vv. 19-20 as: "Therefore, brethren, since we have confidence to enter the sanctuary by the blood of Jesus, by the new and living way which he opened for us through the curtain,

---

19 Bruce, p. 51.

20 Philip Edgcumbe Hughes, *A Commentary on the Epistle to the Hebrews* (Grand Rapids: Eerdmans, 1977), p. 117.

21 Martin Luther, "Lectures on the Epistle to the Hebrews, 1517-18", in *Luther: Early Theological Works*. Ed. and trans. James Atkinson (Philadelphia: Westminster Press, 1962), p. 56.

22 Ibid., p. 65.

23 Spicq, Vol. 2, p. 46.

24 G. Delling, "ἐπιλαμβάνω," *TDNT*, Vol. 4, p. 9.

25 Hagner, p. 35.

that is, through his flesh..." The question is, does "flesh" qualify
the "veil" or the "new and living way"? RSV identifies "flesh"
with the "veil," whereas NEB chooses the opposite: "the new and
living way which he has opened for us through the curtain, the
way of his flesh."[26] Calvin is among the commentators who
equates the "veil" with the "flesh." Although the veil covered the
access to the sanctuary, it was also a door to it. So also is Christ's
flesh, which both covers the majesty of God and is our access to
him.[27] Davidson relates the "veil-like" nature of Christ's humanity
to the need for his flesh to be rent asunder, as was the veil.[28]
Bruce follows this reasoning, with the added reasons of the word
order and a paradoxical interpretation of the veil. In Christ, that
which kept God and humanity apart now brings them together.[29]
However, it seems that such logical circumlocution is unnecessary
if we see "flesh" as dependent on the "new and living way." As
Montefiore observes, elsewhere in the epistle the purpose of the
"veil" is to hide the sanctuary from view, not to reveal what is
within (9:3).[30] In the context of the great discourses on identification with humanity in chapters two, four, and five, it is much eas-
ier to see the "flesh" as the "new and living way." The author's
passion is to communicate the fact that the pre-existent Son is now
known through the humanity of common human "flesh."

The author takes pains to emphasize the real and total identification of the humanity of Christ with common humanity. This is
not abstract human nature, a kind of platonic ideal, but a human
being in a specific spiritual relation to God, expressed by the ideas
of sonship and faith. Thus, according to Calvin, "the qualities of
our human nature" are found in Christ such as the "emotions of
the soul... fear, dread of death and the like."[31] The necessity of
the qualification "without sin" (4:15) is there because these

---

26   Bruce, p. 247.

27   Calvin, *Hebrews* p. 141.

28   Davidson, p. 212.

29   Bruce, p. 247.

30   Montefiore, p. 173. Cf. Geerhardus Vos, "The Priesthood of Christ in the
Epistle to the Hebrews," *Princeton Theological Review* (1907), p. 445.

31   Calvin, *Hebrews*, pp. 55-56.

emotions are "always sinful in us because of our fallen nature."
Nevertheless, it is interesting to note that Calvin does not consider
"fear" and "dread of death" as necessarily sins. Rissi mentions that
Christ's identification with humanity is so complete that it was
necessary to add the corollary "without sin."[32]

Hebrews is not simply interested in the humanity of Christ in
an abstract sense. The identification of the Son with humanity has
a distinct soteriological purpose. This is a vital part of his qualifications as a high priest in order "to make expiation for the sins of
the people" (2:17). Yet, it is not simply limited to expiation. His
help not only deals with the past, but also with the present and the
future (7:25; 13:8). As 2:18 continues, he is able to help those
who are tempted because he has suffered and has been tempted.

INCARNATION AND ATONEMENT

What is the relationship between the Incarnation and atonement in Hebrews? If the sum of soteriology in Hebrews is not
only "expiation," what part does the death of Christ play? Some
refer to the Incarnation as the "necessary preliminary to the sufferings."[33] It may be admitted that Christ fulfilled the destiny of
humanity by redemption and consummation, but the emphasis is
put on his death, not on his life.[34] Yet, is it adequate to say that
the Incarnation is only a "necessary preliminary" to his death?
Incarnation and cross are certainly intertwined, as 2:14 shows
plainly: the one who shares in the same "flesh and blood" is the
one able to destroy him who has the power of death through his
own death. Could it be that the death of Jesus should be seen as a
part of the larger redemptive power of his humanity, as we have
seen in the theology of John McLeod Campbell? The death of
Christ is a part of his identification with humanity. As Bruce puts
it, "If his fellow men, entering this earthly life by birth, leave it in
due course by death, it was divinely fitting that He too should

---

32 Matthias Rissi, "Die Menschheit Jesu nach Hebr 5, 7-8," *Theologische
Zeitschrift* 11 (1955), p. 35.

33 Davidson, p. 68.

34 David C. Peterson, *Hebrews and Perfection* (Cambridge: Cambridge University
Press, 1982), p. 101. Cf. James Denney, *The Death of Christ.* ed. R. V. G.
Tasker (London: Tyndale Press, 1951), p. 121.

die."[35] However, should it be said, as Bruce states, that this is "the purpose of the Incarnation"? This deserves a closer look at the relationship between Incarnation and atonement through the "perfection" of Jesus "through suffering" (2:10).

"PERFECT... THROUGH SUFFERING"

Hebrews 2:10 (RSV) declares,

For it was fitting that he, for whom and by whom all things exist, in bringing many sons to glory, should make the pioneer of their salvation perfect through suffering.

In this context, the identification of Christ with humanity is not seen in his teaching, nor in the revelation of his nature or of the will of God, but in suffering.[36] But is it suffering for suffering's sake, or as a part of the wider "redemptive power" of the Son's participation in humanity?[37]

What is meant by the incarnate Son of God being made "perfect through suffering"? Cullmann believes this to be nothing less than "moral perfection."[38] This is because it "happens in a really human life." Hebrews "had the courage to speak of the man Jesus in shockingly human terms." Cullmann seeks to unite the other meaning of τελειῶσαι, "completion," with the meaning of moral perfection: "Because he himself is 'perfect,' Jesus as the High Priest brings humanity to 'perfection.'" However, it is hard to see what would not demand the "perfected" humanity to be morally perfect, if this is demanded of the "perfect" Jesus.

Many arguments can be raised against ascribing "moral perfection" to the meaning of τελειῶσαι in 2:10. Ladd points out that the teaching on the pre-existence of the Son certainly argues

---

[35] Bruce, p. 49.

[36] E. F. Scott, *The Epistle to the Hebrews* (Edinburgh: T. & T. Clark, 1922), pp. 98f. Cf. William Manson, *The Epistle to the Hebrews: An Historical and Theological Reconstruction* (London: Hodder and Stoughton, 1951), p. 100.

[37] Robert Jewett, *Letter to Pilgrims: A Commentary on the Epistle to the Hebrews* (New York: Pilgrim Press, 1981), p. 44,

[38] Oscar Cullmann, *The Christology of the New Testament*, pp. 92-93.

against such a meaning.[39] David Peterson argues for a
"vocational" rather than a "metaphysical" meaning of perfection.[40]
He grants that the "functional" or "vocational" meaning should not
be understood to preclude the personal development of the man
Jesus. However, the perfecting of Christ has to do primarily with
his "perfection" as a savior, not as a man, according to Peterson.
The latter is a "subsidiary theme." It is difficult to agree with him
in light of the extensive emphasis Hebrews puts on the humanity
of Christ throughout the epistle. He is right to emphasize the
salvific sense of "perfection," but he seems to err in setting it
asunder from its context in the humanity of Jesus. The human nature of Jesus is not just a "prerequisite" to salvation but belongs to
the *essence* of salvation. The suffering of Jesus is an essential part
of his identification with humanity in all of its facets. In addition,
an allusion to the implications of Christ's suffering for Christian
existence is found in 10:34: Just as Christ was "perfected...
through suffering," so also his brethren are to be involved in suffering with the plights of others: "For you had compassion on the
prisoners" (τοῖς δεσμίοις συνεπαθήσατε, literally, "suffered
with").[41] The reality of salvation for Hebrews is integrally related
to the "completeness" of God's plan of salvation in the humanity
of Jesus.[42] This sense of "completeness" of God's plan entails an
involvement of Christians in the plight of those suffering under the
bonds of injustice, as seen in 10:34.

THE FAITH OF JESUS

This comprehensive, soteriological view of the humanity of
Jesus is seen all the more in the emphasis the author places on the
faith and obedience of Jesus. This is particularly seen in 12:2
(RSV): "...looking to Jesus the pioneer and perfecter of our
faith..." This passage follows the classic roll call of examples of
faith in chapter eleven. However, according to T. E. Pollard, it is
"almost universally mistranslated by the unwarranted insertion of

---

39   Ladd, pp. 578-579.
40   Peterson, p. 121.
41   Rissi, p. 38.
42   Hagner, p. 26.

'our' before 'faith.'"[43] There is no possessive pronoun in the
Greek. The emphasis is not on "our" faith, but on the faith of
Jesus, according to Pollard. Jesus both *originated* (ἀρχηγὸν) faith
and *summed up* (τελειωτὴν) the faith of all those who have lived
by faith (ch.11). Is Jesus the *source* of faith or its greatest exemplar in 12:2?[44] Pollard's view is the former, but it is definitely in
the minority. Graham Hughes believes that one of the reasons for
the majority opinion is a "partly subconscious unwillingness to see
that Jesus can be spoken of in the New Testament, albeit infre-
quently, as a participant in faith as well as the object *of* faith."[45]

The majority viewpoint relies on several arguments. Bruce
contends that the definite article before "faith" needs to be represented by the possessive pronoun "our."[46] Montefiore admits that
it is "possible" that this verse refers to the faith of Jesus, but since
the next clause is only concerned with his death, this meaning is
"improbable."[47] However, this would not be true if the cross was
seen, as we have argued, as the climax, as well as an integral part,
of the Incarnation.

In addition to the above mentioned reasons for this verse to
refer to the faith of Jesus, other reasons may be offered. It must be
remembered that this phrase is dependent on its antecedent in verse
one:

> Therefore, since we are surrounded by so great a cloud
> of witnesses, let us also lay aside every weight, and
> sin ...and let us run with perseverance (or *endurance*:
> ὑπομονῆς) the race that is set before us, looking to
> Jesus, the pioneer and perfecter of (our?) faith, who
> for the joy that was set before him *endured*
> (ὑπέμεινεν) the cross... (12:1,2)

---

43   Pollard, pp. 81-82.

44   Graham Hughes, *Hebrews and Hermeneutics: The Epistle to the Hebrews as a
     New Testament Example of Biblical Interpretation* (Cambridge: Cambridge
     University Press, 1977), pp. 79-80.

45   Ibid., p. 80.

46   Bruce, p. 351

47   Montefiore, pp. 214-215.

Jesus becomes the source of the endurance of his followers through his own endurance.[48] While the "exemplar" motif may be included here, the concept of "source" seems to provide a much more satisfactory understanding of the epistle's teaching on the implications of the pre-existent Son taking on human flesh. A dual understanding of both "source" and "example" is particularly attractive when one observes the use of ἀρχηγός throughout Hebrews. Jesus, the ἀρχηγὸν τῆς σωτηρίας (2:10) is also the τὸν τῆς πίστεως ἀρχηγὸν (12:2). Certainly, 2:10 includes the aspect of "source": "By His suffering He accomplishes His work as the 'Author' of salvation."[49] It would be unlikely that the author would not be thinking along similar lines later on in the epistle in 12:2, when he again uses ἀρχηγὸν for Jesus.

THE OBEDIENCE OF JESUS

There is a very concrete form of faith in the epistle which speaks of the life of Jesus as a life of total obedience to God. This should not be seen as a contrast to the faith of Jesus, but rather as a concrete working out of that faith in God in the context of earthly existence.

2:6-9 presents an interesting example of the obedience motif in Hebrews. By borrowing Psalm 8, the author takes a passage about the majesty of humanity and turns it into a statement paradoxically ascribed to the humiliation of Jesus.[50] This is another obvious example of the two facets of the person of Christ in Hebrews: both the pre-existent Son and the humiliated Man.

The unique feature about this passage is the presence of an Adam Christology in Hebrews by the use of Psalm 8.[51] Although Psalm 8 speaks of the glory and majesty of humanity given by God, yet, as it is, "we do not see everything in subjection to him" (2:8). The author of Hebrews is using the psalm to ask the question of the reality of salvation: Where is the reality of salvation to

---

[48] G. Hughes, p. 80.
[49] G. Delling, "ἀρχω," *TDNT*, Vol. 1, p. 488.
[50] C. Colpe, "ὁ υἱὸς τοῦ ἀνθρώπου," *TDNT*, Vol. 8, p. 464. Cf. O. Michel, "Son," *NIDNTT*, Vol. 3. pp. 632-633.
[51] Dunn, p. 109.

be found today? His answer is Christological, in an eschatological sense:

> But we see Jesus, who for a little while was made
> lower than the angels, crowned with glory and honor,
> because of the suffering of death, so that by the grace
> of God he might taste death for everyone (2.9).

"The risen Christ is crowned with the glory that Adam failed to reach by virtue of his sin."[52] It is instructive to note, as Dunn observes, that the humanity of Jesus was a necessary prerequisite for Christ to play the role of the "last Adam."[53] He must have become like the first Adam before he could have become the last Adam. Also important to note is the unity between the earthly and exalted Jesus in this passage. The same Jesus who was "made lower than the angels" and partook of "the suffering of death" is now "crowned with glory and honor," as was supposed to be the destiny of humanity (Adam) (2:7). The author does not understand the psalm primarily in messianic terms, but in the sense of Jesus as Archetypal Man.[54] However, if "son of man" had messianic overtones in the first century, it would certainly carry over into this passage (v. 6). Regardless, it would at least remind its readers of its use by Jesus as a title for himself.[55]

The second major passage which speaks of the obedience of Jesus is 5:8, 9:

> Although he was a Son, he learned obedience through
> what he suffered; and being made perfect he became
> the source of eternal salvation to all who obey him.

Michel believes that the roots of "learning obedience" comes from Isaiah 50:4-5.[56]

---

[52] Ibid.

[53] Ibid., p. 110.

[54] Hagner, p. 24.

[55] Ibid., p. 25.

[56] O. Michel, *Der Brief an die Hebräer,* 12th ed. (Gottingen: Vanderhoek and Ruprecht, 1966), p. 224.

The Lord has given me the tongue of those who are taught, that I may know how to sustain with a word him that is weary. Morning by morning he wakens, he wakens my ear, to hear as those who are taught. The Lord has opened my ear, and I was not rebellious, I turned not backward.

In this passage the author continues his teaching on the "developmental" humanity of Jesus. In this case it involves Jesus "learning obedience" through suffering. It is interesting to note how closely he ties this together with his idea of salvation: On the basis of this "learned obedience" Jesus becomes "the source of eternal salvation." As Hagner states, "source" (αἴτιος) can also be translated as "cause" and is reminiscent of the word ἀρχηγὸν in 2:10 and 12:2.[57]

This passage stresses the importance of the "developmental" aspect of Jesus' humanity to the author's teaching on the full identification of Jesus with humanity as expressed in the soteriological significance of his obedience. Therefore, it seems to blunt the force of the author's thrust if the "learning" is a perfunctory task of the earthly Jesus, a kind of "going through the motions," as Bruce seems to suggest.[58] A genuine "learning" takes place in the author's thought which expresses both Jesus' identification with humanity and the accomplishment of faithfulness and obedience to God which was Adam's failure (2:6-9). This is an integral part of the saving significance of Jesus' obedient life.

The third passage which directly concerns the obedience of Jesus is 10:5-10 (RSV):

Consequently, when Christ came into the world, he said, 'Sacrifices and offerings thou hast not desired, but a body hast thou prepared for me; in burnt offerings and sin offerings thou hast taken no pleasure.' Then I said, 'Lo, I have come to do thy will, O God, as it is written of me in the roll of the book.' When he said above, 'Thou has neither desired nor taken plea-

---

57 Hagner, p. 65.
58 Bruce, p. 103.

> sure in sacrifices and offerings and burnt offerings and
> sin offerings' (these are offered according to the law),
> then he added, 'Lo, I have come to do thy will.' He
> abolishes the first in order to establish the second. And
> by that will we have been sanctified through the offer-
> ing of the body of Jesus Christ once for all.

Bruce stresses that the offering of Christ in this passage is not restricted to his "blood," as in vv. 19 and 29. "The offering of His
body is simply the offering of Himself.... Whether our author
speaks of His body or His blood, it is His incarnate life that is
meant, yielded to God in an obedience which was maintained even
to death."[59] Yet it is worth observing that it is "sacrifices" and
"offerings" which are not desired. In other words, the reality of
salvation for Hebrews is centered on the obedient will of Christ.

G. Hughes points out, Hebrews is usually seen to affirm
without question the Old Testament view that sacrificial blood has
a mysterious, expiatory power, e.g., "without shedding of blood
there is no forgiveness" (9:22). But this is questionable. The
phrase in 9:22 is describing the old dispensation: "Under the law
almost everything is purified with blood, and without shedding of
blood there is no forgiveness of sins."[60] The lack of efficacy of
this system is stated in 10:4: "It is impossible that the blood of
bulls and goats should remove sins." The "sacrificial ritual" has
been replaced with the "sacrifice of the will." "In his [the author's]
understanding, the sacrificial worth of Jesus' death therefore consists not so much in his physical death as in the sacrifice of his
human will which that death presupposes."[61] However, as
Davidson is quick to point out, the saving worth of obedience is
only in the context of the Son's offering of himself.[62] There is no
intrinsic worth of obedience apart from the offering of the Son
made flesh.

The significant title of Jesus as "High Priest" in Hebrews
can be discussed in light of his obedience. As Hagner comments,

---

59 Ibid., p. 236.
60 G. Hughes, p. 89.
61 Ibid.
62 Davidson, pp. 193-194.

this title brings together many different themes in the Christology of Hebrews: his humanity, his unique sonship, his exaltation, as well as his ability to help Christians under temptation.[63] The origins of its usage by Hebrews have been explained in several ways. Goppelt argues for a liturgical origin.[64] There is much evidence for this in the Apostolic Fathers (Ign. Phld. 9:1; Pol. Phil. 12:2; Mart. Pol. 14:3), and above all, in I Clement 61:3 (cf. 64:1): "We praise Thee through the high priest and guardian of our souls."[65] Goppelt believes that it is likely that this is a tradition which was already familiar to the readers of Hebrews. In 2:17, the idea "was introduced quite spontaneously and was presupposed as familiar to the readers."[66]

Cullmann believes that we find the significance of the obedience of the high priest in the Old Testament image of the Servant of Yahweh (Isa. 53:12; cf. Heb. 7:27; 9:28). "Only by connection of the High Priest concept with that of the *ebed Yahweh* is the insufficiency of the Jewish high priestly office overcome."[67] Nevertheless, Cullmann admits that there is a dialectic here between "deepest humiliation" and "highest majesty" which goes beyond the meekness of the "Servant of Yahweh."[68]

Ladd summarizes the mission of the high priest in three areas: purification, sanctification, and perfection.[69] The work of Christ is efficacious to "*purify* your conscience from dead works to serve the living God" (9:14; cf. 10:2; 9:26; 10:22). His work also accomplishes the sanctification of his brethren: "We have been *sanctified* through the offering of the body of Jesus Christ once for all" (10:12; cf. 13:12). This does not necessarily mean sinlessness, but dedication to God (9:13). "Perfection" sums up

---

[63] Hagner, p. 59.

[64] Leonard Goppelt, *Theology of the New Testament,* Vol. 2. trans. John Alsup, ed. Jürgen Roloff (Grand Rapids: Eerdmans, 1982), p. 251.

[65] *The Apostolic Fathers,* trans. Kirsopp Lake (London: William Heinemann, 1912), p. 121.

[66] Goppelt, p. 251.

[67] Cullmann, p. 91.

[68] Ibid., p. 92.

[69] Ladd, p. 581.

the completeness and sufficiency of the work of Christ which was unattainable under the old covenant (7:11). "By a single offering he has perfected for all time those who are sanctified" (10:14). As Ladd comments, "He has enabled those who have been purified and dedicated to God to realize all that mankind ought to mean-- complete reliance and trust in God."[70]

A unique feature of the author's teaching on the high priest is his bringing together concepts of sonship and priesthood. James Moffatt speaks of this as "something vital" for the author.[71] This is seen when one observes that in 5:5

> he quotes his favourite text from Ps. 2:7 ("Thou art my Son, today I have begotten thee") before the more apposite one (in v. 6) from Ps. 110:4 ("Thou art a priest forever, after the order of Melchizedek") implying that the position of divine Son carried with it in some sense, the role of ἀρχιερεύς.[72]

It is Hebrews' teaching on the relationship between sonship and priesthood in Jesus as high priest which emphasizes the salvific importance of the humanity of the high priest with those for whom he ministers. The concept of the sonship of Christ is certainly a stratum of continuity which Hebrews shares with the earliest church.[73] An echo may even be seen of Mark 12:2-6 in the distinction between the servants and the son (3:5). However, according to Dunn, Hebrews appears to be the first New Testament writing to have embraced a specific thought of a pre-existent sonship.[74] The interweaving of theological innovation with a grounding in the tradition is an important feature of our author's thought.

Sonship speaks explicitly of Jesus' religious experience. John Knox makes some astute observations concerning Jesus' sonship, his religious experience, and his sharing human nature with common humanity, which emphasize once again the depth of

---

70   Ibid.
71   James Moffatt, *A Critical and Exegetical Commentary on the Epistle to the Hebrews* (Edinburgh: T. & T. Clark, 1924), p. 64.
72   Ibid.
73   Dunn, p. 55.
74   Ibid.

Hebrews' concern with the total identification of Christ with humanity. The religious life of Jesus was not as unique as one might expect.[75] It is "in the midst of the congregation," that is, amongst common humanity that Jesus praises God, and, like common humanity, says, "I will put my trust in him" (2:12-13; cf. 5:7). One would think that reflection on pre-existence would drive the author to find something unique in Jesus' humanity. However, that would separate him from his brethren, which is precisely what the author refuses to consider.[76]

Hagner comments on the importance of the "eschatological dimensions of 'inheritance' and its connection with sonship" for the author of Hebrews (6:12, 17; 9:15; 10:36; 11:8).[77] This is common to other strata in the New Testament (Rom. 8:17; I Pet. 3:17). In 2:11, the author states, "For he who sanctifies and those who are sanctified have all one origin. That is why he is not ashamed to call them brethren" (RSV). The meaning of $\dot{\epsilon}\xi$ $\dot{\epsilon}\nu\dot{o}\varsigma$ has been interpreted in various ways. Spicq considers God to be the source of the common origin of "he who sanctifies and those who are sanctified" because sanctification is a divine prerogative (cf. John 8:42 "If God were your Father, you would love me, for I proceeded and came forth from God").[78] However, Calvin contends that $\dot{\epsilon}\xi$ $\dot{\epsilon}\nu\dot{o}\varsigma$ speaks of a common nature between Christ and his brethren.[79] Interestingly enough, for Calvin, the center of sanctification is not in the power of God *per se*, but in the recreation of human nature:

> It is not only that He sanctified us inasmuch as He is God, but the power of sanctification lies in our human nature, not because it has it of itself, but because God pours into our nature the whole fullness of holiness so that we may all draw from it. That is the meaning of the sentence (John 17:19), "For their sakes I sanctify myself." If we were sinful and unclean, the remedy is

---

[75] Knox, p. 42.
[76] Ibid., p. 43.
[77] Hagner, p. 7.
[78] Spicq, vol. 2, pp. 40-41.
[79] Calvin, *Hebrews,* p. 26.

not far to seek, because it is offered to us in our flesh.[80]

In light of the context of the Son partaking of the same "flesh and blood" as the children, this seems to be more correct interpretation.[81]

THE PRESENT, ESCHATOLOGICAL CHRIST

We have seen that it would be mistaken to assume that the humanity of Jesus in the Epistle to the Hebrews has only an exemplary purpose, e.g. Jesus as the model which we are to follow. That thought is present, but in a rich context from which it should not be separated. This is particularly seen in the author's teaching on the place of the exalted humanity of Jesus. The neglect of this aspect of New Testament Christology has affected the way in which we perceive the significance of the humanity of Christ.

What is this significance? First of all, Cullmann comments that the teaching in Hebrews is on the exalted, eschatological, yet present intercessory ministry of Jesus.[82] He can only intercede for us today if he is the same Christ who was on earth, the one who was tempted in all respects as we are. Hugh Anderson points out the implications of this for the life of the early church:

> For the Church knew that the majesty of her Lord in his perpetual ministry in the unseen heavenly world, which becomes real to faith, was rooted and grounded in an earthly life climaxed by his unique act of obedience and sacrifice on the Cross.[83]

This is distinctly related to the *eschatology* of Hebrews. There is no discontinuity between the earthly Jesus and the exalted Christ for our author. As Anderson continues,

> The author is, to be sure, interested in the continuing and present activity of Christ at the heavenly altar. But

---

80 Ibid.
81 Cf. Philip E. Hughes, p. 105.
82 Cullmann, p. 80.
83 Hugh Anderson, *Jesus and Christian Origins* (New York: Oxford University Press, 1964), p. 288.

> for him, in the most realistic sense, it is the past of
> Jesus that is made forever present; it is his manhood
> that is exalted; it is the person he was, and the life he
> lived and the death he died on earth, to which we are
> brought near in the message and in worship.[84]

In this way the author seeks to maintain his emphasis on the
"once-for-allness" of Christ's sacrifice (Heb. 9:12; 10:10), while
equally stressing the continual and present ministry of Christ.[85]
The Adam Christology of 2:8-18 also reflects a desire to unite the
earthly with the exalted Jesus.[86]

It may be asked whether the expression in 5:7, "the days of
his flesh" speaks of a purely temporal aspect of Jesus' humanity.
According to Bruce, this would argue against the author's contention that Christians now have a priest who can sympathize with
them because he has felt their temptations.[87] However, it could be
argued against Bruce that this does not necessarily mean that the
incarnate state continues in the heavenlies. Could not the remembrance of sympathy with the temptations of humanity be sufficient? Still, we believe that Bruce is correct, particularly if we remember the author's eschatology. Salvation, an important word
for Hebrews, is past, present, and future.[88] It is the salvation
promised in the Old Testament, fulfilled in the present time (2:3,
10; 5:9), and to be consummated in the future (1:14; 6:0; 9:28).
For the author of Hebrews, the soteriological reality of the past is
present now in Jesus Christ. The church does not simply
"remember" Jesus. The same Jesus who walked the sands of
Galilee is now present with the church: "Jesus Christ is the same
yesterday and today and forever: (13:8)."[89]

---

84 Ibid., p. 285.
85 Ibid., p. 285.
86 Dunn, p. 111.
87 Bruce, p. 98.
88 Hagner, p. 21.
89 This is the decisive argument against the criticism made of the doctrine of the
exalted humanity of Christ by Anthony Tyrrell Hanson, *The Image of the
Invisible God*. Hanson believes that Hebrews presents a faulty Christology

The writer of Hebrews continually ties together the reality of the exalted Jesus with its implications for his brethren on earth. Because of the fact of the "great high priest" who has passed through the heavens, the readers are exhorted to "hold fast our confession" (4:14). It is with "confidence" that the readers are to "draw near to the throne of grace, that we may receive mercy and find grace to help in time of need" (4:15). This becomes the crux of the author's basis for earning the readers of the dangers of apostasy and return (most likely) to their former Judaism (2:1-3; 3:6, 12-14; 4:1, 11-13; 6:1-12; 10:26-31, 35-39; 12:3-17; 13:9).[90] The source of their "confidence" (10:19) is not just a memory of the earthly Jesus, nor a mystical exalted Christ idea (e.g. the Christ of the "kerygma"), but the continuity between Jesus of Nazareth and the exalted Christ.

The author stresses that the basis of the intercessory ministry of Christ is in his continual presence: "Consequently he is able for

---

with a view of the Incarnation as a "fact-finding mission," telling God something he does not know about the human condition. Elsewhere in the New Testament, and in the Old Testament, God is not deficient in knowledge about the human condition (p. 158). Hebrews does not have an explicit doctrine of the exalted humanity of Christ, but Hanson acknowledges that its Christology implies this since it claims that because of his humanity, Christ intercedes for us (p. 159). But Hanson finds a basic problem with the doctrine: How can Christ's humanity have an effect in the divine sphere if all human nature is finite, let alone be able to mediate with humanity? (p. 39) On the contrary, according to Hanson, *the Spirit,* not the humanity of Christ, mediates between Christ and Christians (p. 44). The human nature of Christ has only an exemplary purpose, as "a symbol or picture" (p. 104).

Both Hanson's criticism of the exalted humanity doctrine and his proposals are extremely unsatisfactory. As mentioned above, such a view rends asunder the unity between the earthly Jesus and the risen Christ. For our purposes, it is questionable how we can speak of the reality of salvation today apart from God taking upon our humanity, certainly through the Spirit, but not a "naked" Spirit devoid of flesh (cf. Ray S. Anderson, *Historical Transcendence and the Reality of God,* p. 183: "For Spirit needs *place* to work out the intra-divine transcendence which belongs to the historical reality of the Incarnate Logos."). Apart from this, we have the danger of both a highly docetic and "memorial" Christology, both of which do not do justice to the significance of the humanity of Christ for salvation.

90 Ibid., xxii.

all time to save those who draw near to God through him, since he always lives to make intercession for them" (7:25). The high priestly ministry of Christ is still in effect.[91] The one who "had to be made like his brethren in every respect" in order to be "a merciful and faithful high priest" (2:17) "is able (δύναται) to help those who are tempted" (2:18). The present tense brings out the continuous sense and the present reality of the intercessory ministry of Jesus: "he is *continually* able..." Westcott notes that in 2:9 ("But we see Jesus, who for a little while was made lower [ἠλαττωμένον] than the angels..."), it is not the aorist but perfect tense which is used. Westcott concludes, "The human nature which Christ assumed He still retains."[92] Still, it may be argued that the temporal phrase "for a little while" seems to suggest the temporal nature of the incarnate state, in some sense. However, this would not preclude the continual force of the perfect. The earthly manifestation of the humanity of Christ may have been "for a little while," but its reality and significance have a continual meaning. Likewise, the present work of sanctification is emphasized by the present participles in 2:11: ὁ τε γὰρ ἁγιάζων καὶ οἱ ἁγιαζόμενοι ἐξ ἑνὸς πάντες.[93] The act of sanctifying and the process of sanctification are both continual and present realities, based on the exalted humanity of Christ, his eschatological destiny.

13:8, "Jesus Christ is the same yesterday and today and forever," is the quintessential text for an understanding of Hebrews' teaching on the present reality of Christ. The "terse, aphoristic form" suggests a "semi-creedal liturgical formula" (cf. Rom. 10:9; I Cor. 12:3), according to Montefiore.[94] At first glance, the verse might be seen to be an example of the often mentioned influence of Platonism in Hebrews. But, as Hagner observes, this is not a description of an "abstract" and "timeless....transcendent and eternal nature of Christ."[95] Rather, it

---

[91] Cullmann, p. 102.
[92] Westcott, p. 45.
[93] Ibid., p. 50.
[94] Montefiore, p. 242.
[95] Hagner, pp. 224-225.

is a declaration of the faithfulness of Christ to meet the needs of
the brethren in the past, present, and future. In addition, we might
add that this faithfulness is based on his faithfulness to the Father
(2:12-13) and his participation in the human nature of his brethren
(2:14).

The theology of the *eschatological* Christ in Hebrews develops out of the author's broader concern for a theology of the *presence* of Christ. Through his flesh, Christ has provided "a new and
living way" to God (10:20). As Bruce observes, it is not only a
"new" way but a "living" way.[96] It is a way which is not simply a
remembrance of an incarnation, but a very present reality. The basis for this is the exalted humanity of Jesus. The importance of
this exalted, present humanity was not lost on John Calvin:
"Those fanatics who imagine that Christ has now put off His flesh
because the days of His flesh are said to have passed are talking
nonsense."[97] While we would hardly wish to label as "fanatics"
those who do not agree with our position, it is nonetheless instructive to see how strongly Calvin felt about the issue.

We believe our study bears out the concern of Cullmann: the
exalted humanity of Christ, an often neglected doctrine, is essential, not only to an understanding of the theology of the Epistle of
the Hebrews, but also for the concerns of dogmatic theology. For
it is in the full identification of Jesus with common humanity that
there resides the possibility for the purifying, perfecting, and
sanctifying work of the Son as our high priest. This is fulfilled in
the continual obedient and faithful life of Jesus, a life which continues up to the present and for all eternity (13:8). Therefore, the
question of the reality of salvation for our author is answered by
an eschatological reality: the reality of Christ our high priest, continually interceding for humanity, because he continually partakes
of our human nature, even in the heavenlies. As there was redeeming power in that humanity, "in the days of his flesh," there
is a redeeming power even in the present. For this reason, the author can exhort his readers to "pay the closer attention to what we
have heard, lest we drift away from it" (2:1). Humanity's high

---

[96]   Bruce, p. 245.
[97]   Calvin, *Hebrews,* p. 63.

priest in the heavenlies is so much superior to the angels (1:5f.) or
Moses (3:3) since he partakes of a common nature with humanity,
yet still sits in the heavenlies, forever interceding for humanity as
the pre-existent Son (9:25). The "poignant dilemma" of Knox and
Dunn is nonetheless the crux of the drama of salvation for the author of Hebrews and his community.

PART THREE

THE VICARIOUS HUMANITY OF CHRIST
AS THE LOCUS OF THE REALITY
OF SALVATION IN THE WORLD:
VICARIOUS HUMANITY AS ECCLESIAL REALITY

Our previous chapters on the "vicarious" humanity of Christ as the basis and source of a new humanity, and its implications for the question of the reality of salvation, have thus far ranged from critiquing the anthropocentric direction of contemporary soteriology (Part One) to presenting the wide-ranging implications of a positive doctrine of the vicarious humanity of Christ (Part Two).

But a problem lies before us if we do not ask ourselves about the *locus*, or the place of the vicarious humanity of Christ in the world today. This is the church, the body of Christ. The place of the church in the question of the reality of salvation keeps us from an "ideal" or "abstract" view of the humanity of Christ, cut off from our present, mundane world. What is the relationship between the church as the body of Christ and the reality of salvation?

However, we must not rush too quickly into ecclesiology if we are to maintain our thesis that the ultimate reality of salvation is in God himself. Too often ecclesiology has the tendency to create and sustain its own place in the world. That is why our discussion of the vicarious humanity of Christ as the *locus* of the reality of salvation in the world begins with "Humanity Displaced" (Chapter Ten): the implications of the radical substitutionary doctrine of the atonement found in the theology of Karl Barth. Only then can we proceed to "Humanity Restored" (Chapter Eleven): the relationship between Christ as the Last Adam and the church as the body of Christ, the *locus* of the reality of salvation in the world, made manifest under the direction and power of the Spirit, and bearing fruit in concrete acts of faith, hope, and love. To put it bluntly, the church must die, die to its own agenda and aims, in order to be raised with the Last Adam, and thus become the locus of the reality of salvation in the world today, the manifestation of the vicarious humanity of Christ.

CHAPTER TEN

HUMANITY DISPLACED:
THE JUDGE JUDGED IN OUR PLACE
(KARL BARTH)

It is not hard to understand why we would turn to Karl Barth for suggestions on the vicarious humanity of Christ. When one even casually looks through the contents of the *Church Dogmatics*, the concepts related to a vicarious sense of the humanity of Christ are easily noticed.[1] "The Mystery of Revelation" in I/2 is the Word made "flesh."[2] In II/2, the divine beauty is seen in the Incarnation as the divine glory of the true man.[3] Jesus Christ as "the one, true Israelite" and as both electing God and elected man has obvious significance for a concept of the vicarious humanity of Christ.[4] Barth's theological anthropology is thoroughly grounded upon the humanity of Jesus as the basis for common humanity. Jesus is the "Man for God,"[5] "the Man for other Men,"[6] and the "Whole Man."[7] The entirety of section fifty-nine is IV/1 is entitled, "The Obedience of the Son of God."[8] Section sixty-one follows with the concept of Jesus as justified

---

[1] These are only representative sections in Barth.
[2] Barth, *CD* I/2, pp. 147-156.
[3] Ibid., pp. 657-666.
[4] Ibid., II/2, pp. 58f., 94-144.
[5] Ibid., III/2, pp. 55-70.
[6] Ibid., pp. 203-221.
[7] Ibid., pp. 325-344.
[8] Ibid., IV/1, pp. 157-357.

man under the heading "The Justification of Man."[9] In IV/2, the
theme of "Jesus Christ, the Servant as Lord" includes "The
Exaltation of the Son of Man" (sec. 64), "The Sloth and Misery of
Man" (sec 65), and "The Sanctification of Man" (sec. 66). "Jesus
Christ the True Witness" is the title of an entire chapter in IV/3. In
IV/4, Barth finds the basis for baptism in the baptism of Jesus.[10]

Because of the extensiveness of material which could be
covered, we have chosen to look in depth at one section in the
Dogmatics as representative of Barth's teaching, "The Judge
Judged in our Place" in IV/1.[11] The reason for selecting this passage is evident. It is this section which explicitly answers the
question, "*Why* did the eternal Son of God become a servant" by
taking on human flesh? What is the purpose of the Incarnation?
What is its end? Or, in Anselm's words, *Cur Deus Homo*? Since
Barth is, in effect, dealing with the heart of his soteriology at this
point, it seems appropriate to use this section to investigate how
the humanity of Christ relates to common humanity and its implications for the reality of salvation. Our thesis is that Barth's theology has a deep understanding of the significance of the vicarious
humanity of Christ which sometimes parallels, yet at times contra-
dicts, what we have discovered thus far in Torrance, Campbell,
Moberly, and the Epistle to the Hebrews. His emphasis is
squarely centered in the solidarity of Christ with humanity, which
is expressed in a radical doctrine of substitutionary atonement. By
viewing the extent of substitution to the point of considering
Christ as "the one great sinner" (cf. Campbell and Moberly on
"vicarious repentance"), Barth signifies a depth to the reality of
salvation which is rare in the history of theology. This has great
implications for his view of the comprehensive nature of the
gospel, as well as the debate over the "objectivity" or
"subjectivity" of the atonement. Because of his concern for the influence of Rudolf Bultmann (which is mentioned in his fore-
word[12], Barth champions the "objective" side of salvation: Salvation is a once for all, completed, God-initiated act to which hu-

---

9   Ibid., pp. 514-642.
10   Ibid., IV/4, pp52f.
11   Ibid., IV/1, pp. 211-282.
12   Ibid., IV/1, ix.

manity cannot contribute at any level. This is usually seen by critics as an over-emphasis which denigrates the place of human responsibility in salvation. Quite the contrary, we will seek to show that this "objectivity" provides a true place for humanity, based on the vicarious humanity of Christ, and thus, a greater and deeper sense of the reality of salvation. The place for true "subjectivity" in Barth is in the trust and obedience shown to the Father by the Son.

However, it will be argued that the force of Barth's teaching on the vicarious humanity of Christ is mitigated by the priority which he gives to the juridical side of the atonement. This seems to be inconsistent with the preceding part in IV/1, "The Way of the Son of God into the Far Country," which speaks of the Incarnation in terms of the eternal relationship between the Father and the Son, rather than in forensic terms. Our approach in this chapter will be to look at the section closely and then offer our critique.

THE PURPOSE AND END OF THE INCARNATION

We have already alluded to how Barth fits "The Judge Judged in our Place" into the larger context of chapter fourteen, "Jesus Christ, the Lord as Servant," and section fifty-nine, "The Obedience of the Son of God." Barth states that the preceding part of the section, "The Way of the Son of God into the Far Country," explains who the servant is.[13] But another question remains, "Why did he become a servant?"[14] In other words, *Cur Deus Homo?*[15]

---

[13] Ibid., p. 211.

[14] Ibid., p. 212.

[15] Note G. W. Bromiley's interesting comment on how striking it is that Barth has left out any substantial discussion of the history of the doctrine of the atonement (apart from Anselm), with corresponding emphasis on biblical exegesis. His conclusion has implications beyond this topic: "On the whole this is probably a gain, for while we cannot afford to ignore the work of the past, constructive thinking on the atonement is often crowded out by a hackneyed historical survey." "The Doctrine of the Atonement: A Survey of Barth's *Kirchliche Dogmatik* IV/1," *Scottish Journal of Theology,* 8, No. 2 (June, 1955), p. 175.

Barth proceeds to mention several points which he will reiterate throughout this discussion. One, is that the Incarnation and the atonement reveals the depth of Deity, i.e. God is *pro se*: "God vindicates Himself, and is therefore Himself the meaning and basis and end."[16] There is no necessity beyond the atonement apart from the vindication of God himself. He himself is "The meaning and basis and end." Otto Weber considers this part, along with the preceding part, "The Way of the Son into the Far Country," as both dealing with the deity of Christ.[17]

But within this vindication of himself, God has chosen to act *propter nos homines et propter nostram salutem*.[18] The order here is very important for Barth. The act of salvation does not exist as a necessity which God is compelled to fulfill. It is purely an act of grace. As such, there is no necessity for it apart from the meaning which God gives to it. This is not to be reduced to any idea of God, the world, or a principle.[19]

GOD *PRO NOBIS*

The "how" of God "for us" *(pro nobis)* is dealt with next by Barth in the context of two statements: One is that God makes the situation of humanity his own situation.[20] The "mortal peril" of humanity becomes the mortal peril of God. This is the first of several statements which Barth will preface by saying, "We should be explaining the Incarnation docetically..." if this was not so, thus continually stressing the importance of the humanity of Christ, even with his emphasis here on the act of God. His concern is to leave no doubt as to the complete extent to which God has identified with the world in Jesus Christ.

But the solidarity between the Son and humanity does not exhaust all there is to say. In the Incarnation there is also the par-

---

[16] Barth, *CD* IV/1, p. 212.

[17] Otto Weber, *Karl Barth's Kirchkliche Dogmatik: ein einführender Bericht zu den Bd. I.1 bis IV, 3.2* (Neukirchen-Vluyn: Neukirchener Verlag, 1977), p. 212. Cf. John Thompson, *Christ in Perspective: Christological Perspectives in the Theology of Karl Barth* (Grand Rapids Eerdmans, 1978), pp. 61-62.

[18] Barth, *CD* IV/1, p. 212.

[19] Ibid., p. 214.

[20] Ibid., p. 215.

ticipation of the world in "the history of the inner life of His God-head."[21] This is the beginning of Barth's emphasis on the "objectivity" of salvation. Echoes of the Greek Fathers are to be found at this point also.[22]

In addition, this solidarity is with sinners.[23] Again, Barth warns against the docetism which might creep in if we have any reservations at this point. Solidarity with humanity extends to God taking the risk of facing sin in all its ugliness: its "ingratitude, disobedience, unfaithfulness, pride cowardice, and deceit." Jesus' knowledge of sin is equated with his knowledge of himself. In fact, Barth can say that "He came to closer grips with it than any other man." Jesus becomes "the brother of man" because, and here Barth is making a fine, yet necessary, distinction, "He was not immune from sin. He did not commit it, but he was not immune from it." Barth seems to be saying that whereas Jesus did not actively rebel against God, he was confronted with the effects, the environment, and hostility of the presence of sin in humanity. As much as possible, Barth is seeking to erase any wall between the reality of sin and the presence of the eternal Son of God in human flesh.

The reason for this is that Barth's soteriology is profoundly *ontological* at its core. He says that the purpose of the Incarnation was "to change that status [of humanity in sin] from within."[24] The very situation of humanity has been radically altered by the humiliation of the Son of God. Again, the teaching of the Greek Fathers comes to mind.

GOD AS JUDGE

Yet Barth cautions us not to see this ontological change as the result of "cheap grace."[25] The grace of God is costly, for the

---

21 Ibid.

22 For example, Athanasius, "On the Incarnation of the Word," in *A Select Library of Nicene and Post-Nicene Fathers of the Christian Church.* Second series, Vol. 4. Ed. Philip Schaff and Henry Wace (Grand Rapids: Eerdmans, 1953), sec. 9.

23 Barth, *CD* IV/1, pp. 215-216.

24 Ibid., p. 216.

25 Ibid., pp. 216-217.

Incarnation involves the coming of the Savior as a Judge. This is of essence a part of what it means for Jesus to be the Savior. He cannot be the Savior without being the Judge. There is no salvation apart from the judgment of God upon sin, apart from his declaration of the sinfulness of sin. At this point Barth begins his emphasis upon the forensic nature of the atonement. Despite any hesitations we might have regarding the extent of its use and its place in Barth's doctrine of salvation, it must be admitted that Barth is starting his case for forensic atonement on the strongest possible footing. Salvation must avoid sentimentality and take on adequately and decisively the reality of sin and the condemnation of God upon it in the humanity of Jesus.

Barth cautions that one should not have here an all too limiting view of God as a judge. The primary concern in the biblical context is not the role of pardoning or condemning, but to promote "order and peace."[26] This is a positive function which only on occasion is expressed in a negative way. The examples of the "judges" in the Old Testament come readily to mind.

However, this does not mean that the negative aspect of judgment is ruled out. Yet, in the New Testament it is a judgment which is based on the presence of the obedient Son who has shared in the very same humanity as his sinful brethren. This is the significance of Jesus' baptism by John. What is often left unnoticed by commentators is the surprise which John expressed at Jesus' request (Mt. 3:14).[27] It may be added that, even today, there are still those who express surprise at the idea of Jesus provide a "vicarious repentance." Yet, despite their surprise they rarely follow the Baptist's example of contrition!

The nature of the judgment of God is determined by the fact that it is the judgment *of God*.[28] Since it is the judgment of God, it is the ultimate judgment. There is no judgment which is so decisive and thoroughgoing, because there is no greater rule of righteousness. Again, Barth stresses that there is no law, principle, nor necessity which governs the free action of God.

---

26   Ibid., p. 217.
27   Ibid., p. 218.
28   Ibid., p. 219.

The *nature* of the judgment of God also includes a word which humanity does not want to hear concerning its sin.[29] It is a strange word because the righteousness of God is a stranger to humanity. Here again, Barth makes one of his strongest points for his emphasis upon forensic atonement. The action of grace reveals the reality of judgment, a judgment based on the power of grace to illumine, expose, and judge sin. This certainly must have an important place in any doctrine of the atonement. Barth can even categorically say, "All sin has its being and origin in the fact that man wants to be his own judge."[30] The Incarnation of the Word, "the abasement of the Son," is "the divine accusation against every man and the divine accusation of every man."

The *basis* of the judgment becomes crucial to Barth at this point. The ultimate judgment of God has taken place because the Son shares in our common humanity.[31] It is only because of this shared humanity that he can take the righteous judgment of God upon himself. In other words, at the very basis of Barth's doctrine of the atonement is the necessity of the vicarious humanity of Christ. Our question will be whether Barth's forensic emphasis does justice to the profound soteriological implications of this shared humanity.

At this point, one must not neglect noticing the importance of salvation as an act *of God* for Barth. The *actuality* of the action of Christ creates the *possibility*.[32] There is a genuine initiative of the Son of God to take our place as human beings and to undergo the judgment upon us. This is a part of the true "objectivity" of salvation for Barth.

THE "HISTORY" OF JESUS CHRIST

This judgment is not a purely external act, but that which takes place within the "history" of Jesus Christ. This is the basis for Barth's controversial position on the "objective" and "subjective" aspects of the atonement. Barth can even come to the

---

[29] Ibid.
[30] Ibid., p. 220.
[31] Ibid., p. 223.
[32] Ibid., p. 222.

point of saying, "Everything has happened to us, but in the context of the person of the Son."[33] A careful study of this statement will help us avoid many of the caricatures of Barth's preference for the "objective" position.

A typical criticism is voiced by Donald Bloesch, who criticizes Barth for failing to hold together the subjective and objective poles of salvation.[34] Bloesch accuses Barth of a "theological rationalism" which over-emphasizes the objective pole to the neglect of the subjective. "Even in speaking of the subjective appropriation," writes Bloesch, "Barth has in mind primarily Jesus Christ in humanity and secondarily those who are engrafted into Christ."[35]

But this kind of criticism fails to take into account the aspect of the participation of humanity in the history of Jesus Christ, according to Barth.[36] Barth does not deny the subjective aspect: "Everything has happened *to us*" (the emphasis is mine). He sees the root of our human nature in the "history," the human nature of Christ: "...but in the context of the person of the Son." This is because the history of Christ is "a story which has come to pass," as it is related in the narratives of the Gospels.[37] Within the "fact" of the Gospel narrative lies the "significance." We cannot find the "significance" outside of the reality of the "fact." "significance" is not something which we add on according to our own whims and desires. This is made with a simple, yet profound, boldness in the Gospel narrative, where the gospel story is told without an intended interpretation.[38]

---

33   Ibid.

34   Donald G. Bloesch, *Jesus is Victor! Karl Barth's Doctrine of Salvation* (Nashville: Abingdon, 1976), p. 10.

35   Ibid., pp. 10-11.

36   Cf., Barth, *CD* IV/4, p. 21: Christ "creates in the history of every man the beginning of his new history..." Cf. Bloesch, p. 60.

37   Barth, *CD* IV/1, p. 223. Barth's theology is related to the contemporary concerns of "narrative theology" in David Ford, *Barth and God's Story: Biblical Narrative and the Theological Method of Karl Barth in the "Church Dogmatics"* (Frankfurt am Main: P. Lang, 1981).

38   The fact of the different theologies of the evangelists does not lessen the truth of this statement. Even if these theologies are admitted, the clear *intent* of the

The New Testament description of this "history" speaks of a particular, once for all event which consists of three parts. The first consists of the sayings and acts of Jesus in Galilee, where he is in control, and, in a sense, remote from others in his purity.[39] The second part consists of Gethsemane and the Passion.[40] Jesus is no longer the subject but the object of what happens. A judgment takes place, not upon the guilty, but upon the Judge.

The real commentary is in the third part of the story, the resurrection narrative.[41] It tells us that the gospel story is "significant in itself." There is no power beyond the object which can cause it to become significant. In the case of Jesus, it is the power of the Judge to take the place of those who are judged, "the power of the corresponding becoming." Therefore our subjectivity is not something which could begin to add anything to this greatest of "facts."

> He speaks for Himself whenever He is spoken of and
> His story is told and heard. It is not He that needs
> proclamation but proclamation that needs Him.[42]

In addition, if Christ is present today, one cannot relegate the history of Jesus Christ to the past. No, it is "a history which is the new history for every man."[43] The reality of salvation is found for Barth not in the history of the religious experiences of humanity but in the history of one man, the man who has taken the place of humanity in judgment.

THE MEANING OF "FOR US"

Barth has thus far spoken, in general terms, of the nature of God as *pro nobis*, as judge, and the significance of the "history" of Jesus Christ as the expression of God being for us, the one

---

authors was to simply tell the story of Jesus and let the significance of the story be found within the "fact" of the story itself.

[39] Barth, *CD* IV/1, pp. 224-225.

[40] Ibid., pp. 225-226.

[41] Ibid., p. 227.

[42] Ibid., pp. 227-228.

[43] Ibid., p. 228.

who took our place in judgment. The balance of his discussion will be based on a detailed exposition of the meaning and implications of God being "for us" in Jesus Christ.

Before Barth begins his lengthy exposition of "for us," he prefaces it with a discussion of the meaning of "for us" through looking at what it does not mean. First, "for us" does not mean that what took place in Christ simply "applies to us."[44] As we have seen, for Barth there is a unity between the fact and the significance of the Incarnation. There is no separate "application" of the gospel to humanity apart from the significance which is found within the history of Jesus Christ.

Second, it is not sufficient to say that he is "for us" merely in the sense that he is "with us." The solidarity of the eternal Son with humanity is not simply Jesus walking beside us as our "fellow man" who enters into the redemptive act with us.[45] No, it is his existence which is the basis for the redemptive event. The redemptive event is the happening in which he "embraces us in His existence." The "for us" is prior to the "with us," for he came to us when we were without strength, were godless, and were his enemies (Rom. 5:6f). The event is prior to the question of our obedient or disobedient decision. "For us" means something which takes our place, to which we can add nothing.

THE EXPOSITION OF "FOR US"

Barth states that Jesus Christ is "for us" because he took our place as judge.[46] Instead of the arrogance of humanity which assumes the place of judge, God has intervened in Jesus Christ, having claimed that place for himself, and has judged the sin of humanity. This is not simply an intellectual exposure of the arrogance of humanity, but a taking away of its place by the humanity of Christ. This is the radicality of the vicarious nature of the humanity of Christ in Barth's doctrine of the atonement. Such radicality has great implications for the comprehensiveness of the gospel, since "Jesus as very man and very God has taken the place

---

44   Ibid.
45   Ibid., p. 229.
46   Ibid., p. 231.

of every man." Ethical implications are relevant here, also. This is
a "replacement," not a new prohibition or commandment from
eating the fruit from the tree of the knowledge of good and evil. In
summary, "replacement" speaks of "vicarious humanity."

The result of this "replacement" means not only the
"abasement and jeopardising" of humanity, but also its "liberation
and hope." The "abasement and jeopardising of every man" puts
an end to the arrogance of humanity.[47] It is significant that this is
not by another man, but by "the concrete form of a fellow man."
The "representative" aspect of the atonement, such as we have
found in John McLeod Campbell, has a definite place in Barth.
Since this "abasement" is by "God in the flesh," it is "a dangerous
matter." The result is that I can judge no longer. I am "jeopardised" in my place as judge.

But there is also an "immeasurable liberation and hope."[48]
There is "liberation" from the burden of having to judge. There is
"hope" in that I can trust myself into the hands of a judge who is
able to be far more just than anyone could attempt to be.

The radical nature of what Barth is saying here has at times
eluded some critics. George Hendry claims that the true
"exchange" in the atonement is not, as Barth says, the exchange of
responsibility, the innocent for the guilty, but the exchange of the
debt of humanity to the judgment of God with the forgiveness of
God.[49] The influence of Campbell's emphasis on forgiveness is
obvious here, but without his stress on the vicarious humanity of
Christ. Hendry seems to lessen the radical nature of the
"exchange" when he fails to see that the root issue is the totality of
humanity and its sin, a radicality which Barth is able to perceive. It
is not simply a principle of forgiveness which is exchanged, but
the very humanity of God as it exists in the eternal Son made
flesh.[50]

---

47 Ibid., p. 233.

48 Ibid., p. 233-234.

49 George S. Hendry, *The Gospel of the Incarnation* (Philadelphia: Westminster
Press, 1958), p. 113.

50 Cf. Barth's stimulating essay, "The Humanity of God" in *The Humanity of
God*, pp. 37-65.

A similar problem exists in Colin Brown's study on Barth. Brown criticizes Barth for making Christ "the universal object of judgment" rather than "the universal criterion of judgment."[51] John Thompson has responded to these charges with two points:[52] 1) The universality of the atonement is based on the universality of Christ's judgment in becoming sin for us. If the latter is not so, then Brown must hold to a limited atonement. 2) There is no distinction for Brown between the judgment which Christ bore on the cross and the judgment in the end times. Barth's "universalism" does not exclude the possibility of some being judged at the last. A third response may be added: A criticism such as Brown's does not seem to see the significance of the radical depth of Christ's substitution for humanity. To speak of Christ as simply the "universal criterion of judgment" does not affect humanity in its totality, past, present, and future. A judge may rightly sentence a criminal, but the minute the criminal leaves the courtroom, he is free from any obligation to that judge. The entire autonomous, arrogant existence of humanity as sinners is "jeopardised," to use Barth's word, by the fact that Christ has taken our place, not only at the moment of legal acquittal in the past, but also in the present and in the future.

Barth's second statement concerning "for us" deals with the nature of this place which has been taken by Christ. It is the place of *sinners*:[53] "Jesus Christ was and is for us in that He took the place of us sinners." But how could the Son take "the strange place" of rebellion against God?

In the first place, Christ "accepts responsibility" for what we have done in this place. "And as He does that, it ceases to be our sin." This statement may sound strong, but Barth sees it as a vital implication of what we mean when we say that Christ "accepts responsibility" for our sin. If it is his responsibility now, it no longer belongs to our domain.

Secondly, this responsibility means that Jesus has taken upon himself the condemnation of all humanity. As "the electing God" and "the elect man," he is also "the rejecting God" and "the

---

51   Brown, *Karl Barth and the Christian Message,* p. 134.

52   Thompson, p. 167, n. 38.

53   Barth, *CD* IV/1, pp. 235-236.

one rejected man."[54] Barth's concern here is to have a theology which expresses the movement of "the mystery of the divine mercy" *within* sinful humanity, not external to it.[55] If salvation is going to affect the total human being, it must come from an onto-logical, internal basis, not an external act upon it. Therefore, this necessitates the assumption by Christ of our *fallen* human na-ture.[56]

H. Cunliffe-Jones calls attention to what he considers to be "the disastrous retrogression to the uncritical use of the penal sub-stitutionary theory in the theology of Karl Barth."[57] However, Roger White has pointed out that Cunliffe-Jones is wrong to clas-sify Barth's doctrine as identical with traditional penal theories.[58] White cites Barth's views that Christ's punishment does not spare us from suffering the punishment ourselves, and his reinterpreta-tion of the view that Christ "satisfied" the wrath of God.[59] In ad-

---

54   Ibid., p. 235-236.

55   Ibid., p. 237. Cp. II/2, pp. 103-105, 118-120 and the discussion in G. W. Bromiley, *Historical Theology: An Introduction* (Grand Rapids: Eerdmans, 1978), pp. 430-433.

56   Barth, *CD* IV/1, p. 237.

57   See the discussion of Barth and others on this topic in Harry Johnson, *The Humanity of the Savior*. Johnson's book is a persuasive defense of Barth's position that the humanity which Christ assumed was "fallen human nature." (Cf. Barth's fullest exposition of this in I/2, pp. 151f. Johnson discusses Barth on pp. 167-170.) Both true solidarity with humanity and the "corporate personality" of Christ demand this, according to Johnson (p. 219). If Christ possessed a "perfect human nature," there would still be a "deep and humanly impassable abyss" created by sin (p. 211). Based upon the Pauline doctrine that death came into the world because of Adam's sins Rom. 5:12, 15, 17; 6:23; I Cor. 15:21-22), one cannot explain the atoning death of Christ if it is not the death of "fallen human nature" (pp. 111-112). But he was subject to death because of his assumption of fallen human nature, not because of personal sin. Johnson differentiates between "fallen human nature" and personal acts of sin, relying heavily upon I Corinthians 5:21: "For our sake he [God] made him to be sin who knew no sin, so that in him we might become the righteousness of God" (pp. 101-102).

58   H. Cunliffe-Jones, "The Meaning of the Atonement Today," *Theology* 74 (March, 1971), p. 119.

59   Roger White, "Substitution in Karl Barth," *Theology* 74 (June, 1971), p. 218.

dition, Barth's emphasis on Christ as "rejected man" is rarely found in traditional penal theories.

On the other side of the theological spectrum, David Wells claims that, while Barth affirms the fact that Jesus took humanity's place, doing what humanity could not do for itself, he does not affirm that the atonement is the means by which God's attitude is changed towards humanity.[60] It is true that at this point, Barth is at odds with some conservative theories, but for good reason. Is it really God's attitude, or is it the situation of humanity, that needs to be changed? Barth opts for the latter, for God's attitude towards humanity has always and always will be an attitude of grace.[61] John McLeod Campbell is also in sympathy with Barth when he says that the Incarnation was "a peculiar development of the holy sorrow in which He bore the burden of our sins."[62] As James B. Torrance has shown, "evangelical repentance," the priority of forgiveness before the need for repentance, is rooted in Calvin.[63] If the attitude of God needs to be changed, as Wells contends, could this ever really be possible? What external force or necessity could coerce God to change? The good news is that *God* has made the initiative towards us in his grace, and, as Barth takes pains to show, he does this totally without any help on our part.

According to Barth, when Christ takes our place as sinners, he does not do this as a masquerade, or simply an exchange in appearance.[64] Again, Barth's concern to avoid docetism is obvious. The exchange is rather the "bitter earnest" of God to take up our evil case and to make it "his own."

But what place does Barth have then for the sinlessness of Christ? Surprisingly, it is precisely in consideration of Christ taking the place of sinners, and becoming "the one great sinner" that Barth sees the true meaning of the sinlessness of Christ. The sin-

---

[60] Barth, *CD* IV/1, p. 253.

[61] Wells, *The Search for Salvation*, p. 60.

[62] Cf. Barth on "Creation as the External Basis of the Covenant," *CD* III/2, pp. 94f.

[63] Campbell, *Atonement*, p. 136.

[64] James B. Torrance, "The Contribution of John McLeod Campbell to Scottish Theology," *Scottish Journal of Theology*, p. 307; Calvin, *Institutes*, 3.3.1.

lessness of Jesus is based on the obedience of Jesus, who did not refuse to be delivered up and to take the place of sinners.

Barth's conclusion is that Christ, having taken on the condemnation of the world, has delivered humanity from "the intolerable responsibility" for sin.[65] "Our sin is no longer our own. It is His sin, the sin of Jesus Christ." The implication of this rather startling statement is similar to the doctrine of "vicarious repentance" in John McLeod Campbell and R. C. Moberly. In taking away the sin from humanity, Christ has become "the one great sinner."[66] Barth is able to say this because he has already qualified it in light of his definition of the sinlessness of Christ. The sinlessness of Christ is the action of the obedient Son of God in taking the place of sinners and, therefore, becoming "the one great sinner." In a remarkable way, Barth uses the very argument usually held against "vicarious repentance," the sinlessness of Christ, as foundation for the doctrine.

Barth then encapsulates the "scope" of Christ taking our place as sinners into three directions: 1) There is a knowledge of the true reality and meaning of our sinful situation by the fact that Christ takes our place in judgment.[67] This is the place of confession of sin in a confession of faith[68].

2) As we have seen, Barth is often criticized for overemphasizing the "objective" aspect of the atonement to the neglect of the "subjective" aspect. This is answered to some extent by the second point: We must say most emphatically that the place which he has taken is *our* evil place.[69] It is true that we cannot contribute anything to the work of Christ.

> But it is also true that the place from which we find ourselves crowded out is always our place....To look in faith on the One who took our place means always to see ourselves in Him as the men we are, to recog-

---

[65] Barth, *CD* IV/1, p. 237.
[66] Ibid., p. 238.
[67] Ibid., p. 239.
[68] Ibid., p. 240.
[69] Ibid., p. 241.

nize ourselves in Him as the men for whom He as taken responsibility, who are forgiven.[70]

3) The effect of the substitution by Christ is to remove all ground for our standing as sinners. We have "no other ground to do evil now that the ground has been cut off from under our feet."[71] This is because Jesus Christ has become "the one great sinner." "Vicarious repentance" again plays an important role in Barth's doctrine of the atonement. George Hendry criticizes Barth for saying that Christ took upon himself the responsibility for the sins of humanity.[72] However, as much as it may be true that the recorded words of Jesus do not state this, it is hard to understand the baptism of Jesus, among other acts of Jesus, apart from an idea of "vicarious repentance" ("...for thus it is fitting for us to fulfill all righteousness," Mt. 3:15).

The third aspect of "for us" in Barth's thought is the place of the suffering and death of Jesus: "Jesus Christ was and is for us in that He suffered and was crucified and died."[73] Based upon the previous discussion, this is the "aim" of the Incarnation.[74]

Several features of the meaning behind Christ's suffering and death are elaborated upon by Barth. It is an individual action in history, not the result of fate.[75] This is consistent with his view that the atonement is an expression of the freedom of God, not the result of an external necessity. A similar teaching is found in John McLeod Campbell, where the sufferings of Jesus express "the living will and heart of Jesus," not simply fate or necessity.[76] This

---

70 Ibid.

71 Ibid., p. 243.

72 Hendry, p. 112.

73 Barth, *CD* IV/1, p. 244.

74 Ibid.

75 Cf. Anselm: The "gift" which Christ gives is not simply human obedience to God, which is required of "every rational creature," but "giving his life, or laying down his life, giving himself up to death for the honor of God." "Why God Became Man," in *A Scholastic Miscellany*. Ed. Eugene A. Fairweather (New York: Macmillan, 1970), 2.11.

76 Barth, *CD* IV/1, pp. 244-245.

is "the strength of sonship" for Campbell: "The cup which *my Father* hath given me to drink, shall I not drink it?" (Jn. 18:11).[77]

This passion is also an act of God which forever changes the situation of humanity objectively, whether one knows it or not.[78] However, Barth is quick to add, *contra* many critics, that there is a genuine place for individual faith:

> The knowledge of it as the act of God and the knowl-
> edge of the change in the world situation brought about
> by it can come about individually only in the decision
> of faith....[79]

Donald Bloesch complains that Barth does not give a prominent enough place for faith. But it is highly questionable whether we would want to call faith, as Bloesch does, a "cause" of salvation.[80] Is there any "cause" above the free act of God himself? Bloesch properly describes Barth's definition of faith as the "response" to salvation, but curiously rejects this as a valid definition.

Such a definition of faith is consistent with Barth's position on the "objectivity" of salvation in Jesus Christ, which he continues to explore in this section. At this point, the deity of Christ becomes important. The significance of the human suffering of Jesus is not simply in the degree of suffering. Many others have suffered more, humanly speaking. The significance is in the fact that it is God who has humiliated himself, the judge has let himself be judged.[81] We are dealing here with "the suffering of God," the

---

[77] Campbell, *Atonement,* pp. 251-252.

[78] Barth, *CD* IV/1, p. 245.

[79] Ibid.

[80] Bloesch, p. 109. Bloesch cites Jonathan Edwards approvingly as an example of his position: Faith is "the grand condition of the covenant of Christ, by which we are in Christ." "A Humble Inquiry into the Qualifications of Full Communion in the Visible Church of Christ" in *Works of President Edwards,* Vol. 4, ed. Serano E. Dwight (New York: S. Converse, 1829-1830), p. 321; cited by Bloesch, p. 109..

[81] Barth, *CD* IV/1, p. 246.

excruciating encounter of God with the powers of evil and nothingness.[82]

Then Barth returns to the question of faith, but looks at faith
from the perspective of its object, Jesus Christ.[83] He finds this to
be the approach of the New Testament. This act in space and time
is not simply the result of "the true teaching of pious and thought-
ful people," but an act proclaimed concerning Jesus Christ himself. "In this and this alone, it is the act of God for us. With this
there stands or falls the truth of Christian experience."[84]

This "objectivity" means that the act of God in Jesus Christ
is also "self-explanatory." It does not need our feeble attempts to
understand or explain it. The Lord's Supper is a clear example of
this. "This is my body" simply points to Jesus Christ himself. The
role of faith is to confess that this act of God in Jesus Christ has
happened. It is not "a pessimistic anthropology" or "an exagger-
ated doctrine of sin" which emphasizes the inability of humanity.
It is not simply the act of God, but the vicarious act of God in human flesh, the "flesh" of Jesus Christ which keeps it from being
simply an external act.

> What He has done He has done without us, without
> the world, without the counsel or help of that which is
> flesh and lives in the flesh—except only for the flesh of
> Jesus Christ.[85]

A further implication of the "objectivity" of the act of God in
Jesus Christ for Barth is the comprehensive nature of the gospel.
Since Christ is the One who embraces the Many, reconciliation has
a comprehensive scope, with pronounced universalistic tendencies: "In Him the world is converted to God."[86]

Barth's emphasis on the place of the act of God in the suffering and dying of Jesus is meant to counter the tendency in Latin
theology to regard Christ as a man making atonement on humanity's behalf, but without a strong consciousness of this as also an

---

82 Ibid.
83 Ibid., p. 247.
84 Ibid., p. 248.
85 Ibid., p. 249.
86 Ibid., p. 251.

act of God. Without the place of the act of God in the cross, atonement is merely a human sacrifice and God is not the effective agent of redemption.[87] This emphasis on the act of God in the suffering and dying of Jesus has led Hendry to criticize Barth for ascribing only "an instrumental place" to the humanity of Christ in the atonement.[88] But this is certainly not the case. The essential role of Christ taking upon our fallen human nature and being "the one great sinner," not to mention the entire thrust of Barth's substitution doctrine, Christ radically taking our place in every respect, argues plainly against such a charge. Salvation comes through Christ "treading the way of sinners to its bitter end in death, in destruction, in the limitless anguish of separation from God...."[89]

Penal substitution is revived by Barth, but it is important to notice the context in which he deals with it. The "decisive thing" is not that Christ has endured the punishment which we deserve. But it is true only in the context of the passion taking place "in His own person," making "an end of us as sinners... as the One who took our place as sinners.as that of the one great sinner."[90] Satisfaction is not meant to placate the offended honor of God but to satisfy the radical divine love by "killing... extinguishing... removing" humanity through the passion of Christ.[91]

"Jesus Christ was and is for us in that He has done this before God and has therefore done right."[92] The "for us" in Jesus

---

[87] Ibid.

[88] Hendry, pp. 127-128.

[89] Cf. Irenaeus: "The Word of God, however, the Maker of all things, conquering him [the devil] by means of human nature, and showing him to be apostate, has, on the contrary, put him under the power of man." "Against Heresies," in *The Ante-Nicene Fathers,* Vol. 1. Ed. Alexander Roberts and James Donaldson (Grand Rapids: Eerdmans, 1950), 5.24.4. Gustav Aulén comments: "When Irenaeus speaks in this connection of the 'obedience' of Christ, he has not thought of a human offering made to God from man's side, but rather that the Divine will wholly dominated the human life of the Word of God and found perfect expression in His work." *Christus Victor,* trans. A. G. Hebert (New York: Macmillan, 1969), p. 33.

[90] Barth, *CD* IV/1, p. 253.

[91] Ibid., pp. 253-254.

[92] Ibid., pp. 254-255.

Christ expressed as the judge judged in our place, for Barth, is the negative expression of "a positive divine righteousness" which is identical with the free love of God. As is common to Barth, the "Yes" and "No" of God are not equally substantial opposites but, rather, the "No" is simply "the negative form" of God's constant "Yes" toward humanity. The reality of this negative form is found in the obedience of Christ, the just man who is just for the sake of the unjust (I Pet. 3:18).[93] Atonement for Barth means the presentation of a positive human righteousness before God which actually does right. Similar to Campbell, there is an atoning aspect to the obedience of Jesus, an expression of the omnipotence of God over sin and death, based on Christ's humanity taking our place.

How is the obedience of Christ significant? It is significant as the basis for a radically new human freedom. In sin, in disobedience, humanity loses its freedom. This is a repudiation, not only of its relationship with God, but also a repudiation of the true nature of humanity as creatures of God. In Jesus Christ, his obedience demonstrates the true relationship between obedience and human freedom.

> He is true to his own nature as the creature of God, the creature which is appointed in its own decision to follow and correspond to the decisions of God, to follow and correspond to the decisions of God in its decisions which are its own.[94]

The obedience of Christ is also significant as the basis for the sinlessness of Christ in Barth's thought. The sinlessness of Christ is not a kind of abstract purity but "the act of His being," a positive obedience in the face of temptation.[95] Sinlessness is something active, not passive, for Barth. This is expressed in the life of Jesus and explicitly in the temptation narrative and the scene in Gethsemane. He is "the one great sinner" who confesses the sins of humanity and becomes the one lost sheep, the one lost coin, the lost son (Lk. 15:3f.) in order to take their place in judgment.

---

[93] Ibid., p. 257.
[94] Ibid.
[95] Ibid., p. 259.

Barth demonstrates through his perceptive exegesis of the temptation narratives in the Gospels how deeply woven is the theme of the vicarious repentance of Christ into the Gospel narratives themselves. He believes that it is significant that the temptation narratives are placed directly after the baptism of Jesus.[96] In this way they serve as expositions of what it means for Jesus to confess the sins of humanity. Even the reference to the fasting of Jesus points to humanity's acknowledgement of its unworthiness to life, and, therefore, to repentance.

The central theme of the temptations, according to Barth, is the temptation not to go the way of sinners, the way of a great sinner repenting.[97] Either to use the power of God to save his own life, to acknowledge the lordship of Satan, or to become the "religious person," throwing himself down from the temple on the basis of "his own robust faith," would mean a denial of both a genuine repentance before God of humanity's sins and a genuine solidarity with humanity in its sinful situation. Both aspects are important to Barth: Jesus Christ is "the one great sinner *repenting*" and "the one great *sinner* repenting." Both obedience and solidarity are involved in Barth's doctrine of vicarious repentance.[98]

The total inability of humanity which brings about the need for vicarious repentance, and the total obedience of Jesus, the basis of vicarious repentance, is also expressed in the episode of Gethsemane. In the midst of Jesus' darkest hour, the disciples left him, that is, "the apostolate, the community, Christendom, the Church" failed him.[99]

> If there is anything which brings out clearly this simple "for us" as the content of the Gospel, then it is this aspect of the event in Gethsemane, in which the act of God in Jesus Christ had absolutely nothing to corre-

---

[96] Ibid., p. 260.

[97] Ibid., p. 261,

[98] In Irenaeus, Christ's victory over the devil is the victory of the human race: "Against Heresies," 5.21.2. Cf. Franks, *History*, Vol. 1, p. 40.

[99] Barth, *CD* IV/1, p. 267.

spond to it in the existence of those who believe in
Him.[100]

But at the same time, in the midst of the total inability of humanity,
there is expressed the total obedience of Jesus, the response of
"Thy will be done" (Mt. 26:42).[101] This is an obedience which
may only receive "the sign of Jonah," but it still praises and
knows the One who transcends our thoughts and is "holy, just,
and gracious." In this prayer Barth finds the "completion" of the
penitence and obedience which was begun at the Jordan and which
was maintained in the wilderness.[102] Therefore, this prayer is the
"positive content" of the suffering and death of Jesus. As in
Campbell's thought, the atonement is not seen as an autonomous
event, but as the "development" of the Incarnation.[103]

CULTIC AND FORENSIC APPROACHES COMPARED

The last part of "The Judge Judged in our Place" is a section
that seems to be almost an afterthought by Barth on the relationship between the cultic and forensic approaches to the atonement.[104] After a short description of other alternatives, the
"financial" imagery and the "military" view, which Barth says
both lack comprehensiveness, he proceeds to a discussion of the
cultic approach. This approach has a "sufficient distinctness and
importance to merit a special appraisal." This merit derives from
its pervasiveness in the New Testament, particularly in Hebrews,
Paul, and John, a pervasiveness due no doubt to its relation to Old
Testament cultic language, e.g., "the Lamb of God," "His blood."
However, Barth decides not to emphasize this approach because
of its remoteness from the contemporary situation, and because the
forensic teaching is more "distinct" and "comprehensive" than the
cultic view.[105]

---

100 Ibid., p. 268.
101 Ibid., p. 271.
102 Ibid., p. 272.
103 Campbell, *Atonement*, xx.
104 Barth, *CD* IV/1, p. 274.
105 Ibid., p. 276.

Nevertheless, Barth proceeds to delineate ways in which the cultic approach expresses the same ideas as his four points which define the meaning of "for us." The first point, "Jesus Christ took our place as Judge" is expressed in cultic language as the priest who represents us.[106] The work of Christ is "at once the essence and fulfillment of all other priestly work but also that which replaces it and makes it superfluous."[107] As the judge takes the place of humanity in the area of judgment so, also, the priest take the place of all priestly work by humanity.[108]

The second and third forensic points of "for us" are combined into one from a priestly perspective: As the one "accursed, condemned and judged in the place of us sinners," he is also the "sacrifice to take away our sins."[109] The judge who is judged is also the priest who is sacrificed.[110] Again, the importance of atonement as the act of God is stressed by Barth, this time in terms of sacrifice as an actual response to the commandment of the living God, provisional in the Old Testament, fulfilled in Jesus Christ, where "God's own activity and being" takes place.[111] In Jesus Christ as the priest who gives himself to be sacrificed, "God not only demands but He gives what He demands." It is important to note that Barth sees the significance for the cultic approach also in Christ's solidarity with sinful human nature to the point of his becoming "the greatest of all sinners" (vicarious repentance).[112]

Barth's fourth point, "Jesus Christ was just in our place," which speaks of the obedience of Christ, is also fulfilled in the motif of sacrifice. In Christ the priest has been offered as a perfect

---

[106] Ibid.

[107] Ibid., p. 276.

[108] Ibid., p. 277.

[109] Ibid.

[110] Cf. Calvin, *Institutes,* 3.15.6. Again, it is curious that Barth does not mention the history of doctrine at this point. Cf. G. W. Bromiley, "Atone, III. The History of the Doctrine," *International Standard Bible Encyclopedia, Revised,* Vol. 1, p. 358; Francois Wendel, *Calvin: The Origins and Development of His Religious Thought,* trans. Philip Mairet (New York: Harper and Row, 1963), p. 226.

[111] Barth, *CD* IV/1, pp. 278-280.

[112] Ibid., p. 281.

sacrifice.[113] The will of God has been obeyed. "The time of being has dawned in place of that of signifying." The sacrifice which God will not despise has been lifted up: a broken spirit and contrite heart (Ps. 51:9). Judgment now runs down like waters and righteousness as a mighty stream (Amos 5:24). The evil works of humanity are removed from God's sight. "The doing of evil ceases. It has now learned how to do good." The right is now regarded, violence is restrained, and the orphans and widows taken up (Isa. 1:16f.). "All these things have now taken place: 'by the one which will (the taking place of the sacrificial action of Jesus Christ) we are sanctified.'"[114]

"THE JUDGE JUDGED IN OUR PLACE" AND THE REALITY OF SALVATION

Some concluding remarks are now in order. We will relate the substance of Barth's presentation to the question of the reality of salvation under four headings: 1) The act of God and vicarious humanity, 2) The radical substitution by Christ, 3) The question of "objective" atonement, and 4) The emphasis on forensic atonement.

The Act of God and Vicarious Humanity

Barth takes pains to emphasize the importance of atonement as an act of God. Here we have no bare anthropological, sociological, or cultural myth, but an actual interaction of God with human history. In the obedience of his Son, God has gone into "the far country" of sinful human flesh. This comes from an initiation of God alone. Certainly this is related to the prominence of grace in Barth's theology. At every point, Barth seeks to demonstrate that, from a theological point of view, salvation is God's act alone, not half God's and half humanity's. Jesus Christ has radically destroyed the place of humanity's arrogance in desiring to be its own Judge. Certainly this primacy of the act of God in salvation is for Barth an indication of the priority of forgiveness in his

---

[113] Ibid.

[114] Ibid., p. 282.

theology, *contra* George Hendry.[115] The emphasis on the act of God, an act motivated by his grace, means that the forgiveness of God is not contingent upon the penal act of atonement. The penal act of atonement is thus the *result* of the forgiveness of God, not the cause of it.

Yet this humanity is not left without a replacement, according to Barth. This is the place of the vicarious humanity of Christ in Barth's doctrine of the atonement. Barth's doctrine can certainly be misunderstood without taking this aspect into account. "New humanity" has taken the place of "old humanity." The seriousness with which Barth takes the Apostle Paul's teaching in Romans 6 is quite obvious here.

Since Christ has taken the place of the "old humanity," salvation has a comprehensiveness which extends to all humanity. This presents an interesting perspective on Barth's well known universalistic tendencies. Whatever conclusions we may draw concerning the truth of Barth's teaching on the comprehensiveness of the gospel, it must be admitted that Barth grounds his "universalism" on an understanding of the vicarious humanity of Christ. God did not take on only the flesh of some particular human beings, but of all humanity. So also, Christ took the place of every human being: "Jesus Christ as very man and very God has taken the place of every man."[116] Likewise, since conversion is the act of God and not simply the act of humanity, he can say, "In Him the world is converted to God." Bernard Ramm has rightly seen this emphasis in Barth as an expression of Barth's emphasis upon the lordship of God, a desire to be faithful to Paul's Christ-Adam teaching, and a Christian sensitivity to the billions of people who have never heard the gospel.[117] As Barth has made it very clear in "The Judge Judged in our Place," God is not tied to any external necessity. His grace is under his control alone. To quickly write off the fate of myriads of people is to reject the freedom and limit the love of God. In addition, Barth's emphasis on Christ as the Last Adam indicates the profound biblical basis of his

---

[115] Hendry, p. 133.

[116] Barth, *CD* IV/1, p. 232.

[117] Bernard Ramm, *After Fundamentalism: The Future of Evangelical Theology* (San Francisco: Harper and Row, 1983), pp. 170-172.

teaching.[118] This is clearly related to the direction in "The Judge Judged in our Place." If Christ is the Last Adam, then as the first Adam was the representative of all humanity, so also is the Last Adam. All people, of all races and nationalities are now included in his humanity. Their lives have significance because of Jesus Christ, even before they make a personal faith commitment.

The Radical Substitution by Christ

This discussion naturally leads us to the significance of the radical nature of the replacement of humanity by Christ in Barth. *Contra* Campbell, Barth is able to use substitution as a workable expression of the atonement, if it is understood radically enough. For this purpose, it must be integrally related to the vicarious humanity of Christ. Substitution means that the whole human being is replaced by the new human being, Jesus Christ. Substitution does not simply occur at a moment of time on the cross, but partakes in the entirety of the relationship between Christ's existence and our existence. To leave one area to human autonomy is to presume that sinful humanity can add to the inexpressible reality of the grace of God.

The reality of salvation as expressed by substitution is demonstrated by Barth in several ways. The solidarity of Christ with humanity through substitution, solidarity in humanity's sinful situation, is a profound expression of the depth of God's love. The reality of salvation is not be found in platonic forms, but in human flesh, the humanity of "the Word made flesh."

The extent to which Christ is in solidarity with sinners, according to Barth, is seen in Christ as "the one great sinner" (Barth's doctrine of vicarious repentance). As in Campbell and Moberly, in Barth this is integrally related to the inability of humanity. God in Christ undertakes to do himself "what the world cannot do, creating and reversing its course to the abyss."[119] This is the meaning of the disciples sleeping while Jesus prays at Gethsemane. The disciples represent "the apostolate, the commu-

---

[118] Karl Barth, *Christ and Adam,* trans. T. A. Smail (New York: Macmillan, 1968).

[119] Barth, *CD* IV/1, pp. 267-268.

nity, Christendom, the Church." They can contribute nothing to
the prayer of Jesus. "In doing this for Himself Jesus does it for
them, and 'for them' in the strictest sense, in their place."[120] This
is the whole point of Barth's major exposition on the four aspects
of what it means for God to be "for us" in Jesus Christ. There is
nothing that we can add to the "for us."[121]

Barth's unique contribution to the doctrine of vicarious repentance is in his treatment of both the *solidarity* of Christ with
sinners and the *obedience* of Christ as atoning work. In other
words, Christ is both the one great *sinner* who repents (in solidarity with humanity) and the one great sinner who *repents* (obedient
to the Father to the point of repenting for the sins of the world). It
is in this sense that Barth speaks of Gesthemane as the
"completion" of the penitence and obedience which had begun at
the Jordan with Jesus' baptism. Solidarity with sinners and
obedience to the Father are knit together.[122] "In Him God not only
demands but He gives what He demands."[123]

The Question of "Objective" Atonement

As we have seen, Barth is often criticized for overemphasizing the "objective" aspect of the atonement. The result of this, it
is claimed, is that there is no place for the atonement to affect humanity, nor is there a place for faith. In other words, Barth's
stress on the "objective" aspect makes it much more difficult to
speak of the reality of salvation. Indeed, the thesis throughout this
study that the place of the reality of salvation is in God himself
could come under this criticism.

Our contention is, quite the contrary, that Barth has provided
a decisive insight into the reality of salvation through his
"objective" approach, when it is seen in light of the vicarious hu-

---

[120] Ibid., p. 268.
[121] Ibid., p. 273. According to Bromiley, for Barth, "the fourfold act of the 'for
us'... constitutes the center not only of the theology of reconciliation but of
all theology," *Introduction to the Theology of Karl Barth* (Grand Rapids:
Eerdmans, 1979), p. 182.
[122] Barth, *CD* IV/1, p. 272.
[123] Ibid., p. 280.

manity of Christ. Because the humanity of Christ, which is the
basis for our humanity, is a part of "the history of Jesus Christ," it
transcends the dualism of the typical dichotomy between
"objective" and "subjective."[124] The "fact" of Jesus Christ brings
with it its own "significance"[125] because we are no longer speaking about that which only "signifies," as in the Old Testament sacrifices, but "being" itself, the Being of God in the flesh. Within
the Being of God exists our humanity. Therefore, Barth's emphasis on the "objectivity" of the atonement speaks of a reality which
goes beyond the shifting sands of human experience and perception into the reality of God himself. The reality of God is the reality of salvation. And where is the reality of God to be found? It is
found in the history of Jesus Christ alone.

This means that the reality of evil and the reality of faith are
to be understood in a radically different way. Barth speaks of the
loss of "the ground to do evil" when one looks at Jesus Christ.[126]
Barth is not ignoring the actual fact of evil. What he is saying is
that in Jesus Christ the possibilities for evil have lost their foundations. As the individual and the world increasingly participate in
Jesus Christ, there is no place for evil to go. Christ is progres-
sively "squeezing" evil out of the world.

So also, faith is radically qualified by substitution. Barth
does have a place for individual faith, but it is faith devoid of any
"ground" for it to stand on by itself.[127] As he explains concerning
the self-explanatory nature of the saying of Jesus, "This is my
body," there is a power in this event itself which does not need
faith to bring meaning to it. Faith can (and must) simply confess
the truth of the event.[128] The redemptive event means that we are
embraced by his existence.[129] Therefore, Barth can say rather
boldly that justice has come, the orphans are comforted, salvation
has arrived, but only as we see it *in Christ*, not merely in the phe-

---

124   Ibid., p. 223. Cf. the critique of "objectivity" and "subjectivity" as a
       dichotomy in modern thought in T. F. Torrance, *Theological Science*, p. 1.
125   Barth, *CD* IV/1, p. 223.
126   Ibid., p. 281.
127   Ibid., p. 243.
128   Ibid., p. 245.
129   Ibid., pp. 245-246.

nomenal world, and least of all, in our own abilities and accomplishments. This is the Christian's "liberation and hope."[130]

The Emphasis on Forensic Atonement

Some concluding remarks need to be made concerning Barth's emphasis upon the forensic aspect of the atonement. Is this emphasis justified? As we have seen in the work of John McLeod Campbell, the use of forensic language for the atonement has certainly taken a beating in contemporary theology. Barth's emphasis in the contemporary context is quite rare.

It must be said at the outset that Barth has indeed presented some strong reasons for reviving the use of juridical language. If we accept Barth's understanding of the salvation of the whole person through radical substitution, which we do, our view of God's judgment upon sin must be as radical. Barth's view is much more comprehensive than Campbell's at this point. Campbell's view of vicarious repentance includes a place for judgment upon sin (Christ's confession was "a perfect Amen in humanity to the judgment of God on the sin of man"[131]), but his lack of substitutionary doctrine does not allow him to see that it is the entire "old human being" who is replaced, the first Adam by the Last Adam. Jesus is the one great sinner, the one lost sheep, the one lost coin, the lost son, as the judge who is judged.[132] The judgment of God upon sin in the atonement emphasizes that the Incarnation is saying something which we do not want to hear.[133] The Incarnation is God's judgment on the inability and folly of humanity's attempts to judge itself instead of allowing God to be the judge. This is a valuable insight into the meaning of the atonement.

However, it may be that there is a problem owing to the undue emphasis which Barth puts on the forensic aspect. Barth starts out section fifty-nine, "The Obedience of the Son of God" with the theme, "The Way of the Son of God into the Far Country." But

---

130 Ibid., p. 229.
131 Campbell, *Atonement*, p. 136.
132 Ibid., p. 233.
133 Ibid., p. 259.

then, quite inexplicably, "The Judge Judged in our Place" follows. This contrasts with John McLeod Campbell, who maintains throughout his soteriology the atoning significance of the relationship between the Father, the Son, and the sonship in which we share. This is not to say that the forensic aspect should be neglected. We have already seen how Barth has successfully revived its importance. But it seems rather questionable that, having started out with a soteriology of atoning sonship, Barth should leave the concept of sonship if he is endeavoring to answer the question, Why did the Lord become the servant, *Cur Deus Homo?* "With what purpose and to what end does God will this and do this?"[134] According to Paul, the answer is, so that we might become sons and daughters through the Son:

> But when the time had fully come, God sent forth his Son, born of woman, born under the Law, to redeem those who were under the Law, so that we might receive adoption as sons (Gal. 4:4-5).

The overemphasis on the forensic aspect seems to lead to the neglect of another picture of the atonement which is quite prominent in the Old Testament, as well as the New: the cultic. In fact, in coming across Barth's extended notes on the cultic view at the end of the section, one gets the impressions that in the last stages of his writing Barth realized his mistake and hurriedly inserted a rather forced defense for not emphasizing the cultic, while admitting its "distinctness" and worth for serious attention. Certainly his reason for not dealing with it in detail because of the distance of its Old Testament language and culture from us is quite meager, given Barth's own detailed exegesis of the Old Testament throughout the *Dogmatics*, not to mention his most emphatic stand in "The Way of the Son..." that "the Word made flesh" must be understood as "Jewish flesh."[135]

Notwithstanding these criticisms, Barth's presentation of the atonement provides unique insights into the significance of the vicarious humanity of Christ, not only for the question of the reality of salvation, but for all of theology.

---

134 Ibid., p. 201.
135 Ibid., p. 212.

CHAPTER ELEVEN

HUMANITY RESTORED:
CHRIST AS THE LAST ADAM
AND THE CHURCH AS THE BODY OF CHRIST

Amid the varieties of the issues which cause division among New Testament theologians on the nature of the atoning work of Christ, few have been more hotly contested than the role of Jesus Christ in the atonement. Is Jesus the representative of all humanity before God, and therefore our new humanity is grounded in his representative work, or is he the substitute for all humanity, the one who dies in our stead? Our thesis is that this discussion usually becomes trapped in lexical gymnastics and does not take into account the great implications of Christology and ecclesiology, seen in the context of salvation history. For this reason, we shall examine the relationship between the themes of Christ as the last Adam and Paul's idea of the church as the body of Christ for a possible fresh approach to the representation/substitution question, which particularly takes into account the problems which existed in Paul's churches, and most notably, in Corinth. Our hope is to use such a focus as a way to flesh out the *locus* of the reality of salvation in the world as found in the vicarious humanity of Christ expressed in the church as the body of Christ. As we have seen in the previous chapter, the first step in understanding the *locus* is to see "humanity displaced" in Christ as "the judge judged on our place," in a sense of radical substitution in the church. Our next step is to propose "humanity restored" in the flesh and blood existence of the empirical church, where, nevertheless, the reality of salvation is still found only in God himself, known in Jesus Christ.

Romans and I Corinthians are distinctive in the New Testament in that they are the only letters of Paul which share explicitly his teaching on Christ as the Last Adam and the church as the body of Christ. W. D. Davies suggests that the church as the body of Christ is based on Paul's teaching on Christ as the Last Adam.[1] If I Corinthians 12-15 is best interpreted as a unit, then it is likely that chapter 13 (on faith, hope and love) is to be understood in light of both chapter 12 (the church as the body of Christ) and chapter 15 (Christ as the Last Adam). Therefore, we propose that Christ as the Last Adam in Paul is the basis in his thinking for his ethical exhortations to the Corinthians. Paul is able to include chapter 13 because it is sandwiched between his teaching on the body of Christ (ch. 12) and Christ as the Last Adam (ch. 15). Christ is the representative of the new humanity, but this must be understood in tandem with Christ as substitute. The chaotic situation in Corinth makes plain to us that the church must allow Christ as the Last Adam to take their place, not only in death, but in life, in order for faith, hope, and love to be created in their own humanity.

Our discussion will begin with surveys of Adam in the Old Testament, with its basis and expression in the concept of the One and the Many in the Old Testament, the intertestamental period, hellenistic and rabbinic background, culminating in the place of Adam in Romans and I Corinthians. We will move to a similar survey of the church as the body of Christ in the New Testament, with a particular look at σῶμα. The last third of the study will summarize the relationship between Christ as the Last Adam and the church as the body of Christ, "the community of the Last Adam." Instrumental to this community is the work of the Spirit and thus, the ability to manifest concrete acts of faith, hope, and love as a witness to the reality of salvation. The atoning work of Christ as representative and substitute is the basis for this hope.

---

[1] W. D. Davies, *Paul and Rabbinic Judaism* (Philadelphia: Fortress Press, 1980 [1948]), p. 57.

CHRIST AS THE LAST ADAM

Adam in the Ancient World

1. Adam and the One and the Many in the Old Testament

'*Adam* is used over five hundred times in the Old Testament in the generic sense of "humankind."[2] The rare occurrence of a personified individual man is found in Genesis 1-5 and I Chronicles 1:1.

References to Adam as an individual person are scarce in the remainder of the Old Testament, but this is only true in an explicit sense. The sense of Adam as a "corporate personality," as the man who includes all humanity in his person, the "One in the Many" and the "Many in the One" finds expression throughout the Old Testament. Just as Adam is humankind, so also Israel exists in both the name of the patriarch and that of the nation.[3] The histories of the patriarchs, Moses, and David, seem to merge together with the contemporaneous experience of the people, as seen in this exhortation in Isaiah 51:1-2:

> Hearken to me, you who pursue deliverance, you who seek the Lord, look to the rock from which you were hewn, and to the quarry from which you were digged. Look to Abraham your father and to Sarah who bore you: for when he was but one I called him, and I blessed him and made him many.

Manifestations of the relationship between the One and the Many are predominant throughout the Old Testament: the remnant in Israel, the solitary figure in the Psalms, Second Isaiah's

---

[2] B. S. Childs, "Adam," *The Interpreter's Dictionary of the Bible,* Vol. 1, p. 42.

[3] Alan Richardson, *An Introduction to the Theology of the New Testament* (London: SCM Press, 1958), p. 248. The standard studies on "corporate personality" are H. Wheeler Robinson, *Corporate Personality in the Old Testament* (Philadelphia: Fortress Press, 1964) and Aubrey Johnson, *The One and the Many in the Isrealite Conception of God* (Cardiff: University of Wales Press, 1961). A caveat has been offered by Rogerson, "The Hebrew Conception of Corporate Personality—A Re-examination," *Journal of Theological Studies* 21 (1970), pp. 1-16, who claims that the place of the individual in the OT should not be forgotten.

"servant" on behalf of the people, and the "son of man" in the apocalypse of Daniel (7:13-27).[4] The high priest and the king are paramount examples in the Old Testament, according to James Torrance.[5] The high priest was both the "inclusive" and "representative" person for the people of Israel.[6] This role arose out of the consciousness of Israel's election as the nation chosen out from among the peoples of the earth. So also, the high priest was consecrated to perform vicarious acts for the people of Israel. It is important to note, Torrance says, that this thought of "inclusive" and "representative" humanity is not just the platonic concept of the Ideal Man which is behind the Many in the sensible world.[7] The historical importance of the individual priest or king in Israel is radically different from such a Greek concept. For Israel, the historical existence of the king means that from a historical point ("Zion," Ps. 2:6) the king will vanquish Israel's foes (Ps. 2:19).

Alan Richardson also cautions us not to confuse "corporate personality" in the Old Testament with modern social psychological theories such as "the group mind," or "the instincts of the herd."[8] He prefers to speak of "representative man," if that is understood to be more than a metaphor (e.g. "John Bull" or "Uncle Sam"). Ultimately, analogies fail us when we seek to describe the Hebraic truth that Adam is mankind. However we choose to understand it, the common use of the One and the Many in the Old Testament must be recognized.

---

[4] Ralph P. Martin, *The Spirit and the Congregation: Studies in I Corinthians 12–15* (Grand Rapids: Eerdmans, 1984), p. 23.

[5] James B. Torrance, "The Vicarious Humanity of Christ," in *The Incarnation,* ed. Thomas F. Torrance (Edinburgh: The Handsel Press, 1981), p. 137.

[6] Ibid., p. 138.

[7] Ibid., p. 140.

[8] Richardson, p. 248.

2. Intertestamental Usage

The intertestamental period brings a flowering of interest in Adam in a distinctly eschatological sense.[9] Adam is seen as both the originator of sin and death and as the model of the intended existence of humanity.

Adam becomes focused as the origin of sin and death (IV Ezra 3:7). This signifies a growing interest in the results of Adam's act rather than in Adam himself.[10] Death,[11] corruption of life in this world,[12] and the growth of sin[13] are held to be the result of Adam's fall, but not to the exclusion of individual responsibility (with the possible exception of IV Ezra).

At the same time, Adam's image as the intended existence of humanity becomes magnified.[14] Adam is considered to be the first father of Israel.[15] He is exalted a king,[16] possesses glory,[17] and is considered a "second angel."[18]

It has been easy for some scholars to see a connection between the developing "Son of Man" title in the intertestamental period and Adam. Often the antecedent for "Son of Man" is seen in the Gnostic "redeemed redeemer" or *Urmensch* myth particularly set forth by Egon Brandenburger and Ernst Käsemann.[19] The

---

[9] Robin Scroggs, *The Last Adam: A Study in Pauline Anthropology* (Oxford: Basil Blackwell, 1966), p. 16. John R. Levison argues that early Judaism had a vastly more complex usage of Adam than those aspects simply used by Paul. *Portraits of Adam in Early Judaism: From Sirach to 2 Baruch* (Sheffield: JSOT Press, 1988).

[10] Scroggs, p. 18.

[11] Sirach 14:23; Apoc. of Moses 28; IV Ezra 3:7; 7:116-126; II Baruch 17:3; 18:8; 23:4; 54:15; 56:6.

[12] Sirach 40:1-11.

[13] Sirach 25:24.

[14] Scroggs, p. 21.

[15] Sirach 49:16.

[16] Jub. 2:14; II En. 30:12; IV Ez. 6:57f.; Apoc. of Moses 24:4.

[17] II Ez. 30:11.

[18] Ibid.

[19] Egon Brandenburger, *Adam und Christus: Exegetish-Religiongeschichtliche Untersuchung zu Rom 5:12-21 (1 Kor. 15) (Neukirchen-Vluyn: Neukircherner*

widespread nature of this myth is said to include influence upon
the Indian Yama-Yami and the Iranian Gayomart, as well as the
Adam of Genesis and later ideas of the "Son of Man."[20] As
Seyoon Kim has pointed out, however, it is doubtful that "Son of
Man" and Adam speculations came from the *Urmensch* myth.[21]
"Son of Man" is not connected with Adam in Jewish writings,
and, in fact, is usually described as a heavenly, non-human char-
acter (Daniel 7:13; I En. 46:1ff.; IV Ezra 13:2ff.).[22]

It has been suggested by some that Jesus' own use of "Son
of Man" is the direct source for Paul's Adam-Christ analogy.[23]
Evidence for this comes from Paul's references to the parousia of
Christ. These contain imagery and ideas connected to the Son of
Man in the Gospels (I Cor. 4:5; 15:23; II Cor. 5:10; Phil. 3:2).[24]
The Semitic image *bar-('e)nasha'*, which is the basis of ὁ υἱὸς
τοῦ ἀνθρώπου in the Gospels, can also mean simply "man." This
is its usage in Paul (Rom. 5:15; I Cor. 15:21, 47). While there
may be some truth to these claims, Kim cautions that there is no
direct evidence that Paul renders Jesus' self-designation of "Son
of Man" as ὁ ἄνθρωπος. Kümmel remarks rightly that there is no
parallel between the earthly and heavenly man in Jesus' "Son of
Man" self-designation.[25]

3. Near Eastern and Hellenistic Background

As we have cited previously, the popular view is that the
widespread use of the *Urmensch* myth in the Near East accounts
for Jewish thought about Adam. Such views of a "heavenly man"

Verlag, 1962) and Ernst Käsemann, *Leib and Leib Christi* (Tubingen: J. C. B.
Mohr [Paul Siebeck], 1933).

20 Seyoon Kim, *The Origin of Paul's Gospel* (Tubingen: J. C. B. Mohr [Paul
Siebeck], 1981), p. 179.

21 Ibid., p. 182.

22 Ibid., p. 183.

23 The arguments are summarized by Kim, p. 184.

24 Cf. the use of Ps. 8:6 in I Cor. 15:27.

25 Werner-Georg Kümmel, *The Theology of the New Testament,* trans. John E.
Steely (Nashville: Abingdon Press, 1973), p. 156.

seemed to have reached an apex in the Hellenistic Judaism of Philo of Alexandria.[26] James D. G. Dunn believes that Gnostic use of the *Urmensch* ideas encouraged Paul to develop his concept of Jesus as representative man.[27]

However, Robin Scroggs' investigation of Gnostic texts does not find the parallelism between Adam and Christ which one finds in Paul. "What is lost is mankind's good. Nothing is said about Adam's recovering this good."[28] Scroggs accuses Brandenburger, who holds to the belief, along with Dunn, that Paul developed the Adam-Christ analogy because of his Corinthian opponents, of denying the creative impetus of Paul's great theological themes expressed in I Corinthians, such as the resurrection, and being in Christ.[29] These themes are much more likely to be the source of Paul's Adam-Christ teaching. Brandenburger has not understood Paul in the context of Paul's own eschatological soteriology.[30] This seems true, yet one must still not deny the influence of other cultural factors. Davies' perspective is a good reminder:

> It is fair to infer that in Paul's day throughout the cultured Mediterranean world the Heavenly Man or the First Man, however he might be termed, was the source of a perpetual interchange of thought and discussion.[31]

4. Rabbinic Teaching

Although Davies reminds us that we must be open to the mutual interchange of ideas during Paul's day, his examination of

---

26 References cited in James D. G. Dunn, "I Corinthians 15:45—Last Adam, Life-giving Spirit" in *Christ and Spirit in the New Testament,* ed. Barnabas Lindars and Stephen S. Smalley (Cambridge: Cambridge University Press, 1973), p. 135.

27 Ibid.

28 Scroggs, xiv.

29 Ibid., xxi.

30 Ibid.

31 Davies, p. 49.

rabbinic sources uncovers a great Jewish preoccupation with Adam that could not be ignored by the Pharisee Saul.[32] This body of literature is enough to account for Paul's Adam-Christ analogy.

Davies claims that, in the rabbinic teaching, the persistent attention to the consequences of the Fall created a simultaneous fascination with the perfect pre-fall state of Adam. His pre-fallen condition "should be more and more glorified in order to heighten the tragedy of the Fall."[33] Adam takes on superlative characteristics. He is so glorious that he is worthy of worship by the angels.[34] He has great wisdom. He is known for his pious acts (as a *hasid*).[35] But most dominant among the great attributes of pre-fallen Adam is his enormous size, "the body of Adam."[36]

The significance of the body of Adam in rabbinic teaching is not clear, despite the frequent mention by the rabbis. Scroggs identifies two separate traditions concerning the bodily size of Adam before the fall.[37] One asserts that Adam was one hundred cubits tall, a size that will be restored to him in the end times. The other tradition makes him even larger, extending from one end of the world to the other. What its function was in Jewish theology is not clear, according to Scroggs. He is not convinced by the claim of Davies and others that Adam's great size was emphasized in order to heighten the tragedy of the fall.[38] It may have connections to the *Urmensch*, but this does not explain its theological function within Judaism.[39]

---

[32]   Ibid., p. 45.

[33]   Ibid.

[34]   For rabbinic references, see Ibid., p. 46.

[35]   See rabbinic references in Scroggs, p. 42.

[36]   Davies, p. 45.

[37]   Scroggs, p. 49.

[38]   Ibid., p. 50.

[39]   Despite claims that the origins of Adam's great size came from Gnosticism, Susan Niditch has found the proof texts wanting; "The 'Cosmic Adam' Man or Mediator in Rabbinic Literature," *Journal of Jewish Studies* 34 (Autumn, 1983), p. 138. "The immense, immobile man reported by Irenaeus is not like that of the Rabbis, a macanthropos stretching from one end of the world to the other, filling the cosmos" (p. 139).

Seyoon Kim is not satisfied with the attempts to limit the origin of Paul's Adam-Christ analogy to Jewish sources. Kim suggests instead the conversion experience of Paul on the Damascus road as the main source.[40] He argues that the experience of "the man from heaven" (I Cor. 15:47) on the Damascus road was interpreted as a vision of the renewed image of God in humanity, an image which was reduced by the fall of Adam. "Paul's descriptions of Christ as the Last Adam all point to his Damascus vision of the exalted Christ."[41] Attractive as this thesis might sound, the accounts of Paul's conversion experience in both Acts and his own letters do not give any evidence that the experience impressed upon him definite ideas of the *imago Dei*.

Romans 5: Christ as Justified Adam

At first glance, the Adam-Christ analogy seems to be limited in the New Testament to Romans 5:12-21 and I Corinthians 15:44, 49. But there have been several suggestions of other possibilities, not as explicit perhaps, but still, real possibilities of an Adam-Christ analogy behind the tradition. Philippians 2:5-11 comes readily to mind, according to A. M. Hunter,

> Its theme is Jesus, the Second Adam, who, conquering the temptation to which the First Adam fell, chose the role of the Suffering Servant and for his obedience unto death was highly exalted by God, and made "Lord" of the whole cosmos.[42]

R. P. Martin sees the μορφῇ θεοῦ in 2:6 as the equivalent to the ἐικών or δόξα θεοῦ which the first man possessed at creation (Gen. 1:26, 27). It is only natural that Paul would have been familiar with the rabbinic teaching on the "glory" of pre-fallen Adam, which we have previously noted.

> What Paul had learned at the feet of Gamaliel about the "glory" of the first Adam—the idealized picture of the

---

[40] Kim, p. 262.

[41] Ibid., p. 263.

[42] A. M. Hunter, *Paul and His Predecessors* (London: Nicholson and Watson, 1940), p. 46. Cf. Davies, p. 41.

Rabbinic schools—he transferred to the last Adam as
He had revealed Himself to him in a blaze of glory.[43]

Other passages such as Mark 1:13, Jesus with the wild
beasts, and Galatians 3:28, the unity of humanity in Christ, have
possible Adam-Christ backgrounds. Davies believes that in the
Marcan account of the Temptation the scenery is the Garden of
Eden and Christ is placed in the same background as was the first
Adam, with the implication that Christ, unlike Adam, was victorious over temptation.[44] Alan Richardson sees Adam as a similar
backdrop for Galatians 3:28:

> There can be neither Jew nor Greek (as Adam was
> neither), bond nor free (Adam was God's free man),
> male nor female ("Adam" is common gender), you are
> all one in Christ Jesus.[45]

"Adam plays a larger role in Paul's theology than is usually
realized," claims James Dunn. "Adam is a key figure in Paul's attempt to express his understanding of Christ and of man."[46] Dunn
buttresses this claim by tracing the Adam theology implicit
throughout the letter to the Romans: In chapter one, "they" can be
replaced by "Adam" as the one who enjoyed the knowledge of
God (1:19, 21), but did not honor God or give thanks (1:21).[47]
Romans 3:23, "All have sinned and lack the glory of God" is often
thought by modern exegetes to refer to the glory of God which
was forfeited through the fall of Adam.[48] The perennially difficult
chapter seven is possibly interpreted as Paul thinking of Adam as
the one who was once alive apart from the law, but the coming of
the commandment brought sin and death (7:9f.)[49] The traditional

---

43 Ralph P. Martin, *Carmen Christi: Philippians 2:5-11 in Recent Interpretation
    and in the Setting of Early Christian Worship (Revised Edition)* (Grand
    Rapids: Eerdmans, 1983), p. 119.

44 Davies, p. 42.

45 Richardson, p. 246.

46 James D. G. Dunn, *Christology in the Making,* p. 101.

47 Ibid.

48 Ibid., p. 102.

49 Ibid., p. 104.

rabbinic view that creation was involved in the fall of Adam is seen in 8:19-33, "the creation was subjected to futility."

These passages may give us glimmers of an Adam theology in the early church, but Romans 5:12-21 and I Corinthians 15:44-49 remain the only explicit passages which develop the Adam-Christ relationship in Paul.

In Romans 5:14, Adam is the τύπος τοῦ μέλλοντος. As Cranfield remarks, τύπος means here a mark made by striking which causes an impression, a type which is a mold prefiguring something else.[50] In this case, it pertains to eschatological fulfillment. The type points to something besides itself.[51]

Karl Barth has raised some exegetical eyebrows with his novel interpretation of the relationship between Adam and Christ in Romans 5. Romans 5:10 states that humanity is reconciled with God through the death of Christ. "That means that in His own death he makes their peace with God—before they themselves have decided for this peace and quite apart from this decision… it was settled without and in spite of them."[52] Barth's point is that Adam is not "the fundamental truth of anthropology" which determines the nature of relationship between Adam and Christ.[53] Adam has nowhere to stand by himself,

> Man's essential and original nature is to be found, therefore, not in Adam but in Christ. In Adam we can only find it prefigured. Adam can therefore be interpreted only in the light of Christ and not the other way around.[54]

Rudolf Bultmann, among others, has taken sharp exception to Barth's exegesis. According to Bultmann, Barth fails to see chapter 5 in the context of the entire letter to the Romans and therefore misses Paul's chief concern: the presence of salvation

---

50 C. E. B. Cranfield, *A Critical and Exegetical Commentary on the Epistle to the Romans,* Vol. 1 (Edinburgh: T. and T. Clark, 1975), p. 283.

51 Ibid., p. 295. Cranfield admits his indebtedness to Barth at this point.

52 Barth, *Christ and Adam,* p. 34.

53 Ibid., p. 39.

54 Ibid., p. 40.

and the paradoxical situation of the Christian life.[55] "Paul says nothing about whether the Adamic mankind stood within the rule of Christ."[56] Bultmann may be right that Paul says nothing explicitly about Adam standing under the rule of Christ, but it seems hard to understand the Adam-Christ analogy if this is not implicitly understood. The "free gift in the grace of that one man Jesus Christ" (5:15), which brings "justification" (5:16) and "life" (5:17) is the "fundamental truth" (Barth) about humanity. Human existence as "ungodly" (5:6), "sinners" (5:8) and "enemies" (5:10) tells us nothing about Christ. But Christ tells us everything about what it means truly to be human. In the time line of salvation history, Adam precedes Christ. But in the intent of God, the true priority is Christ before Adam.[57]

I Corinthians: Christ as Eschatological Adam

Interpreters have sought lately to understand Paul's teaching on Adam and Christ in I Corinthians in light of possible misunderstandings which the Corinthians have had concerning Paul's teaching. Margaret Thrall proposes that the source of the Corinthians over-realized eschatology was their understanding of Christ as the Last Adam. They understood Paul to mean the risen Christ as bestowing all wisdom and blessings of eschatological existence fully in the present.[58] In I Corinthians 15:44-49, Paul does not deny his Last Adam teaching, but the Corinthians' interpretation of it. For Paul, "conformity to the likeness of the heavenly man is not a matter of present realization but a hope for the future."[59]

In a similar vein, W.D. Davies suggests that the Corinthians' familiarity with Alexandrian thought (Apollos had preached

---

55 Rudolf Bultmann, "Adam and Christ According to Romans 5," *Current Issues in New Testament Interpretation,* ed. William Klassen and Graydon F. Snyder (New York: Harper and Brothers, 1962), pp. 150, 162.

56 Ibid., p. 162.

57 Scroggs, p. 101.

58 Margaret E. Thrall, "Christ Crucified or Second Adam? A Christological Debate between Paul and the Corinthians," in *Christ and Spirit in the New Testament,* ed. Barnabas Lindars and Stephen S. Smalley, pp. 145-146.

59 Ibid., p. 148.

there—I Cor. 3:4f.; Acts 18:29f., 19:11) makes it probable that they would have confused Paul's Adam-Christ teaching with Philo's heavenly/earthly man ideas.[60] The Heavenly Man of Philo, divorced from contact with earthly existence, could provide an excuse for the Corinthians to continue their bickering and immorality, since it is heavenly concerns which are important, not the earthly.

If either or both of these two hypotheses are true, they would call to question James Dunn's thesis that Paul, in using the Adam-Christ analogy in I Corinthians 15, "is referring primarily to Christ risen and exalted."[61] This is the essence of the eschatological nature of Paul's Adam Christology. "His role as last Adam begins with and stems from his resurrection, not from pre-existence, or even from his earthly ministry."[62] Certainly Paul emphasizes the eschatological in the Adam-Christ argument of I Corinthians 15. But is it necessary to deduce from this that Christ is the Last Adam only as he is risen and exalted? The possibility of distortions of Paul's teaching or confusion with Philo's scheme, based on an over-realized eschatology, would seem to make it unlikely that Paul would view the eschatological aspect so restrictively. Indeed, Paul's emphasis upon "Christ crucified" in I Corinthians (2:2), as Margaret Thrall proposes,[63] would suggest more of a continuity between the earthly and risen Christ. As Donald Guthrie remarks, nowhere does Paul support a lack of continuity between the earthly Jesus and the risen Lord.[64] In addition, the context of Paul's argument for the resurrection body must be taken into account, as R. P. Martin comments:

> It is strange that Dunn should conclude that Paul explicitly denies that Christ precedes Adam *(Christology In the Making,* p. 308, n. 41) when the point is exactly what Paul must make to establish that the resurrection bodies of Christians will resemble and share in

---

60 Davies, pp. 51-52.

61 Dunn, *Christology in the Making,* p. 107.

62 Ibid., p. 126.

63 Thrall, p. 145.

64 Donald Guthrie, *New Testament Theology* (Downers Grove, IL: Inter-Varsity Press, 1981), p. 337.

Christ's body of glory (vvs. 48, 49; Phil. 3:21) in the beginning.[65]

Nonetheless, Dunn is correct when he cites the significance of the death (Adam) and life (Christ) parallel, which signifies the necessity of death before life. We have already noticed the relation of dying and rising with Christ (Rom. 6:24), with Christ as the Last Adam (Rom. 5). This is also true in I Corinthians, where the baptismal theme of Romans 6 is echoed again, this time, in Paul's insistence upon the resurrection *from the dead*. Martin suggests that the Corinthians had claimed that the Spirit and their baptismal experience had inaugurated a heavenly, glorious life for them, in which the fullness of God had already arrived.[66] Paul responds by arguing that baptism is not to be understood apart from the death which one experiences with Christ. "Death is a precondition to new life" for Paul.[67]

THE CHURCH AS THE BODY OF CHRIST

σῶμα *in Ancient Literature*

σῶμα has a rich and complex history which we can only outline here. Its original meaning is not clear. But from its meaning in Homer as "a dead body of a man or animal," the idea developed into the chain or grave which imprisoned the soul, culminat-

---

[65] Martin, *The Spirit and the Congregation*, p. 153. Cf. R. P. Martin, "Some Reflections on New Testament Hymns," in *Christ the Lord: Studies in Christology Presented to Donald Guthrie*, ed. Harold H. Rowdon (Leicester: Inter-Varsity Press, 1982), pp. 47ff.

[66] Martin, *The Spirit and the Congregation*, p. 94.

[67] Ibid., p. 95. The baptismal context of I Corinthians 15 helps us to understand the enigmatic verse, 15:29—"Otherwise, what do people mean by being baptized on behalf of the dead?" (RSV) According to Martin, verse 29 is "a rhetorical rebuke aimed at showing how inconsistent is the Corinthian practice of baptism" (Ibid., p. 121). The Corinthians' celestial restriction of the significance of baptism is counter to the place of death in baptism. Therefore, J. C. O'Neill paraphrases the verse: "Otherwise what do those hope to achieve who are baptized for their dying bodies?" "I Cor. 15:29," *The Expository Times* 91 (1980), p. 311.

ing in its usage by Plato.[68] A more positive use of σῶμα is found in Aristotle who believed that the body and the soul are indissoluble. He even uses it to describe the character of the state as an organism.[69] The Stoics continued the dichotomy between the body and soul, but still maintained a sense of the wholeness of the human person.[70] The rise of neo-platonic thought brought about a corresponding devaluation of the body.[71]

In Jewish thought, the negative place of the body as the seat of the passions begins with Sirach 23:16ff. and 47:19.[72] The influence of Greek thought is obvious in the dichotomy between the mortal body and the immortal soul (Wisdom 9:15). This trend continues into rabbinic literature.

The idea of the body in Gnosticism is well-known. The body is the source of the material world from which humanity must be set free.[73] Redemption from the body is a central theme of Gnostic soteriology.

In the New Testament, σῶμα has a wide range of meanings:[74] a corpse (Mk. 27:52; Lk. 17:37), the body of Jesus (Mt. 27:58; Mk. 15:43; Lk. 23:52, 23:55; Jn. 19:31), or, as R. Gundry rightly emphasizes, the physical aspect of the human being; ("She felt in her body that she was healed of her disease," Mk. 5:29 and "...without giving the things needed for the body," Jas. 2:16).[75]

Despite Gundry's caveat, Bultmann's well-known conviction concerning the body as the seat of the human person's "primary experience of himself" and as a representative of the total

---

[68] S. Wibbing, σῶμα in *NIDNTT*, Vol. 1, p. 232. See Greek references cited therein.

[69] See references cited in Ibid.

[70] Ibid.

[71] Ibid., p. 233.

[72] Ibid.

[73] Ibid.

[74] Ibid., p. 234.

[75] Ibid. Robert H. Gundry, *Sōma in Biblical Theology, with Emphasis on Pauline Anthropology* (Cambridge: Cambridge University Press, 1976), p. 44.

person still has strong New Testament support.[76] A prominent instance, which Gundry does not examine, is Hebrews 10:10, the contrast between "the offering of the body of Jesus Christ once for all" and the temple sacrifices.[77] Hebrews 10:5, "sacrifices and offerings thou hast not desired, but a body thou has prepared for me," appears to be an "interpretive gloss" on Psalm 40:6: "Sacrifice and offering thou dost not desire, but thou hast given me an open ear." The purpose of this gloss seems to be to emphasize the wholistic function of σῶμα (cf. I Pet. 2:24). Wibbing is perceptive:

> Body in these passages denotes not only Jesus' physical body but the total giving of himself in death. It thus contrasts with the merely physical bodies of animals in the sacrificial system.[78]

It may be that E. Earle Ellis' recent suggestion will provide a fresh approach to the issue:

> Paul regards the individual as a unitary being who may be viewed from different perspectives but who exists wholly within the present natural creation. In this context Paul represents the body as the essential person considered from a particular viewpoint. However, in his employment of "body" he speaks not only of individual entities but also of corporate entities.[79]

Thus, the "particular viewpoints" of the faculty anthropology (body, soul, spirit) are respected, but not apart from the individual as a unitary being before God.

---

[76] Rudolf Bultmann, *Theology of the New Testament*, Vol. 1, trans. Kendrick Grobel (New York: Charles Scribner's Sons, 1951), p. 196.

[77] Wibbing, p. 234.

[78] Ibid.

[79] E. Earle Ellis, "*Soma* in First Corinthians," *Interpretation*, 44 (April, 1990), No. 2, p. 138.

σῶμα *in Romans and I Corinthians*

As we have seen, Bultmann considers σῶμα to be "the most comprehensive term which Paul uses to characterize man's existence" in the New Testament.[80] This is no less true of its usage in Romans and I Corinthians, particularly when we examine Paul's use of "the body of Christ."

In Paul's thought, σῶμα is not simply restricted to a figure or a form.[81] This is explicitly clear in Romans 6:12 ("Let not sin therefore reign in your mortal bodies to make you obey their passions") and Romans 12:1 ("Present your bodies as a living sacrifice"). It is the sin of the whole person which he exhorts his readers to forsake in Romans 6:12. Likewise, the "living sacrifice" of Romans 12 is not simply the physical side, but the entirety of the human being.

Donald Guthrie calls "the body of Christ" "the most vivid and expressive" of all Paul's images.[82] One of the main emphases in Paul's use of "the body of Christ" is to underscore the unity of the church.[83] Again, σῶμα seems to mean a sense of wholeness and completeness, although not denying individuality (Rom. 12:4f.; I Cor. 12:12-26). Kümmel sees an echo of the local meaning of "in Christ" in "the body of Christ" as a Christian community: "We, being many are one body in Christ" (Rom. 12:8).[84]

There may be several sources behind Paul's thought on the body of Christ. Richardson believes that the Hebraic conception of the One and the Many lies behind it[85]. Ladd perceives a more direct background in the experience of the disciples with Jesus and in the dominical sayings "He who receives you receives me"

---

[80] Bultmann, *Theology of the New Testament*, Vol. 1, p. 192.
[81] Wibbing, p. 234.
[82] Guthrie, p. 744.
[83] Bultmann, *Theology of the New Testament*, Vol. 1, p. 193.
[84] Kümmel, pp. 218-219.
[85] Richardson, p. 254.

(Mt. 10:40); and "As you did it to one of the least of these my brethren, you did it to me" (Mt. 15:40 cf. Acts 9:4).[86]

As many scholars have suggested, "the body of Christ" is not simply a metaphor for Paul. It is a reality which every Christian participates in, and therefore is the ground for Pauline ethical exhortations.[87] This is never more true than when Paul relates the body of Christ to the Lord's Supper: "The cup of blessing which we bless, is it not a participation in the blood of Christ? The bread which we break, is it not a participation in the body of Christ?" (I Cor. 10:16) A similar thought is found in Paul's admonition to the Corinthians not to unite their bodies with those of prostitutes: "Do you not know that he who joins himself to a prostitute becomes one body with her?" (I Cor. 10:1-7) instructs Christians that "idolatry involves a participatory union that excludes one from union with Christ (I Cor. 10:14-22)."[88] So also, union with a prostitute breaks one from his unity with Christ.

Paul's doctrine of the church as the body of Christ possesses a realism which is explicitly seen in the relationship he repeatedly maintains between the body and death: "Likewise, my brethren, you have died to the law through the body of Christ, so that you may belong to another." (Rom. 7:4). Because of this connection, Paul is able to discourage the speculations which would identify the church with Christ in an exhaustive sense. The tendency in church history when one speaks of the "mystical" body of Christ has implied, as Conzelmann remarks, that "the body of Christ would no longer mean our acceptance into the saving event but our possibility of ascent."[89] In I Corinthians 10:16ff., in particular, the ecclesiological significance of σῶμα is thoroughly intertwined with the sacramental significance of the saving event in the death of Christ. Therefore, Paul can speak very freely concerning the

---

86   George Eldon Ladd, *A Theology of the New Testament*, p. 545. Cf. John A. T. Robinson, *The Body: A Study in Pauline Theology* (London: SCM Press, 1952), p. 58.

87   E. P. Sanders, *Paul and Palestinian Judaism* (Philadelphia: Fortress Press, 1977), p. 455.

88   Ibid.

89   Hans Conzelmann, *An Outline of the Theology of the New Testament*, trans. John Bowden (New York: Harper and Row, 1968), p. 263.

relationship between body and the sufferings and death of Christ: He bears in his body the "marks of Jesus" (Gal. 6:17). His own life of persecution and suffering is described as "carrying in the body the death of Jesus" (II Cor. 4:10).[90] Finally, his cry, "Who will deliver me from this body of death?" (Rom. 7:24), unequivocally relates body and death.

THE LAST ADAM AND THE BODY OF CHRIST

The Community of the Last Adam

We come now to a closer understanding of the relationship between Christ as the Last Adam and the church as the body of Christ. Our proposal is that, theologically, they are much more interwoven than is usually thought. So much so, in fact, that we might call the church, "the community of the Last Adam."

We have seen how closely Paul relates σῶμα with death. This is because, in part, σῶμα as a neutral term has been invaded by σάρξ the domination of human selfishness.[91] Therefore, our hope is for "the redemption of our bodies" (Rom. 8:23), so that we may no longer be under the dominion of the σάρξ. Since "our bodies are dead because of sin" (Rom. 8:10), we must participate in the body of Christ, the community of true humanity, the community of the Last Adam.

Participation in the body of Christ is based on the crucifixion with Christ which destroys the place of our selfishness: our old body, i.e. the totality of ourselves: "We know that our old self was crucified with him so that the sinful body might be destroyed, and we might no longer be enslaved to sin" (Rom. 6:6).[92]

Participation in the body of Christ means a community of unity has been created. Why did Paul use σῶμα in order to stress the unity and interdependence (I Cor. 12:12) of the church? Davies believes that it was because Paul was familiar with the traditional rabbinic teaching on the unity of all mankind in Adam.[93] But this

---

90 Bultmann, *Theology of the New Testament,* Vol. 1, p. 193.
91 Martin, *The Spirit and the Congregation,* p. 135.
92 Cranfield, p. 309.
93 Davies, p. 56.

unity is not something which is innate within σῶμα . That is why, for Paul, the genitive is τὸ σῶμα τοῦ χριστοῦ, not τὸ σῶμα τῶν χριστιανῶν.[94] Christ is the center of the unity, not Christians by themselves.

Likewise, E. Schweizer suggests that "the spatial concept of the body of Christ proclaims in a form conditioned by the age the truth that all the community's life is shaped by the historical act of God in Jesus."[95] He concludes this from the fact that the major Pauline teachings on Christ as the Last Adam and the body of Christ are found in both Romans and I Corinthians.[96]

Ernst Käsemann also makes mention of the stress on the genitive in τὸ σῶμα τοῦ χριστοῦ.

> We do not partake in Christ because we are members of the church. Here the irreversability of the order is of vital importance. Christ is there before the church and he is not absorbed into that church. As creator and judge, he remains the counterpart of his members.[97]

Käsemann believes that the concept of the eschatological Adam was necessary in order to communicate this.

A. J. M. Wedderburn questions such a close relationship between Christ as the Last Adam and the church as the body of Christ.[98] He claims that there is no evidence that Paul links the two together, nor does Paul speak of "the body of Adam" in contrast to "the body of Christ," as one might expect. Nevertheless, Wedderburn will grant that similar ideas probably lie behind the two concepts.

---

[94] T. W. Manson, "A Parallel to a New Testament Use of σῶμα ," *Journal of Theological Studies* 37 (1936), p. 385. Cf. Davies, p. 56.

[95] E. Schweizer and F. Baumgartel, "σῶμα, σωματικός, σύσσωμος," *TDNT* , Vol. 7 pp. 1072-1073.

[96] Ibid., p. 1072.

[97] Ernst Käsemann, "The Theological Problem Presented by the Motif of the Body of Christ," in *Perspectives on Paul*, trans. Margaret Kohl (Philadelphia: Fortress Press, 1971), pp. 116-117.

[98] A. J. M. Wedderburn, "The Body of Christ and Related Concepts in I Corinthians," *Scottish Journal of Theology* 24 (1971), p. 90.

The Community of the Spirit

At another level, Paul emphasizes that the community of the Last Adam should not have its own agenda, because it is the community of God's Spirit. As Brandenburger states, the relation between I Corinthians 15:44b ("If there is a physical body, there is also a spiritual body") to v. 45 ("Thus it is written, 'The first Adam became a living being, the last Adam became a life-giving Spirit'") is crucial.[99] The principle of both precedence (the physical before the spiritual) and contrast (between the physical and the spiritual) tells us something about the rule of the Spirit over the congregation. As Davies observes, the body in Paul receives its source of life from the Spirit. This is the Spirit who manifests itself in many ways in the differing gifts of the body (I Cor. 12:1f.; Rom. 12:4).[100] Without the Spirit, there would be no gifts. Indeed, without the Spirit, the body would be lifeless. "The difference between the Body of the First Adam and that of the Second Adam was for Paul that whereas the former was animated by the principle of natural life, was *nephesh*, the latter was animated by the Spirit."[101] This animation by the Spirit for the Christian involves the imperative to put off the old person and his deeds and to put on the new person.[102]

The leadership of the Spirit in the church is explicitly seen in the close relationship between baptism and the Spirit in Paul's thought (I Cor. 12:13). Baptism means that the church exists only by the eschatological promise of God.[103] The "one Spirit" is the basis of all Christian experience.[104] The Corinthians were certainly interested in πνεῦμα, but, as Martin observes, "Paul has to drive a wedge between aspirations of the human spirit (which may be ill-considered and 'fleshly') and the control of the Holy Spirit."[105]

---

[99] Brandenburger, p. 73.
[100] Davies, p. 56.
[101] Ibid., p. 57.
[102] Ibid.
[103] Wibbing, p. 237.
[104] Martin, *The Spirit and the Congregation,* p. 24.
[105] Ibid., p. 36.

Therefore, James Dunn might well be questioned when he states that "Paul wishes to ground his assertion about the spiritual embodiment of the risen Christ in the experience of the believing community."[106] Is it not Paul's burden to wrest the Corinthians away from their experience-oriented theology and to ground them in the apostolic tradition, particularly concerning the resurrection of Jesus (I Cor. 15:1-11)? Dunn grants that Jesus is the source of these experiences,[107] but have not the Corinthians' problems been based on their uncritical interpretation of religious ecstasies, which have ended up as challenging the authority of the apostle himself? Jesus must not only be the source of religious experience for Paul, but also its Lord (I Cor. 12:3).

The Community of Faith, Hope and Love

The true measure of the reality of salvation for the community of the Last Adam, animated by the Spirit in Paul's thought, is the manifestation of concrete acts of faith, hope, and above all, love. Paul also calls this the fruit of the Spirit or walking by the Spirit (Gal. 5:6-26). As Scroggs observes, "Thus, the Spirit is the source of the radical change which is already beginning to take place, and this change leaves no part of man untouched."[108]

As the community of the Last Adam, the church is confronted with the imperative of love. This is grounded in the nature of Paul's Adam-Christ teaching, according to Davies. Paul was certainly aware of the rabbinic teaching that the duty of love is the fundamental implication of the unity of all humankind in Adam.[109] If this is true in the First Adam, how much more is it true in the Last Adam? If the body of Christ in Paul's teaching is integrally related to Christ as the Last Adam, we can see the theological foundation behind Paul's admonition to the Corinthians concerning the Lord's Supper:

---

106 Dunn, "I Cor. 15:45...," p. 131.
107 Ibid., pp. 132-133.
108 Scroggs, p. 67.
109 Davies, p. 53.

For anyone who eats and drinks without discerning the
body eats and drinks judgment upon himself (I Cor.
11:29).[110]

It makes sense that I Corinthians 13 should not be separated
from Paul's concerns in chapter 12 (the body of Christ) and
chapter 15 (Christ as the Last Adam). In fact, one may see an
implicit Adam-Christ analogy in the play between what love is not
(the First Adam) and what love is (the second Adam). Love is not
"puffed up in arrogance" (I Cor. 13:4) nor is it "self-seeking" (I
Cor. 13:5).[111] This is the basic problem behind the Corinthians'
presumptions that they were "risen and reigning with Christ" (I
Cor. 4:8) and therefore were free to engage in all sorts of
licentious activities.

Certainly, the positive example of Christ, who was not arrogant nor self-seeking, is present here, but it does not seem much
to assume that the negative example of the First Adam, the one
who was arrogant and self seeking, was also behind Paul's mind
at this point. In contrast to the choices created by the First Adam,
it is the task of the Last Adam to bring reconciliation through his
body, the church, but only as it dies to itself, and allows the Spirit
to magnify Christ in its midst through concrete expressions of
faith, hope and love.[112]

The Last Adam: Representative and Substitute

We now return to our initial question: Does Paul speak of a
substitutionary aspect to the work of Christ, and if so, how is it to
be understood?

The representative nature of Christ's work is hardly dis-
puted. Dunn remarks that I Corinthians 15:45b makes it clear that
Jesus has a representative capacity on behalf of humanity as the
One who is the πνεῦμα ζῳοποιοῦν.[113] But does Jesus' atoning
work mean something more? Does Barth give us a clue when he
says that "in His Son God provides this human faithfulness that

---

[110] Ibid., p. 55.
[111] Martin, *The Spirit and the Congregation,* pp. 48-49.
[112] Richardson, p. 249.
[113] Dunn, "I Cor. 15:45...," p. 135.

man has failed to provide"?[114] The faithlessness of humanity
means that Christ's work must be more than that of a representative, although representation is certainly a part of it. Christ must
take the place of the faithlessness of humanity with the perfection
of his own faithfulness toward the Father. Paul uses the relationship between Christ as the Last Adam and the church as the body
of Christ in order to 1) create a concrete, worldly place where the
reality of salvation is seen in acts of faith, hope, and love, and 2)
provide a judgment upon any human endeavor to usurp the head-
ship of Christ over the church.

Therefore, Paul stresses that the body of Christ must die to
itself before it can live with Christ. Our observation concerning the
relationship between body and death is important here. Death is
the presupposition of life. Paul experiences not merely new life,
but also decay and death. But it is important to note that, for Paul,
the death and life experience is based on the death and life of
Christ (Rom. 6:5; Gal. 2:19, 6:14). Even our own putting to death
our sinful selves cannot be done apart from the work of Christ in
our stead.[115]

Despite the similarities, the Adam-Christ analogy in Paul
points out their differences as well as their likenesses. The
difference in the Last Adam is that he is able to be the substitute
for the faithlessness of humanity.[116] Both Adams are
representatives. Only the Last Adam can remove any place for the
immorality and arrogance of the Corinthians to stand, by taking
their place, not just in death, but in death and life, in the fullness
of their humanity.

With Paul, the body of the Last Adam is integrally related to
the church as the body of Christ. The Lord Jesus Christ "will
change our lowly *body* to be like his glorious *body*" (Phil. 3:20).

---

[114] Barth, *Christ and Adam*, p. 96.

[115] Cf. Dunn: "Paul does not usually speak of the believer being patterned
according to the image of the earthly Jesus, his ministry, his teaching. And
he thinks in terms of the believer sharing in Christ's death only because
Christ has lived through Adam's fate to resurrection life beyond."
Christology in the Making, p. 127.

[116] T. F. Torrance, *Space, Time and Resurrection*, pp. 116-117.

According to Barrett, this is Christ as the Last Adam.[117] Certainly the rabbinic tradition concerning the enormous size of the body of Adam influenced Paul in his view of the body of the Last Adam as the many differing members of the church (I Cor. 12:12). If Bultmann's interpretation of σῶμα as representative of the whole person still holds, as we believe it does, it would combine nicely with the enormous size of the body as a pointer to the need for a radical view of the substitution in Paul's thought. The *whole* church, with *all* of its members, needs to be *displaced* by the Last Adam, in order to be *replaced* by his new humanity, the only potential source for faith, hope and love.

Objections are often made to substitutionary atonement because of its usual relation to a penal theory of atonement. As Richardson states,

> The curious notion that God's "justice," which demands the punishment of sinners, could be saved by inflicting the death-penalty upon the one sinless human being who had ever lived on earth is not found in the New Testament and it should find no place in Christian theology.[118]

Whatever part the penal aspect may play in one's theory of the atonement, we have striven to show that one may have a view of the radical substitutionary work of Christ, displacing and replacing our humanity, apart from a traditional penal theory of the atonement. Ladd attempts to answer such critics as Richardson by stressing that, because of the death of Christ, I will not die but will have eternal life with him.[119] That may be true, but a radical view of substitution, as we have presented, involves not only the hereafter, but the here-and-now. We are "taken into the community of Jesus' dying" (Pannenberg).[120] That is why Christ as the Last Adam, expressed in the church as the body of Christ, became such

---

[117] C. K. Barrett, *From First Adam to Last* (New York: Charles Scribner's Sons, 1962), p. 76. Cf. Christ as the "head of the body" in Col. 1:18. Cf. Eph. 1:22-23; 4:15-16.

[118] Richardson, p. 234.

[119] Ladd, p. 427.

[120] Wolfhart Pannenberg, *Jesus—God and Man, Second Edition*, p. 263.

a powerful imperative to turn the Corinthian church from their arrogance and self-seeking ways.

EPILOGUE

SONIA'S ANSWER AND THE VICARIOUS
HUMANITY OF CHRIST IN THE CHURCH

At the beginning of our study, we posed the question of the skeptic Rashkolnikov to the pious Sonia: "And what does God do for you?" This was the question of reality, the reality of salvation. It is only now, after our examination of the vicarious humanity of Christ, that we are able to hear the simple, yet profound answer of Sonia: "Everything!" God does "everything!"

Everything! Can we bear to say something so apparently simple? Should not we be more sophisticated and obtuse in our answer? But perhaps Sonia is a much better theologian than many who have the academic degrees. For she, like Bonhoeffer, has grasped the meaning of the ultimate reality: God. The place of the reality of salvation is in God himself. He does "everything."

Sonia's answer reminds us of a statement of Barth's: "Everything has happened to us, but in the context of the person of the Son."[1] Sonia is able to say "everything" because she believes in the Incarnation, she believes in the God whose "everything" includes human flesh. The reality of salvation is in God himself, but not apart from humanity, because of the vicarious humanity of Christ. The world in which we live is a world of tragedy and chaos. We cannot see salvation in terms of this world apart from God. Yet we can say with the author of Hebrews, "We do not yet see all things subject to him [the tragic world which we experience] but we see Jesus" (Heb. 2:8-9). We are to join the readers of I Peter, Christians who experienced great suffering

---

[1]Barth, *CD* IV/1, p. 222.

(I Pet. 5:9), in loving Jesus Christ apart from the circumstances
we experience in this world:

> Without having seen him you love him: though you do
> not now see him you believe in him and rejoice with
> unutterable and exalted joy (I Pet. 1:8).

What does this have to do with the reality of salvation? Peter adds
in 1:9: "As the outcome of your faith you obtain the *salvation* of
your souls."

We have moved from Sonia's answer to Rashkolnikov to the
Christian communities of Hebrews and I Peter. It is only right that
we do so, for our previous chapter has shown us how integrally
Christ as Last Adam is related to the church as the body of Christ.
The church is the locus of the vicarious humanity of Christ in the
world. But what are the implications of this? We would like to
make one suggestion, by suggesting the pericope concerning
Jesus and the paralytic man in Mark 2.

The encounter between Jesus and the paralytic becomes a
paradigm for the working of the vicarious humanity of Christ in
the church only when we realize that the story includes not only
Jesus and the paralytic, but also those who took the man to Jesus.
For Mark 2:5 says plainly, "And when Jesus saw *their* faith [the
faith of the four men who brought him to Jesus], he said to the
paralytic, 'My son, your sins are forgiven.'" The forgiveness of
sins, the reality of salvation, came to the paralytic in the midst of
his inability to believe. Someone had to believe for him. The
vicarious humanity of Christ exists in the church when we admit
that there are times when we need to die to our individualism and
self-sufficiency and be "carried"(Mk. 2:2) by the church, by the
community of believers, the body of Christ. There are times when
others have to believe for us. Does this mean that the paralytic did
not need to believe in Jesus himself? Certainly not. As our study
on the "vicarious repentance" of Christ has shown, Christ's act of
repentance on our behalf becomes the *mediation* and the *power* for
our personal acts of repentance. This is also true of the paralytic
and the manifestation of the vicarious humanity of Christ in his
"church" of the four men who gently carried him to Jesus.

But we must be careful to emphasize, as we did in the previous chapter, that the church must die to its own agenda and aims,
before it can participate in the vicarious humanity of Christ in the
world. The four men had no power of their own to bring forgive-

ness and healing. Jesus had to be in their midst. They had to bring the paralytic to Jesus. It takes little to be reminded that the church is made of human beings each of whom are *simul justus, simul peccator*. This is portrayed graphically in the scene at Gethsemane, according to Barth. This is "the hard picture of the Synoptics: the complete denial of Christianity and the Church in relation to Jesus," their notorious "non-participation in His decisive action."[2] The disciples refused to die to their own agenda. And Jesus was left alone.

But the four men, the "church" in Mark 2, offer another possibility for the church: the church as the manifestation of the vicarious humanity of Christ in the world today. So also Sonia in *Crime and Punishment* became the "church" for Rashkolnikov. In the midst of his unbelief, Sonia's faith became a constant reminder to Rashkolnikov, moving him toward his own act of faith. Thus, the vicarious humanity of Christ continues to be the place of the reality of salvation in a lost and tortured world.

---

[2]Ibid., p. 268.

Aland, Philip L. "John Hick's Copernican Theology," *Theology* 86, January, 1983, pp. 34-36.

Allison, Dale C., Jr. *The End of the Ages Has Come: An Early Interpretation of the Passion and Resurrection of Jesus.* Philadelphia: Fortress Press, 1985.

Allmen, J. J. *Worship, Its Theology and Practice.* New York: Oxford University Press, 1961.

Anderson, Hugh. *Jesus and Christian Origins,* New York: Oxford University Press, 1964.

Anderson, Ray S. *Historical Transcendence and the Reality of God.* Grand Rapids: Eerdmans, 1975.

_____. *On Being Human: Essays on Theological Anthropology.* Grand Rapids: Eerdmans, 1982.

_____, ed. *Theological Foundations for Ministry.* Grand Rapids and Edinburgh: Eerdmans and T. & T. Clark, 1979.

_____. "Barth and a new Direction for Natural Theology," in *Theology Beyond Christendom: Essays on the Centenary of the Birth of Karl Barth, May 10, 1886,* ed. John Thompson, pp. 241-266.

_____. "Toward a New Basis for Natural Theology in the Tradition of Karl Barth: A Critical Analysis of the Theology of Thomas F. Torrance." Unpublished paper presented to the American Academy of Religion, Group on Evangelical Theology, San Francisco, CA, Dec. 19-22, 1981.

Anselm, "Why God Became Man," in *A Scholastic Miscellany.* Ed. Eugene A. Fairweather. New York: Macmillan, 1970.

The Apostolic Fathers. trans. Kirsopp Lake. London: William Heinemann, 1912.

Barr, James. *The Semantics of Biblical Language.* Oxford: Oxford University Press, 1961.

Barrett, C. K. "The Eschatology of the Epistle to the Hebrews," in W. D. Davies and David Daube, eds., *The Background of the New Testament and Its Eschatology: C. H. Dodd Festschrift.* Cambridge: Cambridge University Press, 1954, pp. 363-393.

_____. *From First Adam to Last.* New York: Charles Scribner's Sons, 1962.

Barth, Karl. *Christ and Adam.* trans. T. A. Smail. New York: Macmillan, 1968.

_____. *Church Dogmatics*. ed. G. W. Bromiley and T. F. Torrance. Edinburgh: T. & T. Clark, 1936-1969.

_____. *The Humanity of God*. trans. John Newton Thomas and Thomas Wieser. Atlanta: John Knox Press, 1966.

_____. *Letters*. 1961-68, ed. Jürgen Fangmeier and Hinrich Stoevesandt; trans. and ed. Geoffrey W. Bromiley. Grand Rapids: Eerdmans, 1980.

Baxter, Richard. *The Saint's Everlasting Rest*. Westwood: Revell (1962).

Beker, J. Christian. *Paul the Apostle: the Triumph of God in Life and Thought*. Philadelphia: Fortress Press, 1980.

Berkhof, L. *Systematic Theology*. Grand Rapids: Eerdmans, 1941.

Berkouwer, G. C. *Man: the Image of God*. trans. Dirk W. Jellema. Grand Rapids: Eerdmans, 1962.

_____. *The Triumph of Grace in the Theology of Karl Barth*. trans. Harry R. Boer. Grand Rapids: Eerdmans, 1956.

Bethune-Baker, James F. *An Introduction to the Early History of Christian Doctrine*. London: Methuen, 1933.

Bewkes, Eugene Garrett. *Legacy of a Christian Mind*. Philadelphia: Judson Press, 1937.

Black, Matthew. *Romans*. Greenwood, SC: Attic Press, 1973.

Bloesch, Donald. *Essentials of Evangelical Theology*. Vol. 1. San Francisco: Harper and Row, 1978.

_____. *Jesus is Victor! Karl Barth's Doctrine of Salvation*. Nashville: Abingdon, 1976.

_____. *Review of On Being a Christian*. by Hans Küng, *Christianity Today* 21, May 6, 1977, pp. 50-51.

Boff, Leonardo. *The Church: Charism and Power*. trans John W. Dierksmeier, Maryknoll, NY: Orbis, 1984.

_____. *Ecclesiogenesis: The Base Communities Reinvest the Church*. trans. Robert R. Barr, Maryknoll, NY: Orbis, 1986.

_____. *Faith on the Edge: Religion and Marginalized Existence*. trans. Robert R. Barr, San Francisco: Harper and Row, 1957.

_____. *God's Witnesses in the Heart of the World*. trans. and ed. Robert Fath. Chicago: Claretian Pubs., 1981.

_____. *Jesus Christ Liberator: a Critical Christology for our Time*. trans. Patrick Hughes. Maryknoll, NY: Orbis, 1979.

_____. *Liberating Grace,* trans. John Drury, Maryknoll, NY: Orbis, 1979.

_____, and Boff, Clodovis. *Liberation Theology: From Dialogue to Confrontation*. trans Robert R. Barr, San Francisco: Harper and Row, 1986.

_____. *The Lord's Prayer: the Prayer of Integral Liberation*. trans. Theodore Morrow. Maryknoll, NY: Orbis Books, 1984.

_____. *The Maternal Face of God: The Feminine and its Religious Experience*. trans. Robert R. Barr and John Dierksmeier. San Francisco: Harper and Row, 1987.

_____. *Passion of Christ, Passion of the World: The Facts, Their Interpretation, and Their Meaning Yesterday and Today*. trans. Robert R. Barr, Maryknoll, NY: Orbis, 1987.

_____. *Salvation and Liberation*. trans. Robert R. Barr. Maryknoll, NY: Orbis Books, 1984.

_____. *The Trinity and Society*. trans. Paul Burns, Maryknoll, NY: Orbis, 1988.

Bonhoeffer, Dietrich. *Act and Being*. trans. Bernard Noble. London: Collins, 1962.

_____. *Christ the Center*. trans. Edwin H. Robertson. San Francisco: Harper and Row, 1978.

_____. *Ethics*. ed. Eberhard Bethge. New York: Macmillan, 1955.

_____. *Letters and Papers from Prison*. ed. Eberhard Bethge, trans. Reginald Fuller, et al. New York: Macmillan, 1971.

Bonino, José Míguez. *Doing Theology in a Revolutionary Situation*. Philadelphia: Fortress Press, 1976.

Braaten, Carl E. "The Christian Doctrine of Salvation." *Interpretation* 35 April, 1981, pp. 117-131.

_____. and Clayton, Philip, eds. *The Theology of Wolfhart Pannenberg*. Minneapolis: Augsburg, 1988

Brandenburger, Egon. *Adam und Christus: Exegetisch— Religionsgeschichtliche Untersuchung zu Röm, 5:12-21 (I Kor. 15)*. Neukirchen-Vluyn: Neukirchener Verlag, 1962.

Bromiley, Geoffrey W. "Atone, III. History of the Doctrine,"
    International Standard Bible Encyclopedia, Revised. Vol.
    1. Grand Rapids: Eerdmans, 1979, pp. 355-360.
_____. "The Doctrine of the Atonement: A Survey of Barth's
    Kirchliche Dogmatik IV.1." *Scottish Journal of Theology*,
    8, no. 2, June, 1955, pp. 175-187.
_____. *Historical Theology: An Introduction.* Grand Rapids:
    Eerdmans, 1978.
_____. *Introduction to the Theology of Karl Barth.* Grand Rapids:
    Eerdmans, 1979.
Brown, Colin. *Karl Barth and the Christian Message.* London:
    Tyndale Press, 1967.
_____. ed. *New International Dictionary of New Testament
    Theology*, 3 vols. Grand Rapids: Zondervan, 1975-78.
Brown, Robert McAfee. "Leonardo Boff: Theologian for All
    Christians." *Christian Century.* July 2-9, 1986, pp. 615-
    617.
_____. *Theology in a New Key: Responding to Liberation
    Themes.* Philadelphia: Westminster Press, 1978.
Bruce, A. B. *The Humiliation of Christ.* Edinburgh: T. & T.
    Clark, 1895.
Bruce, F. F. *The Epistle to the Hebrews.* Grand Rapids:
    Eerdmans, 1964.
Brunner, Emil. *The Christian Doctrine of God.* trans. Olive
    Wyon. Philadelphia: Westminster Press, 1950.
_____. and Barth, Karl. *Natural Theology.* trans. Peter Frankel.
    London: G. Bles, 1945.
Bultmann, Rudolf. "Adam and Christ According to Romans 5."
    Current Issues in New Testament Interpretation, ed.
    William Klassen and Graydon F. Snyder. New York:
    Harper and Brothers, 1962, pp. 143-165.
_____. *Theology of the New Testament*, 2 vols. trans. Kendrik
    Grobel. New York: Charles Scribner & Son, 1951, 1955.
Burleigh, J. H. S. *A Church History of Scotland.* London:
    Oxford University Press, 1960.
Buttrick, G. A. ed. *The Interpreter's Dictionary of the Bible,* 4
    vols. Nashville: Abingdon Press, 1962.
Byrne, Peter D. "John Hick's Philosophy of World Religions."
    Scottish Journal of Theology 35, no. 4, 1982, pp. 289-
    301.

Calvin, John. *The Epistle of Paul the Apostle to the Hebrews and the First and Second Epistles of St. Peter.* trans. William B. Johnston, eds. David W. Torrance and Thomas F. Torrance. Edinburgh: Oliver and Boyd, 1963.

_____. *Institutes of the Christian Religion.* trans. Ford L. Battles, ed. John T. McNeill. 2 vols. Philadelphia: Westminster Press, 1960.

Campbell, Donald. ed. *Memorials of John McLeod Campbell.* 2 vols. London: Macmillan, 1877.

Campbell, John McLeod. *The Nature of the Atonement,* third edition. London: Macmillan and Co., 1867.

_____. *Reminiscences and Reflections, Referring to His Early Ministry in the Parish of Row, 1825-31.* ed. Donald Campbell. London: Macmillan, 1873.

Cant, Bill. "One Foot in Eden?" *New College Bulletin* 13 Sept. 1982, pp. 1-2.

Cobb, John B., Jr. *Christ in a Pluralistic Age.* Philadelphia: Westminster Press, 1975.

_____. *A Christian Natural Theology Based on the Thought of Alfred North Whitehead.* Philadelphia: Westminster Press, 1965.

_____. *God and the World.* Philadelphia: Westminster Press, 1969.

_____. and Griffin, David Ray. *Process Theology: an Introductory Exposition.* Philadelphia: Westminster Press, 1976.

_____. *Process Theology as Political Theology.* Philadelphia: Westminster Press, 1982.

_____. *The Structures of Christian Existence.* Philadelphia: Westminster Press, 1967.

Cone, James. *A Black Theology of Liberation.* Philadelphia: Lippincott, 1970.

Conzelmann, Hans. *An Outline of the Theology of the New Testament.* trans. John Bowden. New York: Harper and Row, 1968.

Cox, Harvey. *The Silencing of Leonardo Boff: The Vatican and the Future of World Christianity.* Oak Park, IL: Meyer-Stone, 1988.

Cranfield, C. E. B. *A Critical and Exegetical Commentary on the Epistle to the Romans*, Vol. 1. Edinburgh: T. & T. Clark, 1975.

Crawford, R. C., "The Atonement in Karl Barth," *Theology* 74, August 1971, pp. 355-358.

Crawford, T. J. *The Doctrine of Scripture Respecting the Atonement*. Edinburgh: W. Blackwood, 1871.

Cullmann, Oscar. *The Christology of the New Testament*. trans. Shirley C. Guthrie and Charles A. M. Hall. Philadelphia: Westminster Press, 1959.

Cunliffe-Jones, H. "The Meaning of the Atonement Today." *Theology* 74, March, 1971, pp. 119-123.

Cunningham, William. *The Reformation and the Theology of the Reformation,* 2nd edition. Edinburgh: T. & T. Clark, 1861.

Davidson, A. B. *The Epistle to the Hebrews*. Edinburgh: T. & T. Clark, n.d.

Davies, W. D. *Paul and Rabbinic Judaism*. Philadelphia: Fortress Press, 1980 (1948).

Davies, W. D. and Daube, David, eds. *The Background of the New Testament and Its Eschatology: C. H. Dodd Festschrift*. Cambridge: Cambridge University Press, 1954.

Davis, Stephen T. ed. , *Encountering Jesus*. Atlanta: John Knox Press, 1988.

D'Costa, Gavin. *John Hick's Theology of Religions: A Critical Evaluation*. Lanham, MD: University Press of America, 1987.

Denney, James. *The Christian Doctrine of Reconciliation*. New York: George Doran Co., 1918,

_____. *The Death of Christ*. ed. R. V. G. Tasker. London: Tyndale Press, 1951.

Denzinger, Heinz. *The Source of Catholic Dogma*. trans. Roy J. Deferrari. St. Louis: B. Herder, 1957.

Diamond, Malcolm L. and Litzenburg, Thomas V., eds. *The Logic of God: Theology and Verification*. Indianapolis: Bobbs- Merrill, 1971.

Dickie, Edgar P. "Introduction to J. M. Campbell." in John McLeod Campbell, *The Nature of the Atonement*. London: J. Clarke, 1959.

"Doctrinal Congregation Criticizes Brazilian Theologian's Book." *Origins*. NC Documentary Service, 14, No. 42, April 4, 1985, pp. 683, 685-687.

Dodd, C. H. *The Parables of the Kingdom*. New York: Scribner's, 1935.

Dostoevsky, Fyodor. *Crime and Punishment*, trans. David Magarshack. Hammondsworth: Penguin Books, 1966.

Dunn, James D. G. *Christology in the Making: a New Testament Inquiry into the Origins of the Doctrine of the Incarnation*. Philadelphia: Westminster Press, 1980.

Ellis, E. Earle. *"Soma* in First Corinthians" *Interpretation* 44, April, 1990, No. 2, pp. 132-144.

Edwards, Jonathan "Satisfaction for Sin." in *The Works of President Edwards,* Vol. II. New York: J. Leavitt and J. F. Trow, 1843.

Feuerbach, Ludwig. *The Essence of Christianity*. trans. George Eliot, New York: Harper and Row, 1957.

Ford, David. *Barth and God's Story: Biblical Narrative and the Theological Method of Karl Barth in the "Church Dogmatics"*. Frankfurt: P Lang, 1981.

Ford, Lewis S. *The Lure of God; a Biblical Background for Process Theism*. Philadelphia: Fortress Press, 1978.

Forrester, Duncan B. "Professor Hick and the Universe of Faiths." *Scottish Journal of Theology* 29, no. 1, 1976, pp. 65-72.

Forsyth, P. T. *The Work of Christ*. New York: Hodder and Stoughton, 1910.

Franks, Robert S. *A History of the Doctrine of the Work of Christ*. London: Hodder and Stoughton, 1918.

Gerrish, B. A. *Tradition and the Modern World: Reformed Theology in the Nineteenth Century*. Chicago: University of Chicago Press, 1978.

Gilkey, Langdon. *Message and Existence: An Introduction to Christian Theology*. Minneapolis: The Seabury Press, 1979.

Gillis, Chester. *A Question of Final Belief: John Hick's Pluralistic Theory of Salvation*. New York: St Martin's Press, 1988.

Goppelt, Leonard. *A Theology of the New Testament*, Vol. 2. trans. John Alsup, ed. Jürgen Roloff. Grand Rapids: Eerdmans, 1982.

Griffin, David. *A Process Christology.* Philadelphia: Westminster Press, 1973.

Gruenler, Royce G. *The Inexhaustible God; Biblical Faith and the Challenge of Process Theism.* Grand Rapids: Baker, 1983.

Gundry, Robert H. *Sōma in Biblical Theology, with Emphasis on Pauline Anthropology.* Cambridge: Cambridge University Press, 1976.

Gunton, Colin E. *Becoming and Being: the Doctrine of God in Charles Hartshorne and Karl Barth.* New York: Oxford University Press, 1978.

_____. *Yesterday and Today: A Study of Continuities in Christology.* Grand Rapids: Eerdmans, 1983.

Guthrie, Donald. *New Testament Theology.* Downers Grove, IL: Inter-Varsity Press, 1981.

Gutiérrez, Gustavo. *A Theology of Liberation.* trans. and ed. Sister Caridad Indu and John Eagleson. Maryknoll, NY: Orbis Books, 1973.

Hagner, Donald A. *Hebrews.* San Francisco: Harper and Row, 1983.

Hanson, Anthony Tyrrell. *The Image of the Invisible God.* London: SCM Press, 1982.

Haring, Hermann, and Kuschel, Kari-Josef, eds. *Hans Küng: His Work and His way.* Garden City, NY; Image Books, 1979.

Hartshorne, Charles. *The Divine Relativity.* New Haven: Yale University Press, 1948.

_____. *Omnipotence and Other Theological Mistakes.* Albany, NY: State University of New York Press, 1984.

Hartwell, Herbert. *The Theology of Karl Barth: An Introduction.* London: Duckworth, 1964.

Hebblethwaite, Peter. *The New Inquisition: the Case of Edward Schillebeeckx and Hans Küng.* San Francisco: Harper and Row, 1980.

Heinecken, Martin J. *The Moment Before God.* Philadelphia: Muhlenberg Press, 1956.

Hendry, George S. *The Gospel of the Incarnation.* Philadelphia: Westminster Press, 1958.

Hengel, Martin. *The Son of God.* trans. John Bowden. Philadelphia: Fortress Press, 1976.

Henry, Carl F. H. *God, Revelation, and Authority.* Vol. 1. Waco: Word Books, 1976.

Hesselink, I. John. "An Interview with Thomas F. Torrance." *Reformed Review,* 38, No. 1, Autumn, 1984, pp. 47-64.

Heron, A. I. C. "Homoousion with the Father." in *The Incarnation,* ed. T. F. Torrance. Edinburgh: The Handsel Press, pp. 54-76.

Hick, John. "Christianity in an Age of Religious Pluralism." *Journal of Theology for South Africa* 15, June, 1981, pp. 4-9.

_____. *The Center of Christianity.* San Francisco: Harper and Row, 1978.

_____ and Hebblethwaite, Brian, eds. *Christianity and Other Religions.* Philadelphia: Fortress Press, 1981.

_____ "Christianity at the Crossroads," in *Prospects for Theology,* ed. F. Healy. London: James Nesbit, 1966, pp. 137-166.

_____. *Death and Eternal Life.* London: Collins, 1976.

_____. *Evil and the God of Love.* London: Macmillan, 1966.

_____. *Faith and Knowledge.* Second Edition, Glasgow: Collins, 1978.

_____. *God and the Universe of Faiths.* London: Macmillan, 1973.

_____. *God Has Many Names.* Philadelphia: Westminster Press, 1982.

_____. *An Interpretation of Religion: Human Responses to the Transcendent.* New Haven: Yale University Press, 1989.

_____. "Jesus and the World Religions." in *The Myth of God Incarnate.* ed. John Hick. London: SCM Press, 1977, pp. 167-187.

_____. "On Grading Religions." *Religious Studies* 17, December, 1981, pp. 451-467.

_____. "Pluralism and the Reality of the Transcendent: How My Mind Has Changed." *Christian Century* 98, January 21, 1981, pp. 45-48.

_____. "The Philosophy of World Religions." *Scottish Journal of Theology* 37, no. 2, 1984, pp. 229-236.

_____, ed. *Truth and Dialogue on World Religions: Conflicting Truth-Claims.* Philadelphia: Westminster Press, 1974.

_____ and Goulder, Michael. *Why Believe in God?* London: SCM Press, 1983.

Hodge, Charles. *Systematic Theology,* Vol. II. Grand Rapids: Eerdmans, 1977.

Hughes, Graham. *Hebrews and Hermeneutics: The Epistle to the Hebrews as a New Testament Example of Biblical Interpretation,* Cambridge: Cambridge University Press, 1977.

Hughes, Philip Edgcumbe. *A Commentary on the Epistle to the Hebrews.* Grand Rapids: Eerdmans, 1977.

Hunter, A. M. *Paul and His Predecessors.* London: Nicholson and Watson, 1940.

Hyers, Conrad. Review of *God Has Many Names* by John Hick. *Theology Today* 40 April, 1983, pp. 68-71.

Irenaeus. "Against Heresies." in *The Ante-Nicene Fathers,* Vol. 1. Ed. Alexander Roberts and James Donaldson. Grand Rapids: Eerdmans, 1950.

Jewett, Robert. *Letter to Pilgrims: A Commentary on the Epistle to the Hebrews.* New York: Pilgrim Press, 1981.

Johnson, Aubrey. *The One and the Many in the Israelite Conception of God.* Cardiff: University of Wales Press, 1961.

Johnson, Harry. *The Humanity of the Savior.* London: Epworth Press, 1962.

Jüngel, Eberhard. *God as the Mystery of the World.* trans. Darrell L. Guder. Grand Rapids: Eerdmans, 1983.

Jüngmann, J. A. *The Place of Jesus Christ in Liturgical Prayer.* 2nd rev. ed. trans. A. Peeler. State Island: Alba House, 1925.

Kähler, Martin. *The So-Called Historical Jesus and the Historic Biblical Christ.* trans. and ed. Carl Braaten. Philadelphia: Fortress Press, 1964.

Kaiser, Christopher B. *The Doctrine of God.* Westchester, IL: Crossway Books, 1982.

Käsemann, Ernst. *Leib und Leib Christi.* Tubingen: J. C. B. Mohr (Paul Siebeck), 1933.

_____. *Perspectives on Paul.* trans. Margaret Kohl. Philadelphia: Fortress Press, 1971.

Kernohan, R. D. "Tom Torrance: The Man and the Reputation." *Life and Work,* 32, No. 5, May, 1976, pp. 47-64.

Kettler, Christian D., "The Atonement as the Life of God in the Ministry of the Church" in *Incarnational Ministry:The Presence of Christ in Church, Society, and Family. Essays in Honor of Ray S. Anderson,* Christian D. Kettler and Todd H. Speidell, ed. Colorado Springs: Helmers and Howard, 1990.

Kettler, F. H. "Versöhnung." in *Die Religion in Geschichte und Gegenwart,* Vol. 6. Tubingen: J. C. Mohr (Paul Siebeck), 1962.

Kim, Seyoon. *The Origin of Paul's Gospel.* Tubingen: J. C. B. Mohr (Paul Siebeck), 1981.

Kirk, J. Andrew. *Liberation Theology: an Evangelical View from the Third World.* Atlanta: John Knox Press, 1979.

Kittel, Gerhard, and Friedrich, Gerhard, eds. *Theological Dictionary of the New Testament.* trans. G. W. Bromiley. Grand Rapids: Eerdmans, 1964-76.

Kiwiet, John. *Hans Küng.* Waco, TX: Word Books, 1985.

Kümmel, Werner Georg. *The Theology of the New Testament.* trans. John E. Steely. Nashville: Abingdon, 1973.

Küng, Hans. *The Church.* trans. Ray and Roseleen Ockenda. Garden City, NY: Doubleday, 1967.

_____. *Does God Exist? An Answer for Today.* trans. Edward Quinn. Garden City, NY: Doubleday, 1980.

_____. *Eternal Life? Life After Death as a Medical, Philosophical, and Theological Problem.* trans. Edward Quinn. Garden City, NY: Doubleday, 1984.

_____. *The Incarnation of God: An Introduction to Hegel's Theological Thought as a Prolegomenon to a Future Christology.* trans. J. R. Stephenson, New York: Crossroad, 1987.

_____. *Infallible? An Inquiry.* trans. Edward Quinn. Garden City, NY: Doubleday, 1971.

_____. *Justification: The Doctrine of Karl Barth and a Catholic Response.* trans. Thomas Collins, Edmund E. Tolk, and David Granskou. New York: Nelson, 1964.

_____. *On Being a Christian,* trans. Edward Quinn. Garden City, NY: Doubleday, 1971.

_____. *Theology and the Third Millenium: An Ecumenical View.* trans. Peter Heinegg, New York: Doubleday, 1988.

The Küng Dialogue. Washington, D.C.: United States Catholic Conference, 1980.

Ladd, George E. *The Presence of the Future.* Grand Rapids: Eerdmans, 1974.

_____. *A Theology of the New Testament.* Grand Rapids: Eerdmans, 1974.

Levison, John R. *Portraits of Adam in Early Judaism: From Sirach to 2 Baruch.* Sheffield: JSOT Press, 1988.

Lewis, C. S. *Mere Christianity.* New York: Macmillan, 1952.

Lindars, Barnabas, and Smalley, Stephen S., ed. *Christ and Spirit in the New Testament,* Cambridge: Cambridge University Press, 1973.

Lipner, Julius. "Christians and the Uniqueness of Christ." *Scottish Journal of Theology* 28, no. 4, 1975, pp. 359-368.

_____. "Truth Claims, and Interreligious Dialogue." *Religious Studies* 12, June, 1976, pp. 217-230.

Lowe, Walter. "Christ and Salvation." in Peter C. Hodgson and Robert H. King, eds. *Christian Theology: An Introduction to Its Traditions and Tasks.* Philadelphia: Fortress Press, 1982, pp. 196ff.

Luther, Martin. "Lectures on the Epistle to the Hebrews 1517-1518." in *Luther: Early Theological Works.* ed. and trans. James Atkinson. Philadelphia: Westminster Press, 1962.

Mackintosh, H. R. *The Doctrine of the Person of Jesus Christ.* Edinburgh: T. & T. Clark, 1912.

_____. *Some Aspects of Christian Belief.* New York: George Doran, n.d.

Macquarrie, John. "John McLeod Campbell, 1800-1872." *Expository Times,* 83 June 1972, pp. 263-268.

Malraux, André. *The Metamorphosis of the Gods.* trans. Stuart Gilbert. Garden City, NY: Doubleday, 1960.

_____. *The Voices of Silence.* trans. Stuart Gilbert. Garden City, NY: Doubleday, 1953.

Manson, T. W. "A Parallel to a NT use of σῶμα," *Journal of Theological Studies,* 37 1936, p. 385.

Manson, William. *The Epistle to the Hebrews: An Historical and Theological Reconstruction.* London: Hodder and Stoughton, 1951.

Martin, Ralph P. *Carmen Christi: Philippians 2:5-11 in Recent Interpretation and in the Setting of Early Christian Worship*. rev. ed. Grand Rapids: Eerdmans, 1983.
_____. *The Spirit and the Congregation: Studies in I Corinthians 12-15*. Grand Rapids: Eerdmans, 1984.
McKim, Donald. ed. *How Karl Barth Changed My Mind*. Grand Rapids: Eerdmans, 1986.
Meeks, M. Douglas. *Origins of the Theology of Hope*. Philadelphia: Fortress Press, 1974.
Michel, O. *Der Brief an die Hebräer*. 12th ed., Gottingen: Vandenhoeck and Ruprecht, 1966.
Miskotte, Kornelis. *When the Gods are Silent*. trans. John W. Doberstein. New York: Harper and Row, 1967.
Moffatt, James. *A Critical and Exegetical Commentary on the Epistle to the Hebrews*. Edinburgh: T. & T. Clark, 1924.
Moltmann, Jürgen. *The Church in the Power of the Spirit*. trans. Margaret Kohl. New York: Harper and Row, 1981.
_____. *The Crucified God*. trans. R. A. Wilson and John Bowden. New York: Harper and Row, 1973.
_____. *God in Creation: A New Theology of Creation and the Spirit of God*. trans. Margaret Kohl, San Francisco: Harper and Row, 1985.
_____. *Theology of Hope*. trans. James W. Leitch. New York: Harper and Row, 1967.
_____. *The Trinity and the Kingdom*. trans. Margaret Kohl. New York: Harper and Row, 1981.
Montefiore, H. W. *The Epistle to the Hebrews*. London: Black, 1964.
Morse, Christopher. *The Logic of Promise in Moltmann's Theology*. Philadelphia: Fortress Press, 1979.
Newell, Robert. *A Passion for Truth: Hans Küng and His Theology*. New York: Crossroad, 1984.
Niditch, Susan. "The Cosmic Adam: Man as Mediator in Rabbinic Literature." *Journal of Jewish Studies* 34, Autumn, 1983, pp. 137-146.
Novak, Michael. *The Spirit of Democratic Capitalism*. New York: American Enterprise Institute/ Simon and Schuster, 1982.
_____. *Will it Liberate? Questions About Liberation Theology*. New York: Paulist Press, 1986.

O'Neill, J. C. "I Cor. 15:29." *Expository Times* 91, 1980, pp. 310-311.

Palma, Robert J. "Thomas F. Torrance's Reformed Theology." *Reformed Review,* 38, No. 1, Autumn, 1984, pp. 2-45.

Pannenberg, Wolfhart. *Anthropology in Theological Perspective.* trans. Matthew J. O'Connell. Philadelphia: Westminster Press, 1985.

_____. *The Apostle's Creed in Light of Today's Questions.* trans. Margaret Kohl, Philadelphia: Westminster Press, 1972.

_____. *Basic Questions in Theology.* 2 vols. trans. George H. Kehm. London: SCM Press, 1970.

_____. "Christologie II. Dogmengeschlichtlich." in *Die Religion in Geschichte und Gegenwart.* Third ed. Tubingen: J. C. B. Mohr, 1956-1962.

_____. *The Church.* trans. Keith Crim. Philadelphia: Westminster Press, 1983.

_____. *Ethics* trans. Keith Crim. Philadelphia: Westminster Press, 1981.

_____. *Faith and Reality.* trans. John Maxwell. Philadelphia: Westminster Press, 1977.

_____. *Jesus—God and Man.* trans. Lewis L. Wilkins and Duane A. Priebe. Philadelphia: Westminster Press, 1973.

_____. "A Liberal Logos Christology: the Christology of John Cobb." trans. David P. Polk, in *John Cobb's Theology in Process,* ed. David Ray Griffin and Thomas J. J. Altizer. Philadelphia: Westminster Press, 1977, pp. 133-150.

_____, ed. *Revelation as History.* trans. David Granskou. New York: Macmillan, 1968.

_____. *Theology and the Kingdom of God.* Philadelphia: Westminster Press, 1969.

_____. *Theology and the Philosophy of Science.* trans. Francis McDonagle. London: Darton, Longman, and Todd, 1971.

Peterson, David G. *Hebrews and Perfection,* Cambridge University Press, 1982.

Pfleiderer, Otto. *The Development of Theology in Germany Since Kant and Its Progress in Great Britain Since 1825.* trans J. Frederick Smith. New York: Macmillan, 1923.

Pittenger, W. Norman. *Christ and Christian Faith.* New York Round Table Press, 1941.

_____. *Christology Reconsidered.* London: SCM Press, 1970.

_____. *The Word Incarnate: a Study of the Doctrine of the Person of Christ.* New York: Harper, 1959.

Plato. *Five Dialogues.* trans. G. M. A. Grube. Indianapolis: Hackett, 1981.

Pollard, T. E. *Fulness of Humanity: Christ's Humanness and Ours.* Sheffield: Almond Press, 1982.

_____ *Puebla and Beyond: Documentation and Commentary.* eds. John Eagleson and Philip Scharper. trans. John Drury. Maryknoll, NY: Orbis Books, 1979.

Rahner, Karl. *The Trinity.* trans. Joseph Donceel. New York: Herder and Herder, 1970.

Ramm, Bernard. *After Fundamentalism: The Future of Evangelical Theology.* San Francisco: Harper and Row, 1983.

Ratzinger, Joseph, with Messori, Vittorio. *The Ratzinger Report- An Exclusive Interview on the State of the Church.* trans. Salvatori Attanasio and Graham Harrison, San Francisco: Ignatius Press, 1986.

Richardson, Alan. *An Introduction to the Theology of the New Testament.* London: SCM Press, 1958.

Ridderbos, Hermann. *The Coming of the Kingdom.* Philadelphia: Presbyterian and Reformed Pub. Co., 1962.

Rissi, Matthias. "Die Menschheit Jesu nach Hebr 5,7-8." *Theologische Zeitschrift* 11 1955, pp. 28-45.

Robinson, H. Wheeler. *Corporate Personality in Ancient Israel.* Philadelphia: Fortress Press, 1964.

Robinson, John A. T. *The Body.* London: SCM Press, 1952.

_____. *The Human Face of God.* Philadelphia: Westminster Press, 1973.

Rogerson, J. W. "The Hebrew Conception of Corporate Personality—a Re-examination." *Journal of Theological Studies* 21, 1970, pp. 1-16.

Rowden, Harold H., ed. *Christ the Lord: Studies in Christology Presented to Donald Guthrie,* Leicester: Inter-Varsity Press, 1982.

Russell, Letty M. *Human Liberation in a Feminist Perspective—a Theology.* Philadelphia: Westminster Press, 1974.

Sacred Congregation for the Doctrine of the Faith. *Instruction on Certain Aspects of the 'Theology of Liberation'*. Publication No. 935. Washington, D. C. : United States Catholic Conference, 1984.

Sacred Congregation for the Doctrine of the Faith. *Instruction of Christian Freedom and Liberation*. Publication No. 995. Washington, D. C. : United States Catholic Conference, 1986.

Sanders, E. P. *Paul and Palestinian Judaism*. Philadelphia: Fortress Press, 1977.

Schilling, S. Paul. Review of *Theology of Hope* by Jürgen Moltmann. *Interpretation* 35, October, 1968, pp. 480-483

Schleiermacher, Friedrich. *The Christian Faith*. ed. and trans. H. R. Mackintosh and J. S. Stewart. Edinburgh: T. & T Clark, 1928.

Schnackenburg, Rudolf. *God's Rule and Kingdom*. trans. John Murray. New York: Herder and Herder, 1963.

Scott, E. F. *The Epistle to the Hebrews*. Edinburgh: T. & T. Clark, 1922.

Scroggs, Robin. *The Last Adam: a Study in Pauline Anthropology*. Oxford: Basil Blackwell, 1960.

Segundo, Juan Luis. *Liberation of Theology*. trans. John Drury. Maryknoll, NY: Orbis Books, 1976.

Senarclens, Jacques de. *Heirs of the Reformation*. trans. and ed. G. W. Bromiley. London: SCM Press, 1963.

Smail, Thomas. *The Forgotten Father*. London: Hodder and Stoughton, 1980.

_____. *The Giving Gift: The Holy Spirit in Person*. London: Hodder and Stoughton, 1988.

Sobrino, Jon. *Christology at the Crossroads: a Latin American Approach*. Maryknoll, NY: Orbis Books, 1978.

_____, ed. *Faces of Jesus: Latin American Christologies*. trans. Robert R. Barr. Maryknoll, NY: Orbis Books, 1983.

Sontag, F. and Bryant, M. D., eds. *God: The Contemporary Discussion*. New York: Rose of Sharon Press, 1982.

Speidell, Todd. "The Incarnation as Theological Imperative for Human Reconciliation: A Christocentric Social Ethic" Unpublished Ph.D. Dissertation, Fuller Theological Seminary, 1986.

Spicq, C. *L'Epître aux Hebreúx,* 2 vols. Paris: J. Gabolda, 1952-53.

Stewart, James S. *A Man in Christ* London: Hodder and Stoughton, 1964 (1935).

Strong, Augustus. *Systematic Theology.* Philadelphia: Judson Press, 1907.

Swidler, Leonard, eds. *Küng in Conflict.* Garden City, NY: Doubleday, 1981.

Taylor, Vincent. *The Person of Christ in New Testament Teaching.* New York: St. Martin's Press, 1958.

Thielicke, Helmut. *The Evangelical Faith,* Vol. 1. trans. and ed., Geoffrey W. Bromiley. Grand Rapids: Eerdmans, 1974.

Thompson, John. *Christ in Perspective: Christological Perspectives in the Theology of Karl Barth.* Grand Rapids: Eerdmans, 1978.

_____. "The Humanity of God in the Theology of Karl Barth." *Scottish Journal of Theology* 29, no. 3, 1976, pp. 249-269.

_____, ed. *Theology Beyond Christendom: Essays on the Centenary of the Birth of Karl Barth, May 10, 1886.* Allison Park, PA: Pickwick Publications, 1986.

Torrance, Iain R.. "A Bibliography of the Works of Thomas F. Torrance 1941-1989," *Scottish Journal of Theology* 43, No. 2, 1990, pp. 225-262.

Torrance, James B. "The Contribution of John McLeod Campbell to Scottish Theology." *Scottish Journal of Theology,* 31, August, 1973, pp. 295-311.

Torrance, Thomas F. *Calvin's Doctrine of Man.* Westport, CT: Greenwood Press. 1977 (1957).

_____. *The Christian Frame of Mind: Reason, Order, and Openness in Theology and Natural Science.* Colorado Springs: Helmers and Howard, 1989.

_____. *Christian Theology and Scientific Culture.* Belfast: Christian Journals Ltd., 1980.

_____. *Conflict and Agreement in the Church,* 2 vols. London: Lutterworth Press, 1959-1960.

_____. *Divine and Contingent Order.* Oxford: Oxford University Press, 1981.

_____. "The Framework of Belief." in *Belief in Science and Christian Life,* ed. T. F. Torrance, Edinburgh: The Handsel Press, 1980.

_____. *God and Rationality.* Oxford: Oxford University Press, 1971.

_____. *The Ground and Grammar of Theology.* Charlottesville: University Press of Virginia, 1980.

_____ed., *The Incarnation,* Edinburgh: The Handsel Press, 1981

_____. "Karl Barth and the Latin Heresy." *Scottish Journal of Theology,* 39, No. 4, 1986, pp. 461-482.

_____"Karl Barth and Patristic Theology" in *Theology beyond Christendom: Essays on the Centenary of the Birth of Karl Barth, May 10, 1886,* ed. John Thompson. Allison Park, PA: Pickwick Publications, 1986, pp. 215-240.

_____. *The Mediation of Christ.* Grand Rapids: Eerdmans, 1983.

_____. "One Aspect of the Biblical Conception of Faith." *Expository Times* 68, 1956-57, pp. 111-114, 221-222.

_____. "The Place of the Humanity of Christ in the Sacramental Life of the Church." *Church Service Society Annual* 26, 1956, pp. 3-10.

_____. *Reality and Evangelical Theology.* Philadelphia: Westminster Press, 19872.

_____. *Space, Time, and Incarnation.* Oxford: Oxford University Press, 1969.

_____. *Space, Time, and Resurrection.* Grand Rapids: Eerdmans, 1971.

_____. *Theological Science.* Oxford: Oxford University Press, 1969.

_____. *Theology in Reconciliation.* Grand Rapids: Eerdmans, 1975.

_____. *Theology in Reconstruction.* Grand Rapids: Eerdmans, 1965.

_____. "Towards an Ecumenical Consensus on the Trinity." *Theologische Zeitschrift* 31, 1975, pp. 335-350.

_____. *The Trinitarian Faith: The Evangelical Theology of the Ancient Catholic Church.* Edinburgh: T. & T. Clark. 1988.

Tracy, David. *The Analogical Imagination.* New York: Crossroad. 1981.

Trigg, Roger. "Religion and the Threat of Relativism." *Religious Studies* 19, 1983, pp. 197-310.

Tupper, E. Frank. *The Theology of Wolfhart Pannenberg.* Philadelphia: Westminster Press, 1973.

Tuttle, George Milledge. "The Place of John McLeod Campbell in British Thought Concerning the Atonement." Unpublished Ph.D. Dissertation, Victoria University of Toronto, 1961.

_____. *So Rich a Soil: John McLeod Campbell on Christian Atonement.* Edinburgh: The Handsel Press, 1986.

Vos, Gerhardus. "The Priesthood of Christ in the Epistle to the Hebrews." *Princeton Theological Review,* 1907, pp. 423-447.

Warren, Max. "Uniqueness of Christ." *Modern Churchman* 18, Winter, 1974, pp. 55-66.

Weber, Otto. *Foundations of Dogmatics.* Vol. 1. trans. Darrell L. Goder. Grand Rapids: Eerdmans, 1981.

_____. *Karl Barth's Kirchliche Dogmatik ein einführender Bericht zu den Bd. I,l bis IV, 3.2.* Neukirchen-Vloya: Neukirchener Verlag, 1977.

Webster's Dictionary of Synonyms. Springfield, MA: Merriam-Webster, 1984.

Wedderburn, A. J. M. "The Body of Christ and Related Concepts in I Corinthians." *Scottish Journal of Theology* 24, 1971, pp. 74-96.

Wells, David F. *The Search for Salvation.* Downers Grove, IL: Inter-Varsity Press, 1978.

Wendel, Francois. *Calvin: The Origins and Development of his Religious Thought.* trans. Philip Mairet. New York: Harper and Row, 1963.

Westcott, Brooke Foss. *The Epistle to the Hebrews.* Grand Rapids: Eerdmans, 1974.

The Westminster Confession of Faith in the Constitution, Presbyterian Church (U. S. A.), Par. 1, The Book of Confessions. New York: The Office of the General Assembly, 1983.

White, Roger. "Substitution in Karl Barth." *Theology* 74, June, 1971, pp. 268-369.

Whitehead, Alfred North. *Adventures in Ideas.* Cambridge University Press, 1933.

_____. *Process and Reality.* New York: Free Press, 1978 (1929).

_____. *Religion in the Making*. New York: Macmillan, 1926.
_____. *Science and the Modern World*. New York: Macmillan, 1925.

INDEX OF NAMES

INDEX OF SUBJECTS

ABOUT THE AUTHOR

Christian D. Kettler is Assistant Professor of Theology and Philosophy at Friends University, Wichita, Kansas, and is an ordained Presbyterian minister. A native of Wichita, he received his B.A. at Friends University and the degrees M.A., M.Div, and Ph.D. (Systematic Theology) from Fuller Theological Seminary. He is the co-editor (with Todd H. Speidell) of *Incarnational Ministry: The Presence of Christ in Church, Society, and Family. Essays in Honor of Ray S. Anderson* (Helmers and Howard, 1990).